Anna's Son
Joyfully Following Hæert to Hæert
By Hart Wiens

2

Table of Contents

3

Acknowledgments

For years I had thought about writing a book chronicling the amazing journey on which God has led my family and me. There is so much to tell, from the beginnings in Russia, the escape through China, pioneering in Paraguay, immigration to Canada and then more than 40 years of engagement in Bible Translation. I had enjoyed writing some publicity pieces in my career in the Philippines and then at the Canadian Bible Society, but writing a book just seemed so daunting. Then, miracle of miracles, my good friend Gayle Goossen, owner of Barefoot Creative, came along and offered to help. I had enjoyed working with Gayle during my career at CBS when she did some publicity work for us. I could not have asked for a better coach and editor for this project. Thanks so much for all your help on this project Gayle.

Every writer needs a good copy editor. In my career at CBS, I was blessed to have Ruth on my team. One of her jobs was copy editor. I have never met anyone with a better eye for detail and a better understanding of what makes a good manuscript. Thanks Ruth, for so carefully reviewing my manuscript and pointing out the areas that needed my further attention. Your contribution was a great blessing.

Another area where I lack expertise is in formatting of the manuscript. Again, I was so fortunate to be able to call on my good friend and former colleague, Tomas Ortiz. He was our publishing expert at CBS and I so valued his contribution on the formatting of this document. Tomas also created my cover design.

A central piece in my story is the great escape of my parents and grandparents from Russia, through China in 1930. I had heard bits and pieces of their story growing up. But the first documentation I saw of this story in print was in the novel, "Blue Mountains of China," written by renowned Canadian author Rudy Wiebe. Then people who participated in that great escape began writing the story in German. My first source was the book written by my uncle Abram Friesen. He wrote "Die Flucht Uber

Den Amur." Then a former neighbour of our family in Alberta, Dick Thiessen, wrote "Beyond Those Mountains." His story concentrated on the part my uncle Isaac played in this story.

Closer to home, my brother Erv wrote "A Dream Come True: Reflections on the Life of Abram and Anna Wiens." I benefitted greatly from the research brother Erv did in the course of writing this story. His reflections were based on his personal interaction with Mom and Dad. Thanks, Erv. Your book helped me a lot. All of my eight siblings play an important role in my story. My older three brothers were examples and mentors to me in many ways. My sisters and my youngest brother Dave were good friends and playmates. Many of my siblings read early versions of my story and gave helpful comments.

Then there were cousins who contributed resources from which I was able to draw. Cousin Isaak Eitzen wrote, "Erinnerungen aus dem Chaco," and "Life of Jacob and Maria Eitzen." Maria is my mother Anna's sister. Then cousin Erv Wiens sent me the hand-written German memories of Grandpa Jacob and cousin Ernie sent me a German version of Tante Lena's memories. Tante Lena is my dad's sister. I translated both stories into English for future generations and included them in the appendix of this book. Then I received a great book about Dad's cousin Abram Ratzlaff entitled "Vater Abram." This book was put out by Abram Ratzlaff's children. I found it fascinating and very helpful in understanding the story of our parents and grandparents. My cousins Gerhard and Mary Friesen patiently answered many questions based on their experience with my grandparents in Paraguay and they supplied some key photos.

Although I am the author of this story, it is not mine alone. It is the story of my heritage and my family, including the ones who follow me. It also chronicles my 40 years of engagement in Bible Translation during which I worked side by side with many remarkable people from around the world. I am grateful to each of the people I worked with as a colleague as well as the people from so many cultural communities who showed me new ways of seeing the world and my place in it.

Most important among the people who share my story is my life partner, Ginny Wichert Wiens. She has stood by me and shared many adventures with me. Through her marriage to this "wandering Wiens" she had to give up her preference for stability and nesting to accompany me on a life that was filled with uncertainty and change. She has also read and given feedback on everything in this book.

Finally, I need to thank my parents, Anna and Abram and my siblings who helped shape me and who encouraged me throughout my life. They gave me the home where I first experienced the meaning of love at home. I am so grateful for the faith and courage of my parents, which motivated them to pursue peace, freedom and opportunity through some of the most trying circumstances imaginable. As a testament to the faith and integrity of my parents' example, all 8 of their surviving children grew up to be people of faith, integrity and service in their communities and in the world. The example of my parents and my siblings inspired me and it is my prayer that it will inspire my children and the generations yet to come.

Introduction

> Shrek: Ogres are like onions.
>
> Donkey: They stink?
>
> Shrek: Yes. No.
>
> Donkey: Oh, they make you cry.
>
> Shrek: No.
>
> Donkey: Oh, you leave 'em out in the sun, they get all brown, start sproutin' little white hairs.
>
> Shrek: No. Layers. Onions have layers. Ogres have layers. Onions have layers. You get it? We both have layers.
>
> Donkey: Oh, you both have layers. Oh. You know, not everybody likes onions.

I could say I have layers. We all have layers.

But I think I am more like a farmhouse, built on a deep foundation. A house that has survived generations of laughter, sorrow and ordinary living. A house where each era defines it and melds together with the next. It cannot be defined by itself or its parts, but by the whole.

I am writing this because it matters to me. I want my children and grandchildren to know the influences that formed me.

Some of my friends and family have challenged me to write it. I admit, it seemed like an overwhelming task. When I started to tell the story, other stories interrupted it, tangled together and I got lost in the memories. These are my words, my memories, my reflections. Many people have shared the scenes with me. They may see them differently. That's because they live in a different house and stand at a different angle.

I am telling my story. But in the process of telling my story, I will tell the story of others because they laid a foundation, hung a sheet of wallpaper, painted a wall, built an addition.... They have been a part of planning, framing, building and decorating that old farmhouse.

The metaphor of the farmhouse may seem unusual for a man who has spent so much of his life living away from the farm or even in urban communities. I want you to know that I am never far from that farmhouse, the place where we milk the cows and get our food, the field, the chicken coop, the barn. The farm provides so many Gospel metaphors: the sheep, the fields, the vineyards, the rain, stony ground and rich fertile soil.

My people are farming people. Even when they were well to do, their life was centred around agriculture. Even when they worked in careers other than farming, their hope was in the land.

There is really no beginning to my story – and the end has not yet been written. But I am starting with Uncle Isaac, my mother's oldest brother. I am writing during a season of fear and change, as COVID-19 threatens what we knew as normal. People are terrified of the change, the isolation, the interruption to all that we see as normal. So, my Uncle Isaac's life seems poignantly relevant today, because he knew nothing but change. The journey he travelled, the life he lived, is a foundation for me. Even though I did not walk with him, the pain resonated through the generations. The traumatic fall and displacement of the Russian Mennonite communities in the early 20th century genetically modified my DNA. It changed the trajectory of my life and my family.

So that's where I will begin….

1: Inspired and Awed

I am writing this during the COVID-19 pandemic of 2020. Holed up at home, I looked to my past for perspective. How might we weather this storm and make the best of a difficult situation. And I looked back to my roots and thought of Uncle Isaac, my mom's oldest brother.

We all like to look into the past and reminisce about life before the complexities of the modern age. Was there a more simple way of life back then? But Uncle Isaac's life was anything but simple.

Born in Russia in 1904, he was a descendant of persecuted Mennonites. They had responded to an invitation about 100 years earlier from Tsarina Catherine the Great, to establish farming communities in Ukraine. Uncle Isaac lived the history I learned in school: on his 10th birthday World War One broke out. Four long years of horrific battle left 22 million people dead. During the war Uncle Isaac's father, my grandfather Jacob Wiens, a peace-loving Mennonite pacifist, was drafted into the Russian army as a medic. This was an early sign of a breach in the freedoms and privileges our people had been promised. Among the many privileges offered to them when Tsarina Catherine had invited them to settle in Russia was freedom from military service. He served in the Russian army for more than a year, leaving his family behind. From the age of 12 to 13, Uncle Isaac was the man of the home while his father was serving in the medical corps. By the end of the war Russia was destroyed. Czar Nicholas, attempting to cling to the traditional autocratic, hierarchical government, was unprepared for the immensity of the impact of the war. Modernization, poor leadership, political instability, and power struggles culminated in the decimation of the peaceful lifestyle the Mennonites had carved out in the Ukrainian steppes and daughter colonies further east.

Uncle Isaac, at 13, was deeply affected by the misguided policies of Czar Nicholas. The instability spawned by these policies culminated in total chaos. Russia erupted into a civil war – a war within a war. On top of the war, the world was struck by a global pandemic known as the Spanish flu. On top of that the revolution brought starvation and outbreaks of typhoid.

During the revolution, unbelievable violence and cruelty were perpetrated on our people in a campaign of ethnocide. The disintegration of the state opened opportunities for marauding bandits to roam freely, inflicting unimaginable cruelties on our people. The terror left an indelible mark on our family. I'll write more about that later.

By the time Uncle Isaac was 19, he couldn't remember peace. Fear and instability reigned over his community. His family had to leave their homes and almost everything they owned and they had migrated East across the Ural Mountains, into Siberia. They had lost everything. The government, led by wealthy aristocrats, was demolished. The new communist government took control of all industry and farmland. Prosperous and productive Mennonite farms were vandalized by bandits and then taken over by the government in their move to collectivize agriculture. All produce was taxed at a rate that left many farmers with not enough grain to plant new crops. The land Uncle Isaac's parents were so proud of, now belonged to the newly formed communist Russia. The German hymn *"Wehrlos und verlassen sehnt sich Oft mein Herz nach stiller Ruh"* [When I'm lonely and defenseless my heart longs for rest and peace] was a constant theme running through their lives.

By now my mother, Uncle Isaac's youngest sibling, was born. With promise of more freedom and opportunity for free enterprise in the Russian Far East, the family moved more than 4,000 kilometers east to the Amur River region, bordering Manchuria—it was as far as they could go to try to escape Stalin's reign of terror. But Stalin's reach was long. Collectivization caught up with them even there.

On Uncle Isaac's 25th birthday, the "Great Depression" hit. Unemployment went through the roof all around the world. A record 25% of employable people in America had lost their jobs. The World GDP dropped 27%.

Life in Russia was unbearable. By now Uncle Isaac had his own family. He was recognized as a leader in the new Mennonite community of Schumanovka, near the Amur River bordering China. Longing for freedom, the community looked to the Blue Mountains of Manchuria, wondering what lay beyond those mountains. The people were desperate for a place of refuge and freedom. It was Uncle Isaac that people implored to help lead them out of their bondage to a new homeland. He, along with William Fehderau, made the initial secret foray across the Amur River into China to scout out the feasibility of the escape plan that was being developed in their village.

My mom was 10 years old. My dad's family had also escaped the horror of their desecrated villages and farmland in Ukraine. They too had settled in Schumanovka, bringing the two Wiens families together. My dad was 12. Dad's father, Franz Wiens, was a lay preacher in the church, which made him an open target of frequent late-night interrogation by the secret police. My dad recalled the interrogations that happened as he lay in his bed. The inquisitors always came to the same conclusion – our people would have to give up their land, their faith and their Bibles for peace in Stalin's Russia.

How I would like to have been a fly on the wall of some of the community's planning meetings and the interrogation sessions. So much was going on in secret. How did a community of impoverished Mennonites, who had lost their homes, their communities and all of their wealth, think they could escape the intrusiveness of Stalin's terrifying regime?

But the thirst for freedom was strong. They decided to slip across the Amur River and cross over the Blue Mountains in search of safety in China and beyond. It was mid-winter and the temperatures dipped well below freezing, frequently falling to minus 40 degrees. It was so cold that saliva would freeze before a spit reached the ground. The Amur River was frozen solid. While China was not under communist rule at the time, it was embroiled in conflict sparked by Japan's invasion. But in a daring escape, thanks to leaders like Uncle Isaac, my parents escaped communist Russia and were given temporary refuge in China. They understood it was temporary – no more than two years. If they stayed longer, they would be deported, back to Russia. Unthinkable!

The escape to China was dramatic. While the entire village of Schumanovka sought freedom from the communist regime, they were assaulted by a different form of imprisonment when they got to China. They were free from Stalin's terror, but China would not offer them a permanent home. They were helpless and marooned. No country would accept them. No one wanted these hapless refugees. They had hoped to get to Canada or the United States where many of them had relatives, but these countries were not accepting refugees due to the collapse of their economies during the Great Depression.

My grandparents had one prayer: the opportunity to start again in a country that would grant them the freedom to worship according to their beliefs. They longed for peace and the ability to till the land and enjoy the fruit of their labours.

The 1930s brought years of excruciating pain and loss.

The global depression had plunged nations into austerity measures to protect their own economic conditions. North America had closed their doors to immigrants. The small band of Mennonites that Uncle Isaac had helped escape Stalin's terror was heartbroken. Many felt hopeless. There was no prospect of getting to North America. In the 1920s, the average income in North America was $3,269. But in the 1930s everything changed. The unemployment rate hovered near the 20% mark and, if they could find work, many people earned as little as $1 a day. There was no capacity for bringing new refugees or immigrants into this calamity.

Desperate to leave China and determined not to return to Russia, they explored, they consulted, they negotiated, they prayed and they sought refuge. The Mennonite Central Committee had been established 10 years earlier to assist desperate and starving Mennonites in Russia. Thankfully the group that reached Harbin in China also found MCC representatives to assist them with their search for a new homeland. They considered various options, including Indonesia, but in the end the only choice open to them was Paraguay, which offered resettlement in the sparsely populated Paraguayan Chaco.

By the time they left China for Paraguay, Uncle Isaac was 27 years old, my mother was 11 and my dad was 13. With support from MCC and the German government, the group travelled by train to the coast, then by ship from Shanghai to France, then by train through France, and again by ship across the Atlantic Ocean to Buenos Aires. From there it was another laborious journey inland by river boat, train and on foot into the heart of Paraguay. At the end of the railroad, they and the rest of the Mennonite families, shouldered their meagre belongings and hiked into the Paraguayan Chaco – a large expanse of open and unexplored land. They arrived at their new home in Paraguay on May 12, 1932, almost three months after their departure from Harbin, China and an agonizingly long 18 months after their escape across the Amur River into China.

They walked through the jungle and into what would come to be aptly called the "Green Hell." The land they had farmed in Russia was rich and fertile. My great-great grandparents had tamed the land. Uncle Isaac only knew the rich fertile fields that yielded excellent harvests. He had never worked virgin soil in such excruciating heat as they had to endure in Paraguay.

The land that had nurtured the Mennonite villages in the Ukraine and further East in Russia, yielded diverse crops. Food was plentiful. Cream, eggs, pork, and a variety of vegetables and fruits were readily available in return for their diligent labour. They had never experienced anything like the sweltering jungles of Paraguay. The climate was semi-arid. After periods of drought, they might get intense downpours of rain, drowning the crops they had worked so hard to seed. Frequently, drought would rob the plants of any nutrition and their crops would wilt in the sweltering sun. Mosquitos swarmed and infected the families with malaria. Often grasshoppers, like the locusts of the Bible stories they knew so well, consumed everything green and growing. They longed for a return to a more productive relationship with the land.

The Russian Mennonite farmers had no idea how to work the land or what crops would thrive here. While they were working to eke out a meagre existence in their new homeland, it startled them to discover that Paraguay was at war with Bolivia in a dispute over their borders. The battlefield encompassed the new homeland granted to our people. Caught in the middle of a war he had no history to understand, Uncle Isaac lived through this conflict. Sometimes his land was claimed by Paraguay, and then again it would come under Bolivian control.

When Uncle Isaac was 36 years old, the world was plunged once again into global conflict. Germany, the nation that had lent our people the money for their journey to Paraguay, swept across Europe in a "blitzkrieg" (definition: an intense military campaign intended to bring about a swift victory) that threatened peace and security everywhere. Uncle Isaac spoke German. His culture, while modified by the Russian experience, still harboured so much from the German "motherland." Our people were considered Germans.

Germany invaded Russia taking control of much of the area where many Mennonites still lived. The Germans were seen as liberators.

In England and most of continental Europe, bombs rained down. Every day tanks and artillery shelled devastated communities. Between Uncle Isaac's 30th and 41st birthday, 75 million people died. His dream to move to North America was once again elusive as the world was obsessed with war. Immigrants were sadly ignored while the world was immersed in a brutal conflict.

For men, women and families with (or perceived to have) German roots, immigration to North America was impossible. The world disdained Germany and all things German, reeling as Hitler attacked, believing that he could overcome his enemies and become the dominant power in the world. Uncle Isaac, a German-speaking, Russian Mennonite, would not be welcome in North America in this climate.

Their dreams died. Hopes of reaching greater opportunity in Canada seemed unreachable.

Then abrupt upheaval and change again.

With the nuclear bomb attack on Japan, killing as many as 200,000 civilians, the war finally ended and the nuclear age was born. Canada once again needed more people and opened its borders to immigrants, including many displaced persons from Germany. Uncle Isaac was 44 years old. By now, my mom and dad had fallen in love, married and started their own family. I was just a little boy. While we were extremely poor, I had no knowledge of our poverty. I was loved; I was fed; I was happy. I was not shaped by the wealth we had left behind in Russia or the horrific tragedy my family lived through as refugees and immigrants. I was a little boy looking forward to a new adventure. The prospect of a move to Canada was exciting.

Several of my Grandma's brothers and sisters had made it to Canada during the great migration from Russia between 1920 and 1926. During those years, Mennonites in North America had banded together to bring 20,000 Mennonites out of Russia, at great effort and expense. A timely election in Canada had delivered the government of William Lyon Mackenzie King, who delivered on his promise to rescind an Order-In-Council banning Mennonite immigration to Canada. Grandma's Friesen siblings, the uncles and aunts of

Uncle Isaac and my mother, had settled in southern Alberta. When Canada opened its doors again to new immigrants, they agreed to sponsor our families.

To us, Canada was a land of unlimited opportunity – the promised land. It even sounded like Canaan to our ears. We didn't understand that our relatives were not rich. Having just gone through the Great Depression and the Second World War, they were struggling to coax a living akin to the prosperity they had left behind in Russia, out of their new Canadian homeland. Canada was a new country, in many ways undeveloped at the time, and counting on hardworking immigrants like the Mennonite farmers to tame the wild prairies.

My Grandma Liese Friesen Wiens, Isaac's mother, died as we were preparing to immigrate.

After so much strife and hardship, our families hungered for new life, peace and freedom in Canada. We had barely arrived when the Korean War broke out. Uncle Isaac is in mid-life by now, 46 years old. Canada, our new refuge, along with their allies, is tangled in another war in Korea, battling the communist aggression our people knew so well. Another five million people died and the economy suffered another setback.

Like so many others, Uncle Isaac, watches with fear and trepidation as the world lurches from one crisis to another:

> – The end of the Second World War did not bring the promised peace our people were longing for. Instead, it inaugurated the Cold War period in which the USA and its NATO allies sought to block the aggression of the Soviet Bloc through a massive nuclear arms race which threatened global annihilation.

> – For more than 20 years the USA was at war in Vietnam. More than 4 million people died. Countless soldiers suffered from the atrocious experience of war in the Vietnam jungles. Social protests rose up. North America was at war with communism, stirring up fears that communism could reach our new homeland, bringing with it the terrors from which our families had fled. Canada became a haven for American draft dodgers.

> – The Cuban Missile Crisis increased global anxiety. Communism was knocking at the door of North America. Could even North

America fall to the communist menace? What if a nuclear war occurred? People were terrified by the real possibility of annihilation.

I chose to focus on Uncle Isaac's life because he experienced so many dramatic changes, literally a life and death struggle. In Russia, he experienced some of the luxury and prosperity of the Mennonite communities that managed their own affairs and had grown rich and influential in the Russian economy. Then, in the bat of an eye, he experienced the terror of war and revolution and the fear of death from disease. Seeking peace and freedom, he travelled through five significant cultural shifts: from southern Russia to Siberia; from Siberia to China; from China to Paraguay; from Paraguay to Coaldale, Alberta; from Coaldale to a dairy farm in northern Alberta. Throughout his tumultuous life, he stayed true to his faith and was relentless in his pursuit of freedom and opportunity.

I am writing from my safe and comfortable home in Waterloo, Ontario. Canada's first fight with COVID-19 has released its grip, at least temporarily. We think we may be hit with a second wave, but no one knows for sure. I can't imagine walking the pathway my family – Uncle Isaac, my mother, my father – walked. It was a heart-wrenching, terrifying journey that paved the way for my privileged opportunity to lay a foundation that will privilege my children and their children for generations to come. They laid the foundation for my future.

Today, July 21, 2020, 612,000 people have died of COVID-19. We can't predict the death toll over the next year, but it will be in the millions. The virus has opened up new controversies around "freedom." "You can't tell me to wear a mask!" some shout, while others demonstrate to remind us that "Black Lives Matter!" All over the world we see refugees clamoring for freedom and opportunity just as our parents did through their long journey from communist terror to freedom and opportunity in Canada.

That is my world at the moment I am writing this.

I wonder, sometimes, if the Mennonite communities in Russia would have had any air time if it had happened today, when the internet and social media are so easily accessed. Families wrote to their relatives in America to share their sorrow and loss. A letter would have taken weeks to travel the ocean. Today we communicate with a quick email, a text message or a tweet.

But even with quick access to information, how many Canadians know that 700,000 people in the Central African Republic have been displaced by civil war and are haunted by hunger? Or that Somalians have experienced conflict for more than 40 years, causing more than 2.6 million people to search for a new home? Or that more than 7.5 million Sudanese refugees are fighting starvation and looking for freedom? Afghanistan, Syria, Colombia, Venezuela.... I could go on. As I look out my front window, I see that the Colombian family, who came to Canada as refugees and then lived with us for seven years, is thriving. I thank God that they too have found peace and a new home right across the street from us. Out of their displacement, they have become like another set of children and grandchildren to us.

Many families are on a journey similar to the one that brought my family to our new home in Canada. They are looking for freedom of religion, a safe place to raise their family, for opportunities for their children, for peace. Some will find their way to Canada. Their journey will be unique, different from mine. I thank God that in a small way we have been able to help two young Filipino families find new homes and opportunities in Canada. They too have been embraced as our children and grandchildren.

All of my siblings have participated in support for refugees and immigrants coming to Canada. In July 2020, together with my seven siblings, we joined in celebration of the 100th anniversary of MCC. In gratitude for the tremendous help MCC was on our journey, we planted a tree at our parents' grave, with a plaque to symbolize our donation of $10,000 to the work of MCC. We did this with great joy, to celebrate the path to peace and freedom on which God had led us.

We are resilient. We are created in the image of God who loves us. The story is not finished. My Uncle Isaac and my parents survived their grueling journey.... God was with them and God is with us.

Uncle Isaac and his family prospered in Alberta. While our parents moved from Alberta to southern Ontario, seeking new and better opportunities for our growing family here, Uncle Isaac settled on a dairy farm near Edmonton, and then retired to a quiet life in Abbotsford, B.C. There he spent his waning years bringing music to the Abbotsford Mennonite Brethren Church as the director of their senior choir. Music was always a rich part of our heritage. Music and songs played an important role in my mother's family and she passed this on to her children.

2: Anna's son

I start this true reflection with something that I wrote some time ago. I am Anna's son.

I've filled out the narrative in other sections, but I wanted to include this short story as an introduction to my own life. It focuses on my mother, my heritage and promise of answered prayer. Much like Hannah's prayer before the birth of her son Samuel, my mother prayed during her pregnancy before my birth. She prayed for my health and she consecrated me to God: a promise for a promise. I believe that God's work in my life in answer to my mother's prayers was what guided me and lead me to the path I chose to follow. Her prayers throughout my life had a profound impact on me.

Anna prayed for me.

And she made a vow, saying, "Lord Almighty, if you will only look on your servant's misery and remember me, and not forget your servant but give her a son, then I will give him to the Lord for all the days of his life, ..." 1 Samuel 1:11

That was Hannah's prayer, which preceded the birth of the Prophet Samuel. How many women have taken that prayer as their liberty to implore God for children yet unborn? That is what my mother, Anna, did. It was 1945. She and my father, Abram, had been married for six years. She was getting used to the rhythms of married life in their new homeland of Paraguay. After a very difficult beginning as immigrants in this "Green Hell," she and Abe were getting accustomed to the hard work required to make a living in the new climate, so entirely different from Russia where they were born. They had three sons now, born in quick succession after their marriage when Anna was just 18.

It had been a cozy Christmas. Although they were now living in Filadelfia, the capital of the Fernheim Mennonite colony, they had gone back to their home village of Orloff. This was the village where their families had settled after their miraculous escape as refugees from Russia in 1930. Anna's parents, Jacob and Liese Wiens, had been allocated a lot in the middle of Orloff (village #15), and Abe's parents, Franz and Anna Wiens, at the far western end. According to some accounts, the two Wiens families were about as different as the distance between the two ends of their village. Anna's parents were open-hearted and generous, especially toward Anna, their youngest. Her father was a deacon in the church. Anna was the sunshine and song bird of her parents' waning years. Her parents and siblings doted on her. Singing and loving engagement were her cherished memories of family life. Abe's memories of family life at home were not as pleasant. His father was a preacher, and life at home was more somber and focused on work and finances. The family's financial viability was a constant source of stress and tension. While Abe was the third of nine children, he often felt that the expectations and burdens of the eldest were laid on him.

So, this Christmas of 1944, Abe and Anna packed up and, with their three little boys in tow, made the 15-kilometer journey from their home in Filidelfia to Orloff, where they had begun their married life in a little house across the path from Anna's family. That is where they would spend Christmas, surrounded by the love and attention of a happy family. Evenings were spent sitting around a campfire at Anna's parents' home, with all her siblings and their families joining in to fill the air with favourite carols, hymns and folk songs. One of Anna's favourites was *"In meine Heimat kam ich wieder"* (I came back to my home). When the singing and reminiscing was done, the little boys were fast asleep. Everyone had retired to their own home and Anna took Abe's hand, suggesting a walk in the moonlight for memory's sake. As they strolled through the village in the soft light of the waxing moon, they reflected on all the ways that God had blessed them since their first secret meeting together as their parents were occupied in a church business meeting. They thanked God for the peace and safety they enjoyed in this new land, and especially for their three healthy and happy boys. With hearts full of memories and love they went to bed.

Early in the new year, as another full moon had come and gone, Anna realized that she had missed her monthly flow. Could she be pregnant again? As the weeks and months went by, the awareness of a new life inside was undeniable. She was 24 years old and expecting her fourth child. She and Abe were excited, but Anna could not entirely get past a nagging worry. Could she really give birth to another healthy child – her fourth? She knew that this could not be taken for granted in a land of limited medical care, where a multitude of strange diseases stalked them at every turn. There were dangers all around. Malaria was rampant in and around the German Mennonite colony of Fernheim. She thought about the time in their early life together when Abe had been picking cotton in their field and a snake had attached to him with its poisonous fangs. With the help of her family, they hitched a horse to their wagon and rushed him to the doctor 15 kilometers away. Another time Abe had been forced to hunker down on the trail at night, as the gleaming eyes of a jaguar peered at him from a nearby tree. There was just one doctor in Filadelfia to serve the 20 villages of Fernheim colony, and important supplies such as medications had to be brought in by ox cart from the end of the railway line, more than a day's journey away. Would this child be born healthy like her other three? If medical help was required, would it be available?

So, Anna prayed. It was not as if prayer was a new experience for her. She had grown up in a close and loving Mennonite family where prayer and singing hymns were part of daily life. Abe and Anna had both been nurtured in the faith, and prayer was a part of their daily routine. But the prayer that Anna verbalized now was different. She needed to give her worries about the child swelling in her womb up to God. So, she prayed. She asked God to grant her another healthy child and she made a promise. If God would grant her request, she would dedicate this child to God in a special way. This child would be raised to serve God in some special mission.

Anna's pregnancy progressed without serious complications and I was born on September 12, 1945, in the small hospital in Filadelfia. I was mostly healthy at birth except for a complication with my urinary tract which required surgery including circumcision. It seemed that Anna's prayer had been answered. She kept her conversation with God to herself and continued to pray for me, as she did daily for each of her children throughout her life.

3: Foundations

I am resisting writing a linear history, where one thing falls neatly in place after the other. But I realize the timeline is the path that will hold it together. Forgive the rabbit trails. While I will tell the story, by and large, chronologically, I will not commit myself to staying clear of rabbit trails.

I want you to understand my grandparents' story.

For a long time, the generation that lived through the Russian Revolution, the Spanish flu and the many challenges of immigration, held much of their experience in stoic silence. The story is difficult. An epic tragedy, the story tells of simple Mennonite families searching for a place of peace and opportunity. The myth has been painted in many colours by past historians and glossed over by theologians. In many ways, my parents and grandparents kept the truth hidden.

As I searched deeper into the stories, some of the piety of the past, the penchant for a "simple" life and the belief that our forefathers in Russia were unaffected by the Russian culture, or compromised by the search of power, wealth and influence, unraveled. Politics did not evade the Mennonite colonies. Powerful men were not protected from ambition or greed.

Unlike the myth perpetuated, they did not live quietly in their estates and farms without intersecting with the Russian population. Bolshevik peasants served as their cooks, gardeners and farm helpers. Mennonite landowners did not always treat their Bolshevik neighbours with grace and generosity. Mennonite men (and some women) were educated in Moscow, Switzerland and other universities. They built schools and hospitals. Their factories produced intricate time pieces, such as the famous Kroeger clocks and modern farm implements. They were engineers, medical professionals and inventors. They were food producers and professors. In 1900, just a few years before all hell broke loose, the community was thriving, thanks in large part to privileges granted them a hundred years earlier by Tsarina Catherine the Great. Part of their initial agreement was that they would hold fast to their religious beliefs in their own communities and would not proselytize the Russian population. They were granted land and special privileges, such as freedom from military service. This resulted in Mennonite communities that were self-sustaining and largely separate from the surrounding community. Their separatism and their relative wealth became a source of resentment against them during the Bolshevik revolution.

While they held fast to their religious identity, their lives were not exemplary exhibits of the Gospel of the Kingdom where Jesus is Lord. Land ownership carried with it special powers and privileges in their communities. With their large families, their population soon outstripped the land available to them. Soon there were large numbers of landless families and individuals living among families with extreme wealth and privilege. Orphans and widows were particularly disadvantaged. Their care was the responsibility of the deacons. The culture was patriarchal. Men who lost their wives could and did remarry. However, when a family lost their father, the fate of the widow and her children was in the hands of the deacons. Everything they owned was first distributed to cover any outstanding debts. After that the widow could be sent to serve in the home of a family of means, and their children could be distributed among other families, where they were often treated more as servants then as children. The poverty and injustice experienced by many of the landless families is believed to have been one of the issues contributing to a religious awakening in the colonies, resulting in the birth of the Mennonite Brethren denomination, the branch of the Mennonite faith in which I was raised.

In response to the growing problem of landless and impoverished families, new daughter colonies were established. One of the daughter colonies in the Ukraine was Sagradovka.

My great-grandfather (my father's grandfather), Johann Julius Wiens, owned one of the many prosperous estates that emerged in the Sagradovka Mennonite colony in Ukraine. He was a proud man, determined to hold on to his wealth and his land, even as he watched his estate being demolished by the revolution. He died of starvation in 1933 on the very land he had coaxed to flourish. He died protecting the idea of wealth and possession. All he had worked so hard to build up was violently destroyed by the enemy he could not conquer. He held on to his earthly gain and lost everything.

My father's story is even more closely linked to his maternal grandfather, Abram Fast who became known among the Mennonites in Sagradovka as "Rich Fast." He chose his son-in-law, Franz Wiens, my dad's father, as the heir apparent for his large estate. When the revolution broke out and the bandit Nestor Makhno and his gang roamed through the Mennonite colonies terrorizing and slaughtering inhabitants at will, they left everything behind and moved to the Amur region of Siberia, where they were offered more freedom. That is how my parents came to live in the same village of Shumanovka in Siberia. My father's family arrived there just in time to participate in the great escape across the Amur River into China.

It's a fantastic story – not so different from the story of the Israelites. My story – like yours – is a story tangled in the human condition. We fight between two vying spirits. "What I don't understand about myself is that I decide one way, but then I act another, doing things I absolutely despise." So says Paul in Romans 7:15. The God-story that is a huge part of our heritage is not about possession or wealth, but about faith. For some, the journey led to greater faith. For others, the journey led to cynicism and fear.

I carry on the story with my mother Anna's family.

Tsarina Catherine the Great saw an opportunity to cultivate the land around the Dnieper River and expand Russia's wealth. She looked for sturdy, hard-working families to settle and work the land. Around 1800, she invited Mennonite farmers from West Prussia to establish colonies in what she identified as large areas of fertile land opened up to immigration by Russia's expansion.

Mennonites, known as radical reformers in the Protestant Reformation, had suffered severe persecution in Europe where the Mennonite faith emerged out of the "radical" Reformation.

Mennonites adopted Jesus' Sermon on the Mount as their constitution. They opposed war and violence. Their obstinate commitment to staying true to their faith was not well received when the Holy Roman Empire fought their way through Europe with war and violence. They actively resisted military activity and refused to join the political movement to conquer Europe. This made them "persona non grata" in the "Holy Roman Empire."

Our Mennonite ancestors sought freedom of worship, first in Prussia, where they were invited to help drain the Delta of the Vistula River. They settled as a community and negotiated the freedom to manage their own villages: electing ministers, appointing teachers and maintaining their own civil society through church leadership. After about a century in Prussia, where they enjoyed freedom and prosperity, they experienced pressure from the government and society around them. Many Prussians resented the fact that they were exempt from military service, and the government began to tax them heavily as compensation for their "conscientious objector" exemption from service.

The invitation from Tsarina Catherine in the waning years of the 18th century was seen as God's answer to their prayers for greater freedom and opportunity. The first colony of Chortitza was established near Zaporizhia (now Ukraine) in 1789, followed in 1804 by the Molotschna Colony about 100 kilometers south.

This began a period of great prosperity, and expansion into Crimea and many new settlements west of the Ural Mountains. Anna's maternal grandparents, the Daniel Friesen family, and paternal grandparents, the Isaak Wiens family, migrated from Molotschna to Crimea. From there, the families moved east to Kaltan in the Neu Samara colony. Anna's father, Jacob, met and then married Anna's mother, Liese Friesen, on October 12, 1901 in the Neu Samara colony.

Because there was not enough land in the Molotschna Colony to support the rapidly increasing population, daughter colonies were established. Among these was the Sagradovka colony some 200 kilometers west of Molotschna. That is where the Johann Julius Wiens family came to live next to the Abram Fast family. One of the Fast sons married one of the Wiens daughters, and in turn two of the Wiens sons, including my grandpa Franz, married two of the Fast daughters, which included my grandma Anna Fast Wiens.

This is where my father Abram was born on April 3, 1918.

For more than 70 years, the Mennonites farmed the land and managed their own society. Over the years, their colonies flourished. In the 1870s the government of Russia intimated the end of self-government for the colonies. It made sense, from a Russian perspective. The Mennonites had grown in numbers and expanded to new territory. Agri-industry and construction industries had emerged, serving not only the Mennonite villages, but engaging in commerce outside of the community. The Russian government wanted to exert more control over these relatively independent communities.

When word from Moscow came that the Russian government would start to influence the schools and civil authority, Mennonites resisted. About 7500 Mennonites emigrated to Canada around the end of the 19th century. While they cited political asylum, many emigrants were from less wealthy families – families without a legacy of land or an estate. They saw Canada, much like the Russian steppes, as a place of opportunity (free land), with freedom to worship, speak their own language and have the privilege of alternative service in times of conscription.

Life in the Russian Mennonite colonies continued. For the next 30 years, estates grew in wealth, and Mennonites were leaders in their communities and influencers in Moscow.

But the Russian political climate was changing for the worse. In the early years of the 20th century Czar Nicholas II demonstrated complete incompetence in governing Russia. Civil strife and turmoil emerged, especially in the areas west of the Ural Mountains.

When the Great War began in 1914, Russia was in crisis. Many Mennonites were beginning to consider whether there might not be more peaceful and stable homes for them elsewhere, either in North America or in other parts of Russia. In Russia, new colonies east of the Urals in Siberia began to look promising, as land west of the Urals was becoming scarce for the growing population. In 1910, looking for new opportunities, Jacob and Liese Wiens packed up their family of four children and moved more than 2000 kilometers across the Ural mountains to the settlement of Barnaul, south of Novosibirsk on the Siberian plain, in search of peace and economic opportunity.

This is where Anna was born on August 8, 1920.

She was born in the village of Schumanovka, part of the German Mennonite colony of Barnaul, about 200 kilometers south of the city of Novosibirsk. The name, Schumanovka would be carried by settlers from this community when they moved further east to the Amur River region about a decade later.

Anna was the youngest of eight siblings, five years younger than her next youngest sibling Abram, and 18 years younger than her eldest sister Liese. She was the love child of her parents' declining years, born after her father returned from service in the Russian medical corps during the Great War.

By this time Russia had come through the disastrous years of the war, the Spanish flu pandemic and the revolution. On March 15, 1917, near the end of WWI, Czar Nicholas II was abducted, marking the end of the ruling Romanov dynasty. The family was taken to the Ural Mountains where they were heavily guarded. Bolsheviks took advantage of a government in chaos and in a bloody clash, overthrew the provisional government.

Vladimir Lenin, in antithesis to the Soviet State managed by Russia's bourgeois capitalists, instated councils led by soldiers, peasants and workers. Lenin became the dictator of the world's first communist state.

All of this was happening in the background. Anna's father had been conscripted into the World War effort as a medic. Original and more established Mennonite colonies in the Ukrainian steppes were savagely attacked. Anna's family, living in Siberia, did not experience the brutal terrorism their friends in the "old" colonies were subjected to. But news of the terror and atrocities reached them and it wrenched their souls.

Communities west of the Urals were especially hard hit by the turmoil. Most feared by the Mennonites in the Ukraine were the bands of roving peasant bandits, especially one led by Nestor Makhno. The large estate owned by my great-grandfather Abram Fast and his son-in-law, my grandfather Franz Wiens, was savagely attacked by the bandits one night when my father was just a toddler. A grenade was tossed through their window, which Grandpa Franz fortunately threw back out before it exploded.

Relatives and families in North America engaged with the plight of the Russian Mennonites. Mennonite Central Committee was established in 1920, the same year my mother was born, to bring aid to their suffering brothers and sisters in Russia.

In the 1920s, after the war, the new Canadian government of William Lyon Mackenzie King rescinded the Order In Council prohibiting immigration of

Mennonites to Canada and immigration was opened again. Mennonites in North America worked together to make it possible for 20,000 Mennonites to emigrate, mostly to Canada. Anna's father, Jacob Wiens, made two attempts to join this migration, but was denied visas for his family. Several of my maternal grandmother's "Friesen" siblings had joined that migration and ended up in southern Alberta.

The other Wiens family, originating in Sagradovka, was desperately petitioning for exit permits in order to join this migration as well. These were my grandparents, Franz and Anna Wiens, my father's parents. David Wiens, the brother of Grandpa Franz Wiens, had succeeded in acquiring the much-treasured exit permit and ended up in Kitchener, Ontario.

Travel documents were denied for both my father's and my mother's families. They felt they had no other option but to join the growing migration east to Siberia. They had heard that in the far east of Siberia there was a new settlement in the Amur River region south of Blagoveshchensk. Far from Moscow and the centre of chaos, they had also heard that they would have more freedom from the worst excesses of communist rule. In the "old" colonies, the land was usurped by the Communist government for communal ownership in collective farms. Along with communal land, industry and employment, the Communists stripped the people of religious freedom. Lenin believed that religion had no place in the new society and that atheism was inseparable from Marxism. His political plan was based on the theory and practice of what he called scientific socialism. The Mennonites' highly religious society, based on the church as a community of faith and practice, had no place in the new Communist state.

Stalin, a young and ambitious party leader, antagonized Lenin. Their clash ended when Lenin died. Stalin's New Economic Policy exacted a heavy tax paid by our people mostly in a forced supply of grain from farmers. This hit the Mennonite settlers especially hard, as many of them were considered to be "kulaks." Despised by Stalin, the direct translation of the word means "fist." A kulak was someone from a peasant or low-class background, not born as a bourgeois, but elevated by growing wealth and ownership of a large farm and livestock. Kulaks were wealthy enough to hire labour. The Mennonites had come to Russia as immigrants from Prussia. Through their industry, along with privileges granted by Tsarina Catherine who had invited them to Russia, many had grown wealthy with large estates and hired

Russian peasant labour. They, especially my father's family in Sagradovka, fit the description of "kulak" to a tee.

When my mother, Anna was six years old, her family decided to pull up stakes again and move more than 4000 kilometers east to the Amur region of Siberia.

The Franz Wiens family, my father Abram's family, like so many others, were denied the much-coveted exit permits to join the migration to Canada. So, they traveled to the Amur region as well, in 1927. Both Anna's family and Abram's family ended up in the same village, the new village of Schumanovka, named after the settlement of the same name in the Barnaul colony where Anna was born. The new village of Schumanovka was about three kilometers south of the Russian village of Klyuchi and about 20 kilometers North of Konstantinovka on the Amur River bordering Manchuria.

Abram's father Franz was a preacher in the community and Anna's father Jacob was a deacon. Life in the new colony was good for a few years. The small community seemed to have found the peace and freedom they were looking for. Once more, the hard-working Mennonite farmers were able to coax rich crops from the fertile soil and the farms were thriving.

They built schools and churches. The children were happy, farmers successful, families blessed to worship freely. Close to rich forests, the industrious Mennonites harvested the trees to build new homes and produced lumber for sale.

But, as is so often the reality in life, peace was fleeting.

The revolution caught up with them. The Russian government sent agents to the community. Leaders – like my grandfathers (a pastor and a deacon) – were interrogated. My father was 12 years old. He had experienced the terror of the marauding bandits in Sagradovka. Just a young boy, he was badly frightened, aware of the pervading tension as he lay in his bed at night listening to the secret police asking question after question. Faith and the Bible always seemed to surface as contentious issues in the interrogations. Past experience taught many hard lessons. Fear – agonizing fear – lurked close to the surface.

Anna was 10 years old. Her older brother Isaac, now a young man, was a respected leader in the community. Isaac, longing for peace, but knowing that immigration to North America was not possible, dreamed of a better way, a peaceful future, a new opportunity. While he worked the land, cared for livestock, went about daily chores, turbulent thoughts of change were swirling about in his mind.

Like many others in his small community of Schumanovka, he looked to the mountains of Manchuria on the other side of the Amur River. What might life be like beyond those mountains? There were rumours of Mennonites having escaped into China.

Isaac joined other community leaders as they began to meet secretly after dark. The conversation was hushed. They had to be very discreet about who was invited to these clandestine meetings. They knew that some in their community had been compromised and had agreed to cooperate with the Russian authorities. They talked late into the night many nights. New laws, social changes at the hands of the Communist Party, and challenges to their freedoms and right to worship worried the leaders. Would they experience another revolution? Would the secret agents sent from Moscow take their land, their profits, their schools, their churches? Increasingly higher and higher taxes of grain were being demanded and the government was insisting on collectivization of their land.

The leaders were determined to save each and every family in the village. No one should be left behind. People were allowed to invite close relatives from neighbouring villages to join the planned escape. There were just a few exceptions. They learned that there were men in the small community who had been compromised. In fear of persecution, they had become informers to the secret police. The leaders were careful that these men were not a part of the secret plans being made.

As the men deliberated, they discovered that leaders in New York, a small community nearby, were also exploring the idea of escape. They wanted to be included in the plans.

By the autumn of 1930, the community was determined to escape. The plans were well thought out. They decided to send two men secretly across the river with Alexander, a travelling Chinese smuggler, who agreed to be their guide. My Uncle Isaac was one of these men.

This was not an easy trip. Isaac, Alexander and the other scout, William Fehderau, were young and healthy. They were strong and quick – not hindered on their journey by women, children, the elderly or possessions. Even so, the trip was not easy. The weather was challenging. In spite of this, Isaac and Mr. Fehderau believed the escape was possible and the right thing to do. They brought their report to the other community leaders and all agreed with trembling knees that it was worth the risk.

They hired Alexander and another Chinese smuggler to be their guides. But they couldn't just pick up and leave. Isaac and the other leaders needed to make sure they thought of everything. Isaac was assigned to hide the Chinese guides in his attic.

And there was an added complication. The settlers from New York asked for a little more time, hoping to sell more of their crop to help finance their trip.

The men continued to meet in secret. The Russian government agents were suspicious. They made regular visits to the community. As much as possible they tried to make their trips a surprise, hoping to catch the farmers, their children or wives off guard, so they would slip up.

The agents watched for any signs of change. They saw all the work the farmers were doing on the sleds and with their horses. They quizzed them. The farmers were quick with their planned response. They showed the agents their contracts from the government to bring logs out of the forests.

Everyone involved in the planning was sworn to secrecy. Those who could not be trusted continued to be left out of the deliberations.

The Chinese guides were anxious to get going. They threatened to abandon the plan if the community was not ready to leave soon. Tensions were high. The leaders in New York were still holding out. They threatened to report the plans to the government if the people of Schumanovka left without them. They were suspicious and untrusting. The leaders of New York posted spies in Schumanovka every night, making sure they would not leave without their neighbouring village.

But the Chinese guides insisted that they needed to leave.

It was bitterly cold – 40 degrees below zero – the night of December 16, 1930. Just before midnight the New York spies went home, abandoning their watch. It was just too cold.

This was their chance.

Just after midnight, in spite of the frigid weather, the leaders of Schumanovka made their move. They gave the entire village 15 minutes to gather their possessions, their children, load their sleds and harness the horses. People dressed in their warmest clothing – fur-lined where possible. Their footwear was lined with felt. Young children and old folks were bundled in blankets. They were all instructed to gather in the centre of the village. There was no time to lose. They had to move.

This was a gut-wrenching decision to have to make – so much was in jeopardy!

Even though it was just over a week until Christmas, few families were thinking about carols, trees and gifts. They were terrified that their fortunes would change. My grandfather, Franz Wiens, a lay preacher in the community, had had regular interrogations from the secret police. Stalin's reign of terror was rising. Just 80 kilometers away, was the city of Blagoveshchensk, the administrative centre under Stalin for the region. A border detachment with machine guns was posted along the Amur River in Konstantinovka, less than 20 kilometers away.

Again and again, Mennonite leaders had answered the questions of their interrogators. They were under constant pressure to renounce their faith. They were being compelled to give up their farms to the collectivization plan of the state. Imagine, this would mean leaving their past behind and wholeheartedly embracing the Bolshevik revolution with all its political, cultural, religious and economic ramifications.

The secret agents were adamant. If they wanted peace, if they wanted protection from the state, they would have to give up their land, give up their faith, and turn over their Bibles. Their schools would be replaced by Russian communist-run schools. Their churches were to be abandoned.

The government did not give up. They came often and stayed late into the night.

The people longed for peace. They were convinced they needed to leave their village and find a new home, new opportunities and new peace. They looked longingly at the Blue Mountains across the Amur River in China. Was there freedom beyond those mountains? Was there a way of escape across the heavily guarded border with China?

It was -40 degrees. The mighty Amur River was frozen solid. This was the best time to escape. The village leaders had devised a daring plan. They prayed that God would be with them. It was a long shot. Children, women and older men would be packed into the newly refurbished sleds and they would travel through the waist deep snow to the border and then across the river. Travelling along the open roads was too risky. They would have to pass two Russian villages along the way. The plan was full of hardship and risk – the snow lay deep in the fields, the weather was frigid, the banks of the river were well guarded. But they were filled with hope –beyond those mountains was their freedom.

My mother, Anna, was just 10 years old. She was the youngest of eight siblings. She was a bright, happy young girl. She was well loved. And she had no idea what lay ahead. She was blissfully unaware of the drama that was unfolding and the scary adventure that awaited her. Her parents picked her up, sound asleep, and tucked her into the sled.

My dad, just a few houses away, had listened to the secret police and his 12-year-old ears picked up threads of the plan. He knew the risk. His father expected a lot of him and pushed him to contribute above his years. He was needed to drive one of the sleds.

The entire village – 217 people, with clothing and food for their journey – packed into 56 horse-drawn sleds. My father was tense, well aware of the dangers. There was not a moment to waste. The men fed the horses, preparing for a long, difficult journey. They opened the barns and let the cattle go free.

15 minutes. Families rushed out of their homes.

10 minutes. Men and women took what they were allowed. Bags of melba toasted "zwieback" were loaded on the sleds. Everyone was wearing their warmest clothing. Half-eaten meals were left on the tables.

5 minutes. Women carried small children. Fathers bundled them into the sleighs. Blankets, warm coats, mittens, scarves, hats and felt-lined boots. Children were packed tightly into the sleds against the cold and to keep them from being heard by Russians in the two villages they would pass along the way and by the agents patrolling the border on horseback. Mothers and fathers were terrified that their children would cry out, giving them away.

In so many ways, the risk before them was terrifying – it must have seemed daunting to these intrepid people. Their only hope was in God. The same God that had rescued the people of Israel from slavery in Egypt.

To avoid being seen by people in the Russian villages they would have to pass, they avoided the roads and set out across the fields. The men took turns breaking the trail through the meter-high snow for the sleds. Riders on horseback rode alongside to keep the caravan together and ensure quiet. All night they trudged across open fields toward the river, with Alexander as their guide. Because of the uneven terrain and obstacles along the way, sleds were toppled and broken. Working quickly, with freezing fingers, they cobbled together hasty repairs. One family had overloaded their sled, including all the meat of a newly butchered cow. It was too much for their sled and everything had to be abandoned in the field.

Finally, they reached the river banks. There was a steep drop of about three meters to the frozen river. The horses stopped at the cliff, trembling with fear. The drop was sharp and they instinctively balked, refusing to budge.

The refugees were desperate. The village of Konstantinovka, housing the feared border guards, was just one kilometer away. They could hear the dogs barking and roosters crowing. As they teetered at the edge of the cliff, Russian guards were patrolling the border and could come upon them at any moment. This was the community's only chance to escape their oppressors, they couldn't wait. Men and boys picked up sleds and threw them up against the backs of the horses, forcing them to move forward down the steep embankments. Sleds were broken and damaged. Goods were scattered on the ice below, but the horses surged forward.

Against all odds, they made it! They were safe on the other side of the Amur River.

When the sun rose and the fog cleared, they looked back across the river. They clearly saw the guards on patrol. They didn't know how they had made it across without being detected. No one had seen a guard the night before. They imagined that cold and fog were part of their protection, but they also thanked God for protecting them.

They had made it safely to China. The Russian guards couldn't hurt them anymore. But now they faced new challenges. They had to find a way to get permission from authorities to remain in China as refugees. This would involve a perilous two-day journey for two of their leaders to a Chinese city where they could plead their case.

As my father told the story of their escape – it was dramatic. He was a boy, doing the work of a man. Like many of the men, they retold the story – of how God had protected them with fog and ice and cold weather.

But no one knew the real story.

Years later, one of the men who had escaped that night, returned to Russia for a visit. By happenstance, he met a man from their neighbouring village of New York, which had been left behind the night of their escape. The conversation quickly turned to the miraculous escape that night of 1930. The man who had escaped marveled at their success, but the one who had been left behind said, "Oh, but let me tell you the rest of the story!

"Soon after that night, I ended up in prison on the Soviet side. There I struck up a conversation with one of the guards. We talked about the escape. I expressed how amazed we all were that the guards had not intercepted the fleeing villagers. They must have seen them.

'Of course, we saw them,' said the guard, 'I was on duty that night, and I watched as they fled. Many other guards saw the same thing. We tried in vain to get to the fleeing group and stop them, but they were surrounded by fiery beings who stood between us and them. The fiery beings would not let us pass.'"

Whether in a pillar of fire or by enveloping clouds, God was with them and rescued them.

China was not the end of their adventure. It was a stopping point, a temporary haven that gave them space to regroup and find a new home.

This is a photo of Mom's family taken in Schumanovka before the escape into China. Mom is the little girl on the right with a white collar standing between Grandpa Jacob and Grandma Liese. Uncle Isaac is in the top left.

4: Chinese Interlude

I can't imagine what they felt when they arrived safely on the Chinese side of the Amur River. Elation? Exhaustion? Fear? Hope? Uncertainty?

While they had successfully crossed the river, the journey was not without sacrifice. At 40 degrees below zero, the cold seeped through their warm clothes and blankets and even their felt-lined boots. Several people suffered severe frostbite. My grandfather Jacob even had to have a toe amputated, as did others. One family made a horrific discovery. When they dug into the blankets in their sled, they discovered that their toddler had suffocated during the night and died.

Alexander and his companion guide needed to be compensated for the risk they had taken. Each family gave their best horse to the Chinese guides as payment for their perilous contribution in the escape. Now that they were across the river, families had no further need for the horses. The remaining horses were sold to help fund the rest of their journey.

The Mennonites were used to organizing, making committees, assigning responsible leaders for specific roles. Once in China, they elected Jacob Siemens as their leader. With the same goal, they agreed to pool their resources to ensure that everyone would be provided for.

The Chinese villagers near the border did their best to accommodate all the refugees. But the Mennonites knew this was not their final stop in China. They had set the city of Harbin as their goal. The city was about 700 kilometers from their border crossing. The city was well known for its Russian population. At this time in history, about 40% of the people in Harbin were Russians. The Russians had been instrumental in building the railway link from Lake Baikal to Vladivostok, passing through Harbin.

One of the larger cities in China at the time, Harbin was well known as a fashion capital. On a highly travelled trade route, new fashions passed through the city from Moscow and Paris before they reached Shanghai. With Russian newspapers, journals, libraries and theatres, Harbin was an ideal place for the Mennonite refugees to regroup and explore their options. Their ultimate goal was to reach North America, and the Mennonite Central Committee (MCC) sent representatives to assist them.

But, before they could even continue their journey from the border to Harbin, they needed to secure some official documentation to allow them to remain in China as refugees. The group appointed three men to travel to the city of Sijiazixiang about 120 kilometers north, up the Amur River, to secure visas for the group. Sijiazixiang lay on the Chinese side of the Amur, directly across from the Russian city of Blagoveshchensk. A local Chinese merchant provided them with a sled and guides and the name of a Japanese hotel manager in Sijiazixiang who would be able to assist them. They skirted towns and villages along the way. It was important to avoid the police. Halfway to their destination they had to stop in the middle of the night to give their horses a break. While they rested and fed the horses, the police appeared. They angrily interrogated the Mennonite refugees, threatening to send them back to Russia. They went as far as to beat their Chinese guides. But, eventually, they let them continue on their journey. Finally, after a night and two days of travel in the bitter cold, the emissaries reached their destination. But their trouble was not over. The police appeared once more, threatening them and beating them again. The Japanese hotel manager finally came to their rescue.

With the help of the Japanese hotel manager, they were able to get visas for the group, and rent eight buses for the overland journey across the mountains to Qiqihar, and then on to Harbin by train. Today, the trip would take about eight hours. But at the time, the roads through the mountains were extremely rugged, and the buses, not well maintained or in very good condition, struggled over the icy mountain roads. For years the suffering Mennonites had looked with longing to the "blue mountains" of China. They saw it as freedom from life under Stalin's terror in Russia. (If you are a brave reader, Rudy Wiebe wrote a romantic, quasi history entitled *The Blue Mountains of China*. Wiebe's work gives an interesting glimpse into this time in Mennonite history. Also, Dick Thiessen, a family friend and neighbour to our family in Alberta, wrote a book entitled *Beyond Those Mountains*, chronicling Uncle Isaac's part in this story.)

Now they were to discover the challenges of crossing over those Blue Mountains to freedom.

Families crowded into the buses, with just barely enough room for everyone. The Franz Wiens family, along with three other families (31 people), was assigned to the largest bus. The buses were not like any you would imagine. Passengers were seated in a narrow passage, a wooden bench on each side. There was not really enough space for all the people and the last little boy had to be pushed in through the rear door, which was then barred from the outside. Their luggage was tied to the roof and on the fenders.

They set off, hopeful to reach Harbin. But it was winter and the roads were slick with ice. Late in the afternoon the bus carrying my dad's family slid off the icy road and tipped over into the ditch. The men in the bus went to the forest and cut logs to help push the bus out of the ditch. The other buses passed by as the men worked. Finally, they maneuvered the bus back onto the road. Within minutes of starting out again, the driver realized that something was seriously amiss. They stopped once more. The driver finally determined that one of the cylinders had cracked. The bus was not going anywhere.

The bus driver wrapped himself in his sheep skins, preparing to spend the night. The conductor started walking in the hope of finding help. The passengers feared they were being abandoned and might freeze to death. They decided to send three young men to follow the conductor, hoping he would lead them to a place where they could find lodging in this bitterly frigid night. After what seemed like a very long walk, the boys following the conductor were ready to give up and go back when they heard a dog bark.

There, in the middle of nowhere, they came upon a Buddhist monastery functioning as a wayside inn. The building was long and sleeping platforms were built along one wall. Under this platform, the exhaust from the fire provided some warmth.

When they reached the monastery, it was already past midnight. The three young men were exhausted. After a brief rest and a cup of tea, they walked back to the bus to tell the rest of the people what they had found. Each of the passengers took warm bedding and some food. Every adult was carrying baggage or a child. Two elderly members of the community could not manage the walk and had to be helped along. It was slow going. They reached the monastery at eight in the morning.

They were drained, but safe and out of the frigid weather. They eagerly waited for the bus to appear. Finally, they saw it coming. The inoperative bus was being slowly towed by two oxen. It was clear that they would not be on their way any time soon.

The driver sent his conductor on ahead with a passing motorist to get a new cylinder. It took several days for him to go to the city, purchase the cylinder and return to the monastery. And, can you believe it – the cylinder was the wrong size! He would have to return to the city, return the cylinder and purchase a new one. The bus driver, hired for this trip, was anxious to make sure the people did not abandon him and hire another vehicle to complete their journey.

The group had packed enough food for a three-day trip. They had rationed their food to make sure they would have enough for the full trip. But the delay – much longer than they expected – meant their food supplies were diminishing quickly. There were no grocery stores or markets in the area. They decided to barter some of their belongings, meagre as they were, for food with the monks at the monastery. The monks were only able to provide them with some kind of slimy gruel of millet, which was almost inedible. They called it "Tschumisa."

They tried to sleep, but discovered the sleeping platform was infested by lice. They had no sanitation, no clean clothing (their suitcases with their clothes were on the other buses), no way to alleviate the agony of the lice crawling over their bodies. The group that had gone on ahead finally decided to send help from their end. Two vehicles arrived to pick up the stranded passengers.

After negotiating with their bus driver and the monks at the monastery about the additional costs, they were once more on their way across the mountains. The one in charge at the monastery had to be satisfied with one of their fur coats as payment, because they were out of money. As they were descending toward their destination, one of their vehicles blew a tire and they were stranded again. This time they negotiated with the owners of some passing two-wheeled farm carts and sleds to take them to the next village. Finally, they reached a place where they could get temporary lodging. By this time, they were discouraged almost to the point of despair.

Many were suffering severe frostbite. Their Chinese hosts helped them by rubbing their limbs with snow.

One of the young men went ahead to the bus station in the next town to arrange for a bus to pick up all the passengers. On his way back to the temporary lodging, he met a man carrying a basket full of bread. With signs and gestures, he understood that the man's wife was the baker and spoke some Russian. When he finally got back to the waiting passengers and told them what he had found, every family took a pillow to trade for some bread.

The trip for the other families was less of an adventure, but not without some drama. One of the buses stopped abruptly, ordering all of the men and children to get out of the bus. The women stayed in the bus and busied themselves to help deliver a baby! On another bus an old man breathed his last breath. The bus stopped briefly, allowing the men to carry the body into the snowy field. They buried their lifeless brother in the snow, prayed together and carried on.

The entire group was united again in Qiqihar, the halfway point to their destination. There the tired and bedraggled refugees were finally able to bathe, change their clothes and eat a decent meal. They dragged their suitcases to their rooms, eager to put on clean clothes. When they lifted the cases, they were much too light. They had been robbed!

The group was held up here for a short while. They were asked to wait in Qiqihar while MCC and the German consulate arranged lodging for them in Harbin. As already mentioned, Russian was commonly spoken in Harbin and many of the refugees were fluent in Russian. It was a large and modern city and they had access to help from the German consulate and MCC.

After their miraculous escape from Russia, it took a grueling two months to cross the Blue Mountains and reach Harbin.

Finally, the refugees felt safe. But they had not yet found a home.

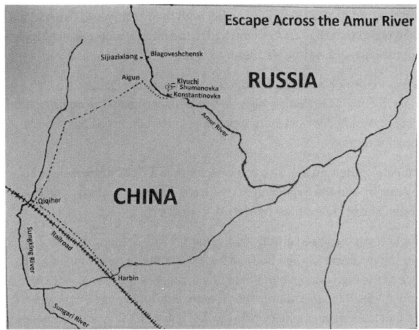

The dotted lines in this map follow the path of my parents escape into China on December 17, 1930. From their village of Schumanovka they travelled by sleds, crossing at Konstantinovka. From there they travelled by bus through Aigun to Qiqihar and then by train to Harbin.

They had successfully escaped the fear and repression they had experienced in Russia. Ultimately, they were looking for the freedom and opportunity they had heard about from their relatives who had been fortunate enough to escape and find new homes in North America.

All of them had friends or relatives who had emigrated during the great migration to North America between 1920 and 1926. Canadian and American Mennonites had worked together to bring 20,000 desperate fellow Mennonites out of their life of repression, fear and starvation in Russia. Many of them, including my dad's uncle David Wiens, ended up in Kitchener, Ontario. From Kitchener many were dispersed as farm hands to Mennonite farms across Canada.

Both my maternal and paternal grandparents had siblings who had made it out of Russia legally during that migration. My grandparents had travelled to Moscow and begged for exit permits to be able to join the migration. But they were denied. Without cell phones, email or even a reliable postal service, they did not have regular contact with their relatives in Canada, but they had heard that the families who had made it to Canada were enjoying freedom and a much better life there.

China was in turmoil because it had just been invaded by Japan. Unemployment was extremely high, so the refugees had to be content with the most undignified jobs at starvation wage in Harbin. It was not an ideal situation for them.

Unfortunately, their escape also coincided with the stock market crash in North America and the beginning of the Great Depression. Both Canada and the United States closed their borders to immigrants.

This shabby and displaced group of Mennonites was desperate. They needed to find a way to keep body and soul together in their time of exile. Because of the high unemployment in China, most of the Mennonite men were not allowed to work there. The women, girls and young boys were able to find low-paying menial work. My dad tells of finding work carrying bags for wealthy Russian shoppers, and even carrying human waste to the fields as fertilizer. The little they earned was gathered together and used for the good of the community.

This is the house at 53 Ji Lin Street in Harbin where 217 refugees lived for more than a year.

With help from MCC and Germany, they rented a large three-story house from a wealthy Japanese businessman. Here the refugees lived in extremely crowded conditions. Sixty-five men, women and children were crowded on each floor, with as many as 32 people to a room. One cooking station had to be shared by the entire floor.

While living conditions were extremely crowded, couples still found time for the joys and pleasure of normal human intimacy. In the midst of their destitution and poverty, Uncle Isaac and Tante Liese welcomed a new daughter into their family, born after almost one year in Harbin.

China had no intention of letting the refugees stay. They were told that they had to leave China within two years or they would be repatriated to Russia.

The dream of freedom, over the Blue Mountains of China, seemed to be eluding them.

In the meantime, the Mennonite Central Committee (MCC) and the German consulate were not idle. They worked diligently in Harbin to find a country that would accept these tired, homeless refugees.

Poor food, overcrowded shelter, little privacy and poor sanitation meant that the Mennonite refugees struggled to stay in reasonably good health. Their health was extremely important, because they would not be allowed immigration to another country if they could not pass the requisite health inspection. So, they hired doctors to treat conditions that might keep them from being accepted as immigrants anywhere else. Because my dad's uncle Abram was so malnourished and anemic, the doctor prescribed for him to go to the market and drink a cup of warm beef blood every day. But not all illnesses could be cured. My dad's youngest brother was the sole survivor of a set of twins born almost two years earlier. He had been sickly since birth. He died and was buried in Harbin.

Week after wearisome week, they waited for good news. Week after disheartening week, there was nothing but disappointment. The MCC reps and the German consulate came up empty-handed at every turn. Finally, in an international consultation, Paraguay agreed to accept some refugees. The Paraguayan government was intent on settling the sparsely populated Paraguayan Chaco. This was not an ideal setting for hard-working Mennonite families used to the fertile soils of the Ukraine. The Chaco is a semi-arid region consisting of more than 60% of Paraguay's land area, but with less than 10% of the population. The government offered resettlement to these hardy and industrious Mennonites who had conquered the

Ukrainian steppes. They were hopeful that the new settlers would master the land and prove beneficial to the economy of Paraguay.

The MCC reps were not unaware of the challenges of settling in Paraguay. They were already working with a group of Canadian Mennonites who had sought refuge in Paraguay in hopes of starting a community that could determine its own government and education, much like they had done when they settled in Russia. The ancestors of these settlers had immigrated to Canada in 1870. Then in the 1920s they had left Canada in protest against the attempt of the Canadian government to integrate Mennonite children into the public school system. Looking for more freedom to maintain their language and culture, they had established the first Mennonite colony – the Menno colony – in Paraguay in 1927.

The Mennonite refugees in Harbin had little choice. No other country opened their doors to them. They agreed to go to Paraguay to settle in proximity to the Mennonite community already there and, hopefully, to establish a safe new home of their own.

After just over one year in Harbin, they began to plan for their departure from China to their new home in Paraguay. The journey would be long and arduous. They travelled over land and sea, passing through China, South Korea, Vietnam, India, over the Indian Ocean to Africa through the Suez Canal, across the Mediterranean Sea to Europe, through France to Le Havre and then across the Atlantic Ocean to South America and then by river and overland to Paraguay.

Financial arrangements for their travel were made by MCC, with a loan from Germany. By this time, the group of Mennonites had grown from the original 273 people who had crossed the Amur on December 17, 1930. A number of other people had also crossed the border individually or in smaller groups. There was even a group from another village in Russia that had crossed the day before Schumanovka's escape.

On February 22, 1932, a total of 373 people crowded into three railway cars. There was very little wiggle room! They traveled 800 kilometers to Changchun, where they changed trains. Japan had recently invaded China, and at Changchun they changed to a Japanese train, which was much more comfortable than the Chinese train.

When they reached the Liaodong Bay, they were packed like sardines into a small Japanese boat for the voyage to Shanghai, where they arrived on February 27. In Shanghai, they boarded the 25,000-ton French ship D'Artagnan for the long and grueling ocean voyage to the south coast of France.

The entire group was assigned a room below deck with bunk beds. They were not impressed with the food. The bread rolls were so hard that they had to break them with a hammer. My dad would horrify us with stories of frequently finding mice in the food.

This is the SS D'Artagnan on which they travelled from Shanghai to Marseille in France.

5: Shanghai to Paraguay

This was an ocean adventure Anna would never forget.

For her, the sea voyage was fascinating. So many people to meet and so many new things to see and experience.

A guilty pleasure she experienced on the ship stayed with her. In an area frequented by the more affluent travelers, she heard loud music coming out of a large room. She peeked in through the open door and saw men and women dancing together. This was an activity strictly forbidden in her devout Mennonite culture, but it looked like such a lively and amusing pastime to her. She was overcome by guilt. It was not until more than 50 years later when she visited us in the Philippines that she got to dance her heart out in a Kalinga feast celebrating my parents' visit.

The journey from Shanghai to Paraguay was nearly 18,000 kilometers! As they traveled, Anna remembers seeing many mountains. As she leaned over the deck of the ship, she watched sharks and dolphins playing in the water. Sometimes, to everyone's surprise, flying fish would actually land right on the deck.

They travelled to Hong Kong, where they had a short layover. Then they sailed on to Saigon, where they spent several days in port. Just imagine this ragtag group of weary refugees meandering through the streets of Saigon. They were able to visit the Saigon Zoo, one of the oldest zoos in the world! At the Zoo, Anna saw animals she had not even heard of or imagined before.

From Saigon, they went on to Singapore and then to Colombo where they spent a day. From Colombo they went through the Arabian Sea and the Gulf of Aden.

They docked at Socotra Island, considered one of the most isolated landforms in the world. From there they entered the Red Sea. As they entered the Red Sea, they celebrated Good Friday. For Anna's family and the Mennonites travelling to their new homeland, the passage was very meaningful. They could not help but marvel at the parallels with the story of the Israelites, as they were led out of Egypt and political bondage. In the same way, the Mennonite families were being led by God, out of the land of Russian bondage, to a new land of opportunity.

They celebrated Easter in the Suez Canal and then entered the Mediterranean Sea. The voyage over the Mediterranean Sea was rough. Huge waves actually came over the side of the ship.

The sea calmed as they passed Sicily. On April 1, they landed at Marseille. There they were met by representatives from the League of Nations and examined by medical staff. The Red Cross had small gifts for the children.

After travelling by ship for over a month, the group of refugees left Marseille very early the next morning and travelled by train across France to Le Havre. Two of the families were unable to continue the journey due to medical concerns.

The group arrived in Paris at seven in the morning. The Red Cross was waiting with breakfast. Anna was impressed by the magnificent buildings and the beautiful cars. Then they boarded another train. This leg was just over two hours and at 1:20 PM they reached their destination. Le Havre, the point at which the Seine River meets the English Channel, is one of the most important seaports in northern France. There, vehicles were waiting to take them to a hotel for lunch. Once they had finished lunch, they were given another medical exam. Then they had dinner and stayed at the hotel for the night.

The next morning, April 3, was my father's 14th birthday! So young, he had already experienced so much!

They ate breakfast, then everyone had a bath – the ladies in one room and the men in another. How glorious it felt to be clean again. After lunch, they had a worship service where they sang, *"Der Herr hat Grosses an uns getan des sind wir fröhlich"* (The Lord has done great things for us and so we rejoice). Based on Psalm 126, the song celebrates the goodness of God.

After the service, Benjamin H. Unruh, representing MCC, spoke to the group. Mennonites from Europe were also present and they distributed clean clothing, especially for the children. Anna got a beautiful new dress. Mr. Unruh retold the story of the complex negotiations for their recolonization to Paraguay. While the families understood the difficulty in arranging the trip, most had no idea just how complicated it was. It touched their hearts to realize how many organizations and individuals were involved. It was humbling to recognize that so many had voluntarily worked together to manage this journey to freedom and new opportunity for them.

Unruh felt it was essential to make it clear to the families that their challenges were not over yet. The team planning the trip had been expecting 60 families and now there were 80 families hoping to find a new life and opportunities in Paraguay. That meant they had to rejig the plan. They had gathered implements, tools and supplies for 60 families. They needed to re-distribute the supplies so that all 80 families would receive what they needed to start.

The families had already self-divided into 4 village groupings. Each group had a preacher and teacher assigned to them. But, in Paraguay, they had only made accommodations for 3 villages. Changes needed to be made here to accommodate the additional numbers and changes would need to be made in Paraguay for an additional village. Mr. Unruh continued to moderate the arrangements and leaders were elected for each village. Farm implements were distributed, and each family received a plow, harrow, saw, axe and hammer. (Remember, they traveled with very little and would arrive at their new home with little but what they could carry.) There was a wagon for every four families. In Paraguay, each family would receive a team of oxen.

The Red Cross gave them some instruction on how to avoid the many new diseases they would face. The German Consul in Le Havre, Dr. Bergfeld, expressed appreciation for the very positive impression the refugees had made on all the people they had encountered in France. He emphasized their discipline and good behaviour, as well as the excellent arrangements that had been made for their resettlement.

But the unexpected arrival of 20 more families than they had planned for was not the only challenge. Argentina demanded an exorbitant head tax on each person who would be travelling through Argentina. The German government and the Red Cross advocated robustly for the refugees and negotiated with the government of Argentina, calling the tax an inhumane "sabotage." It was rescinded.

Then Paraguay insisted on optometric examinations, making sure all refugees were free of infectious disease. The optometrist who had tested the refugees in the port noted 57 mild cases of trachoma. This caused a dilemma for the whole team. Would those 57 individuals have to stay back? That was unthinkable – after they had already come so far?

Mr. Unruh chose to send them all on to Paraguay, with a note from the medical staff that there were no infectious diseases among the refugees. While a few people were held back at the port for medical reasons, when all was said and done, 368 passengers were ready to travel to South America.

The Mennonite families, with new clothes, information and immense hope, lined up to board the ocean liner Croix at 1:30 PM on April 5. They were eager and apprehensive for their transatlantic voyage to Buenos Aires.

For 24 days they lived on the Croix. A few highlights punctuated the long days at sea.

They crossed the equator on April 17. The ocean liner served a feast to celebrate. On April 23, they crowded on deck as they passed Rio de Janeiro. There, from the ship, they saw the giant "Christ the Redeemer" statue on top of the 700-meter Corcovado Mountain. The statue reminded them how Christ had redeemed them from the yoke of bondage and set them on a new path to freedom. On April 28, they made a brief stop in Montevideo, Uruguay. There several Russians boarded the ship and questioned the Mennonite refugees. They were intrigued that this large group of people had left their homeland – the Russian paradise they remembered. Then, at last, on April 29 they entered the port of Buenos Aires, Argentina.

But their journey was hardly over.

Paraguay is a landlocked country with no seaports. This meant that they would have to continue their journey by river and overland travel. In Buenos Aires, they all boarded the small river boat, Roma, and set off up the Parana River. This led to the Paraguay River, which would take them to Asunción, the capital of Paraguay. They made a brief stop in Asunción and were met by a representative from the Fernheim colony in the Chaco region. He came on board to greet and welcome them.

They continued along the river to Puerto Casado, where they transferred with all their luggage to small railway cars. The trip to the Chaco region was 145 kilometers. That was the end of the railway line.

The trip took all day. At Kilometer 145, fellow Mennonites from the Fernheim Colony, who had settled there two years earlier, came to welcome them. Their "brothers and sisters" were there waiting for them with ox carts. They had butchered a cow and were squatting around campfires on which they were cooking a welcome meal. They had brought many wagons with them.

The refugees transferred all their worldly possessions onto the carts provided by their Mennonite neighbours. Travel to their new home was slow. They stopped at every watering hole along the way to let the oxen drink and graze. Children and women filled water containers at each opportunity. They were travelling through a semi-arid region.

Finally, after three days of grueling travel, they reached their new home!

They stopped the ox cart procession beside a brand new well dug in preparation for their arrival. They unloaded their luggage. Then their friends and the ox carts turned around, leaving the refugees to begin their new life – building houses again and planting gardens in what was now to be their home. Initially, many set up housekeeping in crudely built holes in the ground covered by tarps.

The refugees built a fire and cooked their first meal in their new homeland. They ate it under a fresh and clear sky. The Southern Cross, as prominent in the Southern Hemisphere as the Big Dipper is in the northern hemisphere, shone over them as they ate.

They were home!

This was the last night of their epic journey. And it was the first night in what would be an equally epic battle with the Chaco wilderness. Semi-arid, isolated and brutally hot, this place would drive them to their knees. Unlike the "paradise" of pre-war Russia, the land wrestled with the farmers. In a land where thorns and cactus thrived, they would try to grow wheat. Familiar with the seasonal changes of Russia and the Northern Hemisphere, they were tragically unprepared for the burning heat of the desert they had come to. They had to learn to cultivate new crops in an environment totally foreign to them.

This is the SS Croix on which they travelled from Le Havre, France to Buenos Aires, Argentina.

6: The Green Hell

Life in the Chaco was hell.

MCC had promised the new immigrants a place to live, farmland and the equipment to work the land. But when they arrived, there was virtually nothing. Each family received meagre tools. They set up tents. There was no fresh water, and disease was rampant. The soil, sandy and unstable, was treacherous. Digging a new well was terrifying. At any moment the well could collapse.

There was a constant battle with the elements. The climate was so utterly different from what they knew from their experience living in Russia, where the Mennonite people had farmed with great success for more than 100 years. As quickly as possible they cleared some land to plant gardens. Leaf-cutter ants and swarms of locusts consumed their plants. They had never seen anything like it. They had never even heard of these nasty pests. Nothing had prepared them for this.

The land was untamed. Safe drinking water was hard to find. To fight the unbearable heat, they needed cold, fresh water. They worked hard, their bodies literally fighting against the elements. They fought diseases they had never before encountered, especially malaria.

It was critical to dig wells, but digging deep holes in the sandy soil by hand was extremely difficult and dangerous. My family tells stories of people miraculously saved from the collapse of wells being dug. They literally had to eke out a living from an untamed wilderness.

These Mennonite farmers were not quitters! They compared their experiences with the children of Israel. Their God was with them. They were determined, industrious, hardworking and stubborn. With these qualities and with God's help, they transformed this "Green Hell" into what is now regarded as the breadbasket of Paraguay.

The MCC had promised to support the refugees with food aid for their first six months in the Chaco. But they couldn't anticipate the declaration of war between Paraguay and Bolivia. This made it nearly impossible to move supplies inland from Asunción.

The settlers worked as quickly as possible to clear plots of land to plant gardens. They learned from their initial disasters that the plants they had been used to growing in Russia were not viable for this part of Paraguay. Neighbouring Mennonites showed them how to plant manioc (cassava or yuca, an edible root that has to be cooked properly to destroy toxins before it can be safely included in stews and soups), sweet potatoes, sorghum (cereal grain), beans and watermelon. Watermelon thrived in the sandy soil.

The soldiers fighting in the conflict between Bolivia and Paraguay moved back and forth across their land. The Mennonite families learned to live in the space between the warring armies. The Paraguayan army took over their hospital in Filadelfia, promising that the military doctors would also treat the settlers. My father learned that soldiers were happy to accept watermelons in exchange for quinine pills. He needed these to treat frequent bouts of malaria brought on by the ever-present marauding mosquitoes.

As established in France, months before, the refugees settled in four different clearings. There already were 13 Mennonite villages in the region which had been settled by Mennonite refugees who had come 2 years earlier and established the Fernheim Colony.

The Mennonites were organized! The villages were all numbered. The four new villages were Blumenort #14, Orloff #15, Karlsruhe #16 and Schoenau #17. Both of my grandparents settled in Orloff – so my mother and father lived in the same village again!

They structured the villages much like they had in Russia. A street ran down the middle, with homestead lots on either side of the street. They parceled land to the families by drawing lots, a common practice in the Mennonite communities. The street in Orloff ran east to west. My mother's family was granted a parcel of land that was in the middle of the village, on the south side of the main street. The lot next to them was reserved for the school they had yet to build. This was similar to the arrangement they had left in Schumanovka. My father's family were given a lot on the west end of the village.

Dad had turned 14 on the journey to Paraguay and Mom was almost 12 when they arrived in Paraguay. Their family name, Wiens, was the same, but their home lives couldn't have been more different. Although they shared the "Wiens" surname and lived in the same village, the way they experienced life – their home life, the way they experienced the refugee journey, and their homesteading experiences were as different as night and day.

My father, strong and healthy, carried a substantial share of the family's workload. He was more robust than his elder brother and so he was often assigned the heavier end of a task. Just a 12-year-old boy when they fled Russia, he had been given the responsibility to drive the family's second sled across the Amur River into China. While he had been called on to help with chores in Russia, such as feeding fuel to the hungry steam engine that ran his father's threshing machine, the responsibility expected of him during the escape marked the beginning of his father's dependency on him. While he often felt that his older brother got preferential treatment, my father felt an immense burden of hard work without his father's affirmation. He was simply expected to work hard and received very little encouragement.

In Paraguay he was no longer a boy, but a man, and expected to do a man's work. He laboured alongside the men, clearing fields for planting, building homes, planting and harvesting crops. He remembers cutting logs in the forest with his older brother. Because he was bigger than his brother, the heavier end of the log was laid on his shoulders. Again and again, the heavier burden was laid on him. He was convinced that the slipped disc which caused him so much pain throughout his life was a result of experiences like this.

My father felt he carried a healing touch in his strong fingers, much like his cousin Tina who had begun medical training in Russia. He dreamt of becoming a medical doctor. But the dream seemed pointless: he was a poor refugee in a community resistant to new ways; there was no school or university nearby; there was no money to send him to school; and the practice of medicine was not seen as the best way to get ahead in life.

He begged his parents to let him apprentice to their cousin Tina Ratzlaff-Epp, who was applying her medical training from Russia and now served the colony as the chiropractor/herbal healer. But his parents would hear none of it. They saw little opportunity for financial success as a medical professional. On the other hand, as the colony grew, there were increasing opportunities for carpenters to earn extra income.

In the end, his parents decided for him.

Two years after they had arrived in the Chaco, Dad was assigned to serve as a carpenter's apprentice with Mr. Martens in village #8 (Schoenwiese). This village was a distance from my grandparent's home. Mr. Loewen, who lived in nearby village #17 (Schoenau), was also a carpenter, but he already had enough apprentices.

Village #8 was a six-hour walk away from my father's home. As an apprentice, he received room and board, and his training costs were covered, but he was paid almost nothing for the work he did. He worked as an apprentice for three years. If it rained or there was no carpentry work, the apprentice was put to work plowing, planting crops and building fences. If wood was needed, the apprentice was sent into the forest to cut logs. The apprentice provided a significant advantage for the lead carpenter. With no significant cost to the family, they had free labour.

Mr. Martens was very particular and a hard taskmaster. He was a proud man. He drove his "droschkje" (carriage pulled by horses) with a stiff reign. He drove his apprentices with the same rigid control.

My father remembers his first trip home after working with Mr. Martens for a full week. He walked through the bush in the oppressive daytime heat. As the evening set in, the heat began to subside. The Southern Cross constellation guided his way along the narrow wagon trail. While the world was struggling through the Great Depression, Abram was mired in his own depressive thoughts. Cautiously he made his way through the black jungle night.

He didn't really want to be a carpenter. He wanted to study. He knew God had gifted him with a healing hand. Once more, he recalled how he had begged his parents to let him apprentice to the local chiropractor. "If I can't go to school," he pleaded, "at least let me apprentice to learn chiropractic and healing arts with Cousin Tina."

His memory of the argument left him feeling raw as he walked through the woods. Stepping carefully through the darkness, he noticed the dim outline of a large tree branch lying across the trail. As he bent down to pick it up, he suddenly let out a hoarse scream and jumped back in terror. The tree branch was alive and slithered menacingly out of his grasp. With a pounding pulse he charged off for home, making a wide detour around the deadly boa. Thorns and branches tore at his clothes and skin as he charged ahead. His coarse canvas shorts made the insides of his legs raw. Every shadow terrified him.

As he ran, his memory was alive and vivid. His young mind replayed a terrible scene that happened in the first months of their homesteading. Once more he heard the horrific yelping of his young puppy, as a puma, on the hunt in the new village, dragged it out of the newly built make-shift shelter. He couldn't escape the puppy's high-pitched screams as it wrestled in a futile fight for its life. It seemed nothing was safe in this hell called Chaco. The scream of the puppy seemed to awaken a subconscious memory of the horrible night so many years ago in Sagradovka when bandits had attacked his family in their home and his mother had let out a bloodcurdling scream of terror.

If he really was the tough 16-year-old young man his parents insisted he be, then he shouldn't be so afraid in the dark. But he had to admit, he was afraid. Regardless of his family's taunting, he couldn't deny his fear and anger, at least not to himself.

Finally, the dim lights of the kerosene lamps in the windows of Orloff homes came into view. Winded and still shaking, he turned off the dusty track onto his parents' yard, the first home on the western end of the village. As he entered the front room, his mother Anna glanced up from her needlework long enough to stretch out her hand asking for his meagre pay.

His father Franz didn't even look up from the table where he sat preparing tomorrow's sermon. As Abram's trembling hands fumbled through the pockets of his rough canvas shorts, he blurted out the story about his encounter with the boa and how he had almost put his hands into the deadly trap. His mother took the money and ignored her son: "So, you are here now! Go to bed and get ready for tomorrow."

Anger, resentment, and deep sadness surged through my father as he stepped outside to relieve himself before bed. "Dear God," he whispered through clenched teeth, looking up at the starry heaven above, "doesn't anybody care even one little bit who I am and what happens to me?"

In sullen silence he slipped back through the front room to the boys' room in the back of their simple adobe cottage. He was exhausted.

He stretched out on the straw-filled sack. His brothers were sound asleep. From his cot on the other side of the room his 18-year-old brother Hans mumbled something about making too much noise, but Abram paid no attention to him. Although his body was exhausted, his mind and emotions were in turmoil as he stared into the darkness.

Abram grappled with his parents' focus on money. "Why was it that money seemed to be the most important thing for his parents?" he wondered. "Where was the laughter? Where was the joy? Where was the love and concern for each other? For their children?"

Life was tough! The "Green Hell" of Paraguay fought against them at every turn. And from what my father saw, it was winning in his family. But he saw laughter and love in families around him. They faced the same challenges, but their home life was different.

He stretched his youthful mind back to his earliest memories in Russia. He remembered their estate in Sagradovka. It wasn't elaborate, but it was well-kept with pride and hard work. His grandfather Abram Fast, the wealthy father-in-law of his father Franz, had lived in a joint household with his family for as long as he could remember. It was the proceeds from Opa Fast's large estate that had covered the cost of their move to Schumanovka, where his Opa and Oma Fast had died shortly before the great escape.

Even in the times of plenty and safety, there had been little joy and laughter. He remembered his grandfather's intent on wealth – money drove him, possessions claimed him. Abram's father, my grandfather, followed in his father's footsteps. Even in extreme poverty, my grandfather and grandmother had one goal: to become rich again.

My father hardly remembered plenty. He lived through the horrific demolition of his community in Sagradovka. He watched as his grandfather Johann Julius Wiens stubbornly refused to leave his Estate. He saw the waste as he protected something that was destroyed.

He was just a boy in post-revolutionary Russia, but little boys have sharp ears.

The Bolshevik Revolution was not history for him. It had imprinted terror into my father's young life. He was there when his grandfather and father had told the story. He knew what it was like to live in constant fear.

Neighbouring villages were decimated by raging bandits. One day they heard that the dreaded Makhno bandits were in the neighbouring village. Everyone grabbed what they could. They hid in the wheat fields. Mothers, fathers, grandmothers and grandfathers trembled, faces close to the dirt. They shushed the children. And they listened.

All through the night they heard the bandits – shouting, celebrating, and destroying everything. They heard the crackle of fire, the sound of broken glass. Early in the morning, as the sun began to rise, my great-grandfather Fast, Opa Franz's father-in-law, Grandpa Franz and Dad's uncle Abram, slithered through the wheat, keeping their bodies low to the ground, taking shallow breaths, praying for the bandits to be gone. As they reached the edge of the field, they saw the swarthy, strong Russians destroying everything.

There was another memorable day when the bandits actually attacked them in their home. While the men were forced to face the wall, the bandits turned their guns on the women and children, finally leaving with whatever loot they could carry with them.

My father, just a boy at the time, never forgot that day.

As he lay in his lumpy, straw-stuffed cot, Abram conjured memories of his Wiens grandparents. He could hardly remember their faces, but he remembered their pride, their work ethic, their unmovable determination to protect everything they had worked so hard for.

He remembered that they were rich with land, a productive farm, workers, livestock – everything they had hoped for when they first moved to Sagradovka on the rugged Ukraine steppes. They adored Tsarina Katherine the Great, who invited them. They clung to her promises.

But they clung to false hope. Catherine the Great's vision was long forgotten by the Russians. The Bolesheviks wanted revenge. Lenin and Stalin wanted power. What the raging bandits didn't destroy, collectivization did. My great-grandfather Wiens did not waver. He stayed with his land. He let his children go.

Memories of his Opa and Oma Fast were more fresh in his mind. Opa Fast had been one of the wealthiest estate owners in Sagradovka. He had chosen his son-in-law, my grandpa Franz Wiens to manage the estate with him. Together Opa and Oma Fast and my father's family had chosen to sell the estate in search of new opportunities in Siberia. This was the move which had finally brought them to Schumanovka and given them the opportunity to escape into China, although Opa and Oma Fast had died shortly before that momentous night.

While my father and his family struggled to tame the hellish land they were given, they learned that his grandparents who had stayed on their Estate in Sagradovka had died. While one son had migrated to Canada and the others to Siberia, they had stayed on their land. Abram, my father, recalled with a shudder how word had reached his family just the year before, that his grandparents had died of starvation on their Estate. Tenaciously clinging onto what little they had left, my great-grandfather and great-grandmother died as Stalin purged the nation of the bourgeois (1930-1933). The new Russia honoured the worker and the national. They systematically worked to cull the rich capitalists and outsiders. My great-grandparents were just two of the Russian Mennonites who refused to give up the land they loved.

I know my father tried to understand. He carried the weight of striving for prosperity with him his whole life. He wondered if the loss of the dream of prosperity made his parents hard and bitter.

That night, in his cot, while he drifted toward sleep, he visualized a different dream for his life. He saw laughter, lightheartedness, and song. He pictured himself telling stories and reading to his children and grandchildren. If and when he had to discipline them, he would do it in a firm yet loving manner.

My mother's family couldn't have been more different than my father's. Even though they lived just a few houses apart and shared the same last name, they shared little else. I wonder at the choices we make. Comparing my grandparents, I can easily see that circumstance is meaningless. Both families lived through identical experiences. They both lost their homes in the madness of Russia. They both escaped across the dark, deep freeze of

Siberia into China. They both lived through the uncertainty of being refugees with no home. They both travelled from Russia to Siberia to China to Paraguay. They both were trying to eke out some living in this God-forsaken hell.

But their homes were polar opposites.

Jacob and Liese Wiens had a beautiful evening tradition. After supper, when the chores were all done, they lit a fire in the neatly swept yard. The smoke from the fire helped to repel the ever-present mosquito hordes. But more importantly, the fire gathered the family together.

My mother loved the evening fire. Just 14 years old, my mother, Anna, was joy-filled and carefree. Anna was the youngest. Her 19-year-old brother Abram still lived at home and was always around the fire with them. Her oldest brother Isaac, one of the leaders of the exodus from Russia, brought his family to the evening fire. Her 3 married sisters and brother Jacob often joined them as well. They sang, laughed, and told stories. If no one felt like singing, my mother sang alone! In those moments – sitting together on a simple, worn canvas, the harsh life they lived fell away.

Grandpa Jacob and Grandma Liese Wiens in Orloff, Paraguay.

My mother, just a young girl, loved the quiet stability of her family. When tensions rose, she struggled.

She remembers a night that she sang alone, her parents deep in conversation. Suddenly, her parents' soft conversation became an argument and Anna's song was lost. She watched her father stalk off into the dark night.

Anna was full of questions. Her mother refused to say a word and sent Anna off to bed.

Anna remembers lying there, hoping to hear the soft murmur of her parents talking before they fell asleep, as they did most nights. The silence was stark, loud, hurtful.

Anna's life was just as difficult as Abram's, but Anna's parents had built a home in that tiny thatched cottage. Her mother worked in her garden, growing the food so important to their family. Her father owned and managed the small village store. He loved his work there, meticulously keeping records of his meager inventory of sugar, flour, and bolts of cloth. He knew the mounting debts of the struggling settlers. He was generous with them, caring more for the people than building his own wealth. He listened sincerely to their stories of hardship and struggle, and he encouraged them with words of empathy and compassion. My grandfather, Jacob, was a wise man, a man who embraced life, people and, most of all, his family, with love.

Because of Jacob's gentle, pastoral manner he was chosen as a deacon in the fledgling Mennonite Brethren Church in the colony. Although deeply pious, he found this calling on his life difficult. Being in church leadership often required participation in heated discussion with the other men on the leadership team. Especially difficult for him were the discipline cases the leaders had to confront. This was a heavy burden for him. They were miles and miles from any civil court. Miscreant behaviour was dealt with by the church leaders. The small Mennonite village was not immune to the dark nature of people. Unethical deals, immorality and anti-social behaviour came to the church leaders. He shared his concern, his pain and the challenges of leadership with his wife, but it was very difficult for him.

Anna, sensitive and happy, rarely saw her parents upset at each other. Even one night was too many. She didn't understand all of the difficult issues her parents faced or her father dealt with. Her little world was beautiful. As she drifted off to sleep, she turned her mind to dreams of a future filled with unending bliss, dreams expressed in one of her all-time favourite songs, "Wo Die Liebe Wohnt" (Love at Home).

The next morning at breakfast, Jacob and Liese chatted in their usual amiable manner. Anna breathed a sigh of relief. Her dream was once again on track.

After three years my father, Abram, completed his apprenticeship with Mr. Martens. He moved back home with his parents in Orloff.

He remembers baptismal Sunday in the Orloff Mennonite Brethren Church that year. Each candidate walked with slow, nervous steps toward the muddy waters of the village dugout. Some of them had helped to dig the clay out of the pit to make adobe bricks for village building projects. Now, during the rainy season, the pit was filled with stagnant brown water. The little Mennonite Brethren congregation took advantage of the water to baptize a group of young people. It was a tradition in the community: young people were invited into the church through baptism. Baptism and membership in the church were among the qualifications required for permission to marry.

My father had been baptized when he was 14. He had accepted Jesus on the SS Croix as they crossed the ocean to Paraguay. He remembers the older man who came to a group of restless teens. He remembers clearly that he prayed for eternal life and for Jesus to come into his life.

Today, as he watched the young people step into the muddy water, he didn't question his faith in Christ, but he had a lot of other questions.

"Clearly the 'Kirchliche Mennonites' (General Conference Mennonites) have it a lot easier," thought 19-year-old Abram as he stood on the bank and watched the procession. "All they do is sprinkle a little water over their candidates' heads. But then, who said that life is easy, especially the Christian life?" he mused.

Now as he observed the baptismal service at the dugout in Orloff, as he sang with the congregation, listened to the testimonies of the candidates and the sermon, Abram's eyes were riveted on Anna. Anna was 17, the oldest in the group. He had known Anna ever since their families had come to live in the same Siberian village of Schumanovka. But how had he not noticed then how lovely she was? This beautiful young woman in a simple white smock intrigued him now.

They were friends. Just a few weeks ago, they had talked about the baptism while their parents attended a church business meeting. She told him she wasn't sure if she was a Christian. She shared her story with him.

Years ago, in Russia, she was deeply moved by a handsome, young Sunday school teacher. He challenged the girls in his class to accept Christ as their Saviour. Young Anna was spiritually impacted and accepted the challenge. As she skipped home to tell her parents, she was full of joy. When she got home her parents were preoccupied with guests. Then, in the weeks that followed, the tensions in the village multiplied. She never got the chance to share her story with her parents.

She was more concerned when she watched this handsome young man, once a Sunday school teacher, fall into a life-style her parents would never approve of. Suddenly he was drinking and smoking. He lived for parties. The whole community talked of it.

Sensitive young Anna believed he had never even been "saved" in the first place. If her teacher, the man she respected and looked up to, had not really been saved, how could her own "salvation experience" be for real?

She also told Abram about another experience she had never told anyone. On the D'Artagnan, the ship they took from China to France, she had heard music as she passed by a room on the ship. She didn't know any of the passengers, as they were a higher class than the Mennonite refugees. But the loud music tempted her to look in. The people, dressed in beautiful clothes, were dancing and singing. The music and the rhythmic movement looked like so much fun. Yet, in her heart, she knew it was sin. Was it sinful to be attracted to something that was wrong?

This longing to dance freely to the music she loved confused her. How could she be "saved" if she was so tempted by sinful behaviour? For years she had agonized in the depths of her soul, longing for assurance. She had never told anyone.

She had attended a "prophecy conference" with other members of her church. The conference was set up to help people understand the challenges of the 1930s. The group studied charts from Daniel and Revelation. They talked about God's plan for the world. They emphasized the importance of a personal conversion experience to escape judgement.

Anna was moved by the conference. She responded to the invitation to experience salvation. She prayed that she would be pardoned from the coming wrath of God. It was enough for Anna at that time. She was ready to be baptized. But as her son, I know that she struggled with this issue for the rest of her life. The only message she heard, throughout her life, was the "Gospel of Sin Management."

This was not Good News – but protection from a wrathful God. It was not an encouragement into a relationship with a God who loved her, but protection from falling into sin.

My mother was honest with Abram. Right from the beginning of their relationship, he understood that her experience at the prophecy conference had not settled her doubts. She lived with those insecurities her whole life.

My mother and father met in secret. The rules were very strict.

She told him about the many times she did not have enough faith – surely that was sin. She told him that she even felt unsure of her decision to be baptized. She couldn't talk to her parents or another adult in leadership. Everyone else was so sure of their faith. No one seemed to have the same questions as she did. Baptism was important. It was more than acceptance into the church. It was the passage into adulthood. No one could be married in the church without first being baptized. She chalked her doubts and fears up to the temptations of the "Evil One." She finally decided to be baptized, as everyone expected her to do.

My father watched as Anna stepped forward, into the sludge of the pool. She moved with a grace he couldn't explain, and he could never forget it. He no longer saw Anna as a young girl, a neighbour. He saw her as a woman. The white smock clung to her wet body. She was one of the happiest girls he had ever known. Filled with joy and life, she could run and ride as well as he could! She loved to challenge the boys to a race along the centre street in their small village. She laughed as she teased them.

This is the young Anna as Abram saw her when he fell in love with her.

Her laughter and open heart were so different than anything Abram had ever known in his own home. His family didn't laugh, they worked. His family wasn't easy-going, but constantly worried. Her family, as poor as any family in the community, didn't fret but lived each day with gratitude. He saw the dominance of the searching after money and wealth in his own family.

That day, as he watched beautiful Anna walk out of the baptismal waters, he wished he could make a family with Anna.

Dating, as we know it now, didn't exist in the Mennonite villages in Paraguay. At least not at that time. My father was very attracted to Anna. He had completed his apprenticeship and moved back home to live with his parents. He was very dissatisfied with his home life. But he was their son and there was no question that he would join them in working the farm.

One evening, as he led the cows along the main street, he passed Anna's house. She stood at the fence, cheerfully swinging back and forth on the gate. She called out to him. Laughing and teasing him. The attraction drove my father to creativity. While dating was frowned upon, choir practice and Sunday evening services were not. Abram casually asked Anna to ride with him and his sister to choir practice. Then one Sunday evening after church, he shyly asked if he could walk her home. She didn't hesitate. It seemed this shy young man had caught her eye too!

My father looked forward to Sunday evening, walking home in the quiet darkness or the bright moonlight. My mother was never short of words or stories. She was eager to share her ideas. As they walked and talked together, they fell in love.

My grandparents were heavily involved in the church. Dad's father was a lay minister. And Mom's father was the church moderator: the "Gemeindeleiter." My mother's father, with a strong pastoral gift, was also a deacon. On occasion, Abram and Anna's parents were at church meetings together. This provided an excellent opportunity for my father and mother to sneak away, alone and out of the watchful eyes of their siblings and parents.

One evening, the moon full and bright, the harsh landscape was bathed in the magic of the moonlight. In the soft light, even this hell looked beautiful. They walked home and as usual, Abram was overwhelmed with his love for Anna. My father was a shy, nervous young man, tentative as he held Anna and softly kissed her. Anna responded with her whole heart, warm and with the love of a young woman.

Abram could think of nothing else but his Anna, a small home of their own and the beautiful family they would make together. He planned, practicing the words in his head. He chose a Sunday night. And as they walked, his nerves were heightened. He mustered up his courage and asked Anna to be his wife.

Mom and Dad's wedding photo on October 1, 1938.

7: Marriage and Family

My grandparents didn't see the match as made in heaven!

Anna's family, so compassionate, warm and caring, were very concerned that their daughter could not see what kind of family Abram came from. They warned her. They told her that Abram's family wasn't like their family. They talked openly about lack of love or expression of care in Abram's family. Franz Wiens, his father, was a lay minister in the community and was well-known for being hard-working, austere and focused only on regaining his wealth.

Grandpa Jacob, a tiny community general store owner, operated his business with kind generosity. While they had enough to eat, the business barely brought in enough to care for the family. Yet the family was strong, healthy, and openly caring for one another and for others.

Abram's family were very concerned that their second son was marrying a weak woman, one who sang and played, but hadn't done a day's work in her life. They knew she was the youngest, and favoured by her parents and her siblings. Life in Paraguay was almost impossible. It took sterner stuff to tame the jungle. They didn't want their son to be at an economic disadvantage. The women in Paraguay needed to work hard. She definitely wasn't their ideal choice for him.

But, as the saying goes, opposites attract. My mother and father were tenacious and fearless. Perhaps that's the beautiful characteristic of young love. They only saw each other. They were determined to be a family. Abram saw the bright spirit in Anna and he wanted that joy to be his. He was determined to trade the solemn focus on making money for the joy of a family: music, walks in the dark, happy children playing in the yard.

The date was set. On October 1, 1938, Abram and Anna were to be married.

As the time neared, my father, firm in his resolve to marry Anna, was still uncertain about their future. He had worked so hard: building furniture, repairing wagons, building barns and adding on to houses. But he did not have one cent to his name.

During the apprenticeship, he was paid poorly. Even so, every little bit of money he earned went to his parents. Even now as a young man, his parents took every penny he made. Financially, he had nothing to give to his new family. He even doubted that he had much to bring spiritually and emotionally. He felt robbed by his parents. They made no effort to help him out. For as long as he could remember, he felt unloved, uncared for. He thought back to the night when he encountered the snake in the woods. His mother only cared for his pay. She had no kind words for him. His father did not mentor him. He simply expected. As a young boy – just 12 years old – he was tasked with driving one of their sleighs through the deep snow out of Russia. He always felt responsible. He never felt loved.

But he was at a crossroads. He was walking into a marriage with absolutely nothing. He was angry. Why couldn't his parents help get him started? Late into the night, he wondered how he would provide for his beautiful Anna.

"Where is the justice in this life?" he fumed.

His anger intensified with the unfairness of his parents. His parents demanded so much from him. Yet so much less was expected of his older brother Hans. Uncle Hans was weak and could not work as hard as my father. It seemed that Uncle Hans got everything, while our dad got nothing. Just before my father and mother married, my grandparents gave Uncle Hans a team of horses. "Why Hans? Why not me?" Dad thought as he watched them prance in excitement and then pull the wagon with high steps, glossy and strong. The horses were so beautiful, the nicest horses in the whole village.

My father took his parents to task. He humbled himself and went to confront them. It wasn't the first time he had asked for their help in setting up his new home. The conversation was hard and angry. His parents found no joy in helping the young family. In the end, my grandparents offered Dad a young calf as a wedding gift. That one calf was so very little to help him set up a home and get started in his family life.

In stolen moments, Abram built a simple china cabinet as a wedding gift to Anna. It wasn't elaborate or expensive, but it held his heart. His mother, a greedy and jealous woman, insisted he make one for her as well.

Abram couldn't wait to leave his home.

In spite of the parents' concern, the wedding went forward. Guests arrived in Orloff throughout the morning of Saturday, October 1. Abram and Anna chose Genesis 2:18 as the theme for their wedding: "The Lord God said, 'It is not good for man to be alone. I will make a helper suitable for him.'"

Johann Schellenberg led the celebration and Preacher Harder built on the text from Colossians 3:17: "And whatever you do, whether in word or in deed, do it all in the name of the Lord Jesus, giving thanks to God the Father through him." The community choir sang the traditional greeting "Gott gruesse Dich." (God bless you).[1]

The most memorable contribution, especially for our dad, was something Mom's father said to them. He quoted Proverbs 30:8-9:
"Keep falsehood and lies far from me;
give me neither poverty nor riches,
but give me only my daily bread.
Otherwise, I may have too much and disown you
and say, 'Who is the Lord?'
Or I may become poor and steal,
and so dishonor the name of my God."

For our Dad, who had experienced the negative impact of striving after riches in his family of origin, Grandpa Jacob's wise words were like a healing balm to his soul. In this new family that was receiving him as a son-in-law, he would not be judged by how much he would accumulate.

After the ceremony guests, were served zwieback, cold meat, and piroshki (fruit-filled pastry). Once the meal was over, they had the final wedding ceremony: "Kranz und Schleier" (wreath and veil). Anna's oldest sister, Liese, removed the veil and replaced it with a bow. Now Anna was a married woman!

---

[1] (https://www.youtube.com/watch?v=jwMUI3vRHBM)

With the bow in place, the older guests left. The young people stayed to play games as night fell on Orloff. Soon the celebration was over and the guests began to leave. Anna and Abram had no home to go to, no hotel or guest house to spend their first night together. The couple said good night. Then went to their own homes and their childhood beds.

My father was filled with doubts – overjoyed that his Anna had accepted him as her husband and agonizing over the future. They had nothing. After their wedding, he trudged down the street in the dark to his parents' home. The day had been filled with music and laughter. And now? There was nothing. My father was not faint of heart. He had driven a team of horses out of Russia when he was just a young boy. He had travelled from northern China across oceans to Paraguay! He had endured three full years of apprenticeship which seemed like prison. He had lived his whole life in a love-starved home, hoping against hope that he would please his parents. But time after time, it seemed that he fell short of their expectations.

How would he care for Anna? He had nothing.

They weren't entirely at loose ends. The plan was to live with Anna's family until they could set up their own home.

At dawn the day after their wedding, Abram left his home and walked to Anna's house. He was in time for breakfast.

It's hard to imagine two young people who grew up in the same village, less than a mile apart, to have been raised by more different parents. My father struggled to shake off the sense of disappointment he had struggled with his whole life. While he was the son who worked, brought in an income and took on a great deal of responsibility at a very young age, he rarely felt his parents' approval. They made demands and expected so much.... They favoured his older brother, even though he contributed much less to the family. My father constantly felt that he was unable to satisfy his parents.

My mother, Anna, on the other hand, was the youngest in her family. She was the child born out of the love of her parents after her father returned home from his service as a medic in the First World War. Her father delighted in her. Her mother supported her and taught her. The rest of the family treated her like a princess. Her disposition was filled with music and joy.

Even filled with joy, making a living as a pioneer in the Paraguayan jungle was no easy task. My father was strong, determined and hard-working. My mother was optimistic, athletic and forward-thinking.

When the homestead across the road from Mom's parents' family came available, Anna and Abram made arrangements to acquire the land. The family who had established this homestead was leaving to set up a new farm in eastern Paraguay.

My parents looked at the fields, the rawness of the land, the opportunity, and rejoiced. This would be their first home. With the kind of optimism that belongs to the young, Anna and Abram began to build their home and their life together.

When the Mennonite families first came to Paraguay, they tried to grow wheat, sunflowers, oats – the kinds of crops they had cultivated in Russia. But the land and weather patterns were entirely different than in Russia. With some ingenuity and faith, they learned that cotton was a viable cash crop. So they planted their first crop of cotton. It was good to work together as a young couple.

Their first harvest was bountiful. As Abram pitched the fresh cotton into large bags, Anna enthusiastically trampled the fluffy white bolls (cotton fluff), stuffing the bags tightly. Song was as much a part of her as talking and, without thinking, she began to sing. Her feet danced in time with the rhythm of her song.

Abruptly, without any warning, Abram stopped working, setting his pitchfork firmly in the ground. "Anna, do you have to sing so loud?" he scolded. "The neighbours will hear you!"

My mother was stunned. She had been complimented so often on her singing that she never thought it would irritate anyone. At school, Teacher Klassen had nicknamed her "the village canary." She had no words. She stopped singing.

My father refused to relent, but went into his "silent treatment" mode. Although he felt guilty as he watched her work in silence, he didn't say another word. Her enthusiasm was gone. "She should know better than to carry on like that," he sulked to himself. "Why would she embarrass us in the neighbourhood?"

The silence followed them into the house and hung like a dark curtain over their evening meal. Disciplined, but still carrying anger and confusion, they sat down for their nightly Bible reading and prayer. They didn't talk about it. But as they lay in bed that night, side by side, but not together, they each felt the pain of disagreement and discord.

There were no counselling sessions or mentors for young couples in those days. My parents were very different personalities raised in very different homes. They loved each other, but had to work at the rough edges in their relationship. While Anna felt the hurt, she couldn't resist a song. Abram nursed his pain in silence. Like so many of us, they eventually came to accept the contrasts in their characters as a gift. They could accept them and learn from them, or turn them into bitterness. They had to choose. My father, never as free or lighthearted as my mother, learned to love her music. She had a beautiful soprano voice. She was born to sing. And, some days, Dad would join his tenor to her soprano and they would make music together. She did learn to time her outbursts of song more strategically.

The land was rugged and dangerous. The couple continued to pick cotton, rejoicing in the plentiful crop. My father was already figuring out what he could do with the income.

One morning as they worked in the blazing Chaco sun, Dad felt a sharp sting on his leg. This was nothing new. The "Green Hell" had too many insects to count. He scratched his leg, not really thinking too much about it. Restless, he asked Anna if she wanted a drink. She didn't.

She kept working as he went in for water. After what seemed to be a very long time for a drink of water, she wondered what had happened to him. She skipped through the cotton rows to see what was keeping him. To her shock and horror, she found him writhing in pain on the floor of their house. His face was swollen unnaturally. A huge, purple welt stained his leg.

This was not good.

In a small village, news spreads quickly. There was no doctor close at hand, so the neighbours came with their "miracle" cures. One forced sour milk down his throat. Another plastered lard on his wound. Still another had him drink a concoction of raw eggs. One neighbour brought him rubbing alcohol to drink.

My father didn't know what to do. The pain was excruciating. He tried every home remedy! As he choked down horrific concoctions, Anna ran to find help. She needed a wagon and a team of horses to take him to the hospital in Filadelfia. It was 15 kilometers away.

His parents offered to take them to the hospital. They rushed back to the house and loaded Abram into the wagon. By this time, Dad was delirious. He begged his father to drive faster.

In and out of consciousness, Abram was standing on the doorstep of death. They reached the hospital, just in time. The doctor couldn't identify the exact source of the infection, but he quickly diagnosed it as a poisonous attack from a venomous spider or snake – a common plight of the settlers. He gave my father several injections to fight the poison. As his body responded to the medical injections, it violently rejected the many home remedies!

My grandparents returned to Orloff, but my mother stayed by my father's side. Unconscious, his body fighting the infection, Anna was terrified she would lose him. Frantically, hour after hour, she prayed, "Please Lord, don't let him die. I promise I'll be the very best wife I can possibly be."

He passed in and out of consciousness throughout the night. When he still had not regained full consciousness the next day, my mother knew just how serious the episode was.

But my father recovered!

We're unsure what bit my father, but local indigenous observers suggested that the crisis was likely caused by a small spider. They had never known anyone to survive from this bite before. My father experienced a miracle: from the quick, no-nonsense response my mother had, the ride of their lifetime to the hospital and the informed treatment of the doctor. For my mother, her prayer was answered. Such a close brush did not escape my parents. Both vowed they would be the best partner they could be.

So, two young Russian Mennonites from radically different families began their life together. Young and in love, they couldn't imagine the challenges they would face. But their determination was united: they would build a good life together, through thick and thin, for better or worse. Neither shirked their responsibilities or gave up on the other. They were partners, lovers and friends.

Two years later, on a rainy Mother's Day Sunday, Mom gave birth to their first child, a son. According to tradition, he should have been named Franz after his paternal grandfather. But they surprised everyone by announcing that their firstborn would be named Ernst. Their families were baffled. But my parents insisted. They both came from large families. There were too many Abrams, Isaacs, Jacobs and Franzes to count! They decided to choose a fresh course for their family. They showed their commitment to change by naming their children less traditional names.

My father never said too much about it, but I always wondered if he saw this as starting fresh with a positive, forward-looking wife. His own family experience was painful. He never felt loved. His father, my grandfather, never expressed pride in his son. He rarely supported him. My father was expected to comply.

The day Ernie was born was a new day, a day of unspeakable joy. On this day he could begin his lifelong dream of building a home where love, kindness and caring would be the guiding hand. Money and possessions were necessities, but they would never become the idols that he felt captivated his parents and stole their sense of joy.

My mother, the youngest in her family, had never cared for an infant. She was not completely sure she was up to the task. She had a lot of questions (some didn't have answers!). Why was this child so red and wrinkled? Why did he cry through the night? Why could she not produce enough milk to satisfy his screaming hunger? Was she up to the challenge of being both a parent and a loving spouse?

In spite of her doubts, the child gained weight! Anna learned the joy of being a mother and a wife too.

Just three months after Ernie was born, my father's mother, Anna Fast-Wiens, died of cancer. Orloff, the jungle village, had few resources for medical care and my grandmother suffered through intense pain.

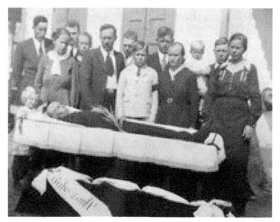

The funeral of Anna (Fast) Wiens, my Dad's mother in 1940. Mom and Dad are the couple, second from right. To Dad's right is his older brother Hans. The young boy in the white jacket in front of Grandpa Franz is Dad's youngest and favourite brother David.

Later that year, my parents decided to move to Filadelfia, the capital of the small Mennonite settlement. This small town was more developed and the settlers had established a cooperative "Industriewerk" to respond to the various needs of the community. Tradespeople and entrepreneurs built and manufactured farm equipment, furniture, wagons and other necessities of pioneer life. They established markets for their produce. Dad worked in the carpentry shop building wagons, furniture and coffins.

With a steady income, life became a little easier for them as a family. My mom felt it was time for another child. They talked about it and their love went to work. Soon a second child was on the way.

Pregnancy was no reason to slow down. My mother was an essential partner in our home. She worked hard. So, large with child, on the morning of March 5, 1942, Anna got up at dawn – like she did every day. She made Dad's breakfast, packed his lunch and saw him off to work. Then she kneaded dough. While it was rising, she scrubbed the laundry by hand, dusted and tidied the house. Then she spread a fresh layer of mud mixed with cow dung over the hard-packed earth floor of their cottage.

She was excited because her oldest brother, Isaac, was coming to town for lunch. He was one of her favourite people! She prepared an impressive meal to serve him for lunch. After lunch, she put Ernie down for his nap and then hurried to her garden to plant several rows of sweet potatoes. At five that afternoon she bathed her toddler and took him to her neighbour's house.

Everything was "schwind, schwind." She didn't have time to waste. She was off! At a brisk pace, she walked a kilometer and a half to the hospital. She knew the baby was coming soon. The contractions were coming in quick succession.

Erwin was born at 6 pm.

The doctor scolded her for waiting until the last minute to come to the hospital. Although Anna was hoping for a girl, she welcomed her new son. He became a good helper and companion to her, as good as any girl could have been.

While my father earned a good living in the larger centre, their dream was to buy land in Orloff. Owning land came with rights and privileges. They saved as much as possible and within a short while they had enough to put a down payment on the land they wanted to buy. It was the same farm they had worked when they were first married. Now, it was available for them to buy.

For my mother this was as close to the fairy tale life she had dreamed of as was possible in the Chaco wilderness. She was very close to her family and the new farm was right across the road from her parents! She loved her strong, quiet husband. She stood by him as he struggled to carve out a viable farm in the harsh scrub land. While Anna was happy here, this move to their own little farm in Orloff was no match for the restlessness that would soon drive Dad to seek new opportunities.

Their love soon brought a third pregnancy. On October 22, 1943, the men of the village called a meeting to discuss community business. During the course of the evening, a severe thunderstorm with gale-force winds blew up. When my father got home from the meeting, Mom was already in advanced labour.

Gritting his teeth, Abram headed back into the stormy night to find his team of horses. He harnessed them to the wagon and set off to the neighbouring village to get the midwife. While the storm raged outside, their third son, Hugo, was born.

78

He was smaller than his brothers. Not only did nature vent her fury at his birth, but his tiny body seemed prone to frequent disease and illness.

This photo is Mom's family in Orloff at Christmas in 1944. Mom and Dad are the couple on the left. Ernie and Erv are the two blond boys in the middle. Hugo was sick and not in the photo.

8: A Mother's Prayer

My mother was still a young woman, married six years with three children. They continued to fight the harsh Paraguayan jungle. Life was not easy.

Living in the "Green Hell" was extremely difficult. My parents worked hard. They were learning the rhythms of the jungle. They understood how to work the land that was so different from the fertile plains of the Russian steppes.

They had moved back to Filadelfia again, but it was Christmas and the family gathered in Orloff. She loved Christmas at her parents' home. It was filled with laughter, songs, stories and love. So, Mom and Dad packed up their three little boys and travelled 15 kilometers to Orloff.

In the evening, they gathered around a captivating fire with all Mom's brothers, sisters and their children. They sang carols, hymns and folk songs. One of Mom's favourites was *"In meine Heimat kam ich wieder"* (I came back to my home). She knew all the hymns of the "Gesang Buch" and many folk songs and carols by heart.

After the singing and reminiscing were done, they put their three little boys to bed under their grandparents' watchful care. Her brothers and sisters had returned to their own homes. With a little quiet time for themselves, Mom took Dad's hand and suggested a walk in the moonlight for memory's sake. As they strolled through the village in the soft light of the waxing moon, they reflected on all the ways that God had blessed them since their first secret meeting together as their parents were occupied in a church business meeting. They thanked God for bringing them safely out of Stalin's terror and for the peace and safety they enjoyed in this new land. Even though life was hard, they were managing to make a living. They especially thanked God for bringing them together and for their three healthy and happy boys. With hearts full of memories and bursting with love for their family and for each other, they went to bed.

Early in the new year as another full moon had come and gone, Mom realized that she had missed her monthly flow.

Could she be pregnant again? As the weeks and months went by, the awareness of a new life inside was undeniable. She was 24 years old and expecting her fourth child. She and Dad were excited, but Mom could not entirely get past a nagging worry. Could she really give birth to another healthy child? She knew that this could not be taken for granted in a land of limited medical care where a multitude of strange diseases stalked them at every turn. There were dangers all around.

Hugo, their third was small and prone to frequent illness. Malaria was rampant in and around the German Mennonite colony, often troubling Dad with severe aching and fever. She thought about the time in their early life together when Dad had been picking cotton in their field and a poisonous spider or snake had injected its poison into his body.

Another time, Dad had been forced to hunker down on the trail at night as the gleaming eyes of a jaguar peered at him from a nearby tree. The medical needs of the colony were served by just one doctor in Filadelfia for the 20 neighbouring villages, along with the services of a midwife. Important supplies such as medications had to be brought in by ox cart from Kilometer 145, the end of the railway line more than two day's journey away. Could another child be born healthy? If medical help was required, would it be available?

My mother remembered Hannah's prayer:

And she made a vow, saying, "Lord Almighty, if you will only look on your servant's misery and remember me, and not forget your servant but give her a son, then I will give him to the Lord for all the days of his life,...." 1 Samuel 1:11

And like Hannah, my mother began to pray for her new child.

It was not as if prayer was a new experience for my mother. In her family, prayer and singing hymns were part of daily life. For both of my parents, faith was a part of their heritage. Their parents nurtured attitudes of prayer. But in this season of life, my mother's prayers changed. She needed to give her worries about the child swelling in her womb to God. So, she prayed. And, as Mom was wont to do, she made a promise along with her prayer. If God would grant her request, she would dedicate this child to God in a special way. This child would be raised to serve God and the world in some special mission. Although she did not tell me about this prayer until much later, it remained with me as my guiding light through my more than 40 years of ministry in Bible translation.

Mom's pregnancy progressed without serious complications. As the due date approached, her mother (my grandmother, Liese) travelled to Filadelfia to help Mom in the last days of her pregnancy. After all, she had three little boys, daily chores and a husband to care for.

My grandmother's presence wasn't assumed. My parents debated the wisdom of her arriving just days before the baby was due. Grandma loved her grandsons, especially Erwin, but she was known for going into bouts of anxiety and fussing when labour set in.

Sometime after midnight on September 12, Mom went into labour. The last thing she wanted was for her mother to wake up and "help." Quietly she woke Dad. They dressed in darkness, took their shoes in hand and tiptoed softly through the front room where Grandma slept.

Once outside, they slipped on their shoes, giggling like little kids who had just escaped to freedom. Mom's contractions were steady as they walked the 1.5 kilometers to the Filadelfia hospital.

They made it!

They had a new son. They called me Hartmut after a young man whom they admired who had come to the colony from Germany.

I was healthy at birth except for a complication with my urinary tract which required surgical intervention and circumcision. Mom's prayers had been answered. She kept her conversation with God to herself. She prayed for her children every day, but her prayers for me were in the context of service and sacrifice.

As I was the fourth boy, there were now four little men to help with the chores. But no daughters to help Mom inside. Our family, democratic in the assignment of chores, assigned my brother Erwin and me as mother's helpers. In our later years, that included milking the cows. In our culture there was a pretty clear division of labour along gender lines. Milking, cooking, baking, laundry and cleaning were women's chores.

I worked alongside my mother throughout my childhood. Mom had a powerful impact on my life direction and choices as I grew up. There is a rumour among missionaries that mothers are the greatest obstacle to children going into missions. My mom actively encouraged me on choosing a career in missionary service. After all, she had promised me to God.

Mom also sang regularly through the hymn book as we worked together. She knew most of the hymns by heart. Today, when singing the hymns that she loved, I rarely need a hymn book!

Throughout her pregnancy, my mother prayed for my health. And, for the most part, I was healthy and strong. But I can't say that I didn't cause my mother a few anxious moments.

When still an infant, Mom packed me in the baby buggy to visit with a friend. They sat nearby, having tea and chatting. I slept quietly in the warm sun. As they chatted, the wind came up and took my buggy for a ride, tossing it over on the ground some meters away. Everyone was terrified! Almost afraid to look, they ran to see if I was alright. No harm was done. But it wasn't the last time my mother's prayers were put to the test.

When I was four weeks old, Dad and Mom decided to move the family to a remote ranch in the wilderness, far from the Fernheim colony. They packed what little they owned into a wagon, along with their four young boys! Uncle Abram (my mom's brother) and his family were already living at the ranch. The colony had acquired the ranch as additional grazing land for the growing herds of cattle the settlers were acquiring. Uncle Isaac and his family managed another ranch nearby.

The ear-splitting buzz of cicadas formed a shrill background to the plodding horses' hooves and the creaking wheels of the loaded wagon. Occasionally, a flock of noisy parrots broke the dreary routine, fluttering and squawking in the trees and breaking the monotony of the shimmering midday heat. As the wagon wheels wound their way along the narrow track toward their new home, Dad and Mom sat, quietly enduring the heat and contemplating the constantly shifting pattern of their young married life.

"Will the moving never end?" wondered Mom. Would her peaceful cottage filled with happy family life ever be a reality again? Once again, she reminded herself not to complain, at least not directly. She was determined to follow through on her promise to be the best wife she could be and to help make the most of every new opportunity. To feed her soul she began singing softly the hymns and folk melodies she had heard and sung so often in her childhood. Dad hummed along in his tenor voice.

The frequent moves seemed easier for Dad. There was by now a noticeable pattern of restlessness in his life. While he worked hard at his various jobs and occupations, nothing seemed to satisfy the unspeakable longing that filled his young life. What was this deep yearning which kept calling him on to another place, another venture?

Perhaps it was a continuation of a pattern begun in his childhood. He thought back to when he was nine years old and remembered how his family had taken that long, long train trip over 8,000 kilometers from Sagradovka in the Ukraine through the Ural Mountains and around Lake Baikal to the distant Amur River Valley in the far eastern part of Siberia. When his father had been refused an exit visa to join the great migration aided by North American Mennonites in the 1920s, the resettlement to Siberia seemed like the only option to escape the worst trauma of the Bolshevik Revolution. He remembered the bitter disappointment his parents and other settlers in Siberia felt when Stalin's regime extended its long arm of control into the newly formed settlement where they had been enticed to move with promises of greater freedom from state intrusion into their lives. He recalled vividly the bitterly cold night in December 1930, when their entire village had fled across the Amur River into China. He recalled how at 12 years old he had been given the responsibility to drive the family's second sled and how he had struggled to control his horses while following his family who were in the large sleigh ahead. He remembered how God had protected them and brought them to safety.

While Mom tried to keep the restless children quiet in the back of the wagon, Dad thought about the difficult years in the refugee camp in Harbin, China. There was so little food, virtually no job opportunities, and worst of all, very little hope. Adult men were not allowed to work at all. While Mom, at 10, like most other young children, attended school in the three-story home rented for the refugees by MCC, Dad was sent out to scrounge all day long for any little source of income. He tried his hand as a shoeshine boy, he carried parcels for wealthy Russian women living in Harbin and collected bottles and scrap newspapers to sell. He even had a job carrying the filth from septic tanks to fertilize the Chinese gardens. Like all the refugees, his family was desperately poor. He was willing to do anything to make a few *yuán*.

Dad wondered how life might have been different for them if instead of coming to this torrid wilderness, they had been allowed to settle in the German Third Reich in 1932. How would the war have affected them? Like so many of the settlers in the Chaco, he respected the German values of discipline, hard work, resourcefulness and sacrifice. Pro-Nazi feelings had run high among the colonists during the early years of the war. Wouldn't it have been something if Germany had been able to wipe out the hated Bolsheviks in Russia! Surely Germany would have extended a generous hand to her scattered peoples, even here in the Chaco. It was, after all, Germany that had lent them the funds for their journey from China to Paraguay.

Meanwhile, as the family's wagon rolled on, I was snuggled comfortably in Mom's lap, secure in her love and feeling calmed and drowsy by her sweet and gentle songs. She sang softly through the Gesangbuch, alternating some of her favourite "Heimatslieder." To this day, I still find myself waking up with a song in my heart.

My three brothers, active young boys, were restless. The ride seemed endless and they were hungry. Dad encouraged the horses to pick up the pace. With what lay ahead, there would be plenty of opportunity to contemplate the mysteries of life and Divine healing. As the setting sun brought some relief to the intense heat of the day, they arrived at the ranch.

Perhaps calling the site a "ranch" conjures the wrong picture. As they rode towards their new home, they saw three low and lonely buildings through the tall bitter-grass. Uncle Isaac and Uncle Abram had quickly built a common kitchen and two thatched-roofed sleeping cottages for their families. The "ranch" was crudely built. There wasn't even a vague echo of the small cottage my mother dreamed of.

Dad took care of the horses. Mom gathered the boys. They were hungry and ready to run. For them, this was another adventure. For my parents, it was a tremendous challenge.

But my mother, who had promised to be the best wife she could be, persisted. Intensely lonely, longing for community, she set out to make this God-forsaken ranch our home. She plastered the walls and floor with a mixture of cow dung and clay. Once she was satisfied, she painted them white with lime. She swept the yard clear of all grass and other debris in order to give the children a safe, snake-free place to play. Evenings, after supper, she lit a fire in the cleanly swept yard and gathered the children around for songs, stories, games and prayers. That was the pattern she had learned in her home.

Life was simple on the ranch, but there was so little protection from the dangers of the untamed wilderness. Snakes were a constant concern. Mom reminded her children often of the dangers of snakes. But, when the attack came, it was not one of the children who was hit, but our dad.

One day, he was digging a new well in hopes of getting a more reliable water supply. After a hard stint of digging, he stepped out of the hole for a break, just as an airplane flew overhead. While glancing upward at the rare sight, he felt a sudden slap against his leg. Instinctively he jerked his foot forward and as he did, he saw a small, brightly coloured snake slither off into the long grass. In an instant, he had his belt off and tied into a tight tourniquet just above the marks of the fangs.

He ran to the house, shouting for Mom to get the horses hitched. As he waited for the wagon, he took a razor blade and made a large cross-shaped cut over the snakebite. As the blood flowed freely, he bent down and sucked vigorously on the wound to increase the flow, spitting out the poison-laden blood.

As Mom's lithe legs flew out to the corral, she cried out in prayer. She prayed that Dad would live. AND that God would help her catch and harness the team of horses. No one is sure which of the two was the greater miracle. Barely conscious, Dad hung on as they rode to the nearest neighbouring ranch. There they had a vial of anti-snake serum. They used a large cattle syringe to inject it into Dad.

They were living in the wilderness, miles away from medical help. The land was untamed and unbroken. It was a daily contest to see which would break first: the rancher or the land.

Living so far from other families, in a land that resisted their efforts to manage it, was discouraging. Mom and her sister-in-law spent many hours cultivating and tending a garden to provide a supply of fresh produce. One evening, shortly before sunset, a sound like a rushing wind came out of the northern sky. Mom recognized it immediately and called all of us children. She gave each of us a tin and a stick and sent us into the garden to make as much noise as possible. We (well, my brothers and cousins) responded enthusiastically – remember, active boys. We beat sticks against the tins, yelling at the top of our lungs and stomping on as many of the green invaders as possible. But the invasion was endless. In the end, we had to go to bed, leaving the swarms of locusts to their feast. And feast they did. The next morning, there was not a green blade or stalk left in the garden. Destroying the garden my mother and aunt worked so hard at, the locusts abandoned our ranch in search of other greens.

An important and valuable food source had vanished. My mother and aunt had to think of another way to feed their growing families.

Toward the end of June in my second year, our family made the dreary journey back to Orloff to await the arrival of my next brother. On June 27, Mom's labour pains began. Even though this was her fifth time, it was more difficult than the previous births. All night long and all day Saturday, the contractions wore on. Throughout the day, the Chaco wind picked up and howled in one of the epic winter blizzards of sand and debris. Finally, as dusk set in on June 28, her fifth son was born. They named my new brother Henry.

We often wonder if that long, hard labour in the midst of the storm was an omen of the pain yet to come. Henry, quiet and gentle, lost his life to cerebral meningitis at age 18.

We happily greeted our new brother. But we left Orloff with tears – Ernie, our oldest brother, was left behind. He was old enough to go to school. But there was no school in the wilderness. So Mom had packed the few clothes he had and left him to live with her parents. My mother's sadness was palpable.

We returned to the ranch. Mom missed her oldest son. Her songs became increasingly melancholy, choosing the melodies of the "Heimatslieder." Dad knew it was once again time to move.

Mom's mother, Grandma Liese, had long dreamed of migrating to Canada. Most of her brothers and sisters had made their way to Canada during the great migration out of Russia during the 1920s. The Second World War was finally over. Canada desperately needed to expand its workforce and was, once again, accepting refugees and immigrants. Grandma Liese's dream was about to move from a wish to a real possibility.

Feeling the pain of having to send their children away to school Dad's affinity to Grandma Liese's dream grew. Together with Mom's parents, Mom and Dad began the legal process for immigration to Canada.

From the stories we heard, Canada was Canaan: a land of milk and honey, abundance of food and opportunity. My father dreamed of freedom, of opportunity and of distance from the family in which he grew up. His dream of his own happy, safe family had wobbled a few times as they faced almost inhumane challenges. Maybe Canada was the place where dreams could come true.

But dreams were only dreams. The harsh reality of daily life threatened to destroy his dream.

Early in September, just before my second birthday, we received the message that Grandma Liese was seriously ill. Mom packed up her youngest three and joined her brother Abram's family for the long trek back to the parental home. She couldn't resist. Not only was her mother in need of care, she could check in on her oldest son!

My brother Erwin stayed at the ranch with Dad. They worked the ranch together with the help of two Lengua Indian assistants. Remember, Erwin was barely five years old! Within two days of Mom's departure, another messenger arrived at the ranch with news that Grandma was on her deathbed. By the time Dad and Erwin were able to get back to Orloff, she had passed on into her eternal rest and her body, which could not be preserved in the harsh environment, had been buried. The only doctor in the colony, an optometrist, declared her death to be the result of a gallbladder infection.

Grandma Liese's untimely death seemed to bring urgency to the plan to migrate to Canada. Her brother in Alberta was sponsoring our immigration.

Sadly, while my parents continued their plans of immigration, my grandmother would be left behind.

There was so much to do.

Letters were written, passports applied for, and resignation notice given at the cattle ranch. Arrangements were made to borrow money for the journey. The family agreed that Mom's father, our Grandpa Jacob, should join the family's migration to Canada. Shortly before he left the "Green Hell" they had called home, his last act of love for his precious life partner was to build a simple wooden marker and picket fence around our grandmother's grave.

These are the five boys with whom Mom and Dad moved to Canada in 1948. The back row left is Ernie and back row right is Erv. Front left is Hugo and I am in the front right. Sitting on the lap of Mom's friend is Henry.

9: The Promised Land

In March of 1948, when I was two and a half, a tense but hope-filled couple set off. With five active and healthy young boys and an aging, grieving father, they were a motley crew. The goal for this first leg of the journey was to travel from our home in Fernheim colony to the rail line at Kilometer 145.

Tired, exhausted and excited, they arrived at the station, bags and kids around their ankles. The train they hoped to catch did not leave until the next morning. They scanned the train station for a suitable place to wait. The grounds were teeming with travelers: Mennonites, Spanish-Paraguayans and indigenous travelers. They were all waiting for the train to Puerto Casado.

Mom tried to settle us down on the hard ground. She did everything she could, with their few possessions, to make us comfortable. Then she lay down beside Dad, hoping to catch a few hours of sleep.

Dad, the leader of our little travelling circus, carried our precious travel documents. In his little package, he had stowed every cent of the money they had borrowed to make this trip. Carefully, he tucked the treasured bag under his makeshift pillow. He tried to sleep, but was always mindful that everything they owned, everything that was so important for this journey, was stashed beneath his head. Finally, he drifted into a fitful sleep.

His subconscious didn't sleep. It was on high alert. In the shadows of the dark night, he awoke with a start. Two men were running by. His first thought was his bag. Without even checking to see if it was safe under his pillow, he leapt into the air. He would not lose that bag. In a flying leap, he tackled the slower of the runners. It still makes me chuckle to think of my quiet, humble father leaping into the air to attack the would-be thieves.

Surprised, the victim denied taking the bag or even knowing it was there. Dad let him go and went after the second runner. He didn't know anything about the bag or the money either.

Sheepishly Dad went back to his makeshift bed. There, under the pillow, right where he had left it, was the bag. But the story is a valuable reminder of the risk my parents took. They were not worldly-wise. They were simple peasants trying to eke out a life with their children in a safe place. There had been more freedom in Paraguay, but not the abundance they were searching for. Together, against all odds, my parents were following a dream that had begun decades ago. They gave up everything, sold what little they owned and borrowed the rest of the money needed to fund their migration to Canada.

That dark night in the train station at Kilometer 145 was only the beginning of a complicated journey. We travelled by rail to Puerto Casado and then by river boat to Asunción. After a few days in Asunción to process the necessary papers, we finally made our way to the airport.

I can't imagine what people thought when they saw our family on that trip. Imagine a harried mother carrying a 10-month-old baby while she corrals five boys under seven into the train. My father stood guard, making the connections, holding the passports, making sure the tickets were in order. Grandpa Jacob was there trying to help, but still mourning the loss of his life partner. Leaving her buried under the soil in the "Green Hell" of Paraguay, while he travelled to Canada, was perhaps the hardest thing he ever did.

Airline service was not streamlined in 1948. We flew from Asunción to Rio de Janeiro; there we deplaned and boarded our second plane which took us to Miami. There we disembarked once more and boarded the next plane that would take us to New York City. Then, once more gathering all our worldly possessions (and making sure all five boys were within sight), we boarded the train for Buffalo.

When we arrived in Buffalo, C. J. Remple, from Mennonite Central Committee, was waiting for us. He packed all seven of us into his car and drove us to Kitchener. My father's Uncle David, Grandfather Franz Wiens' younger brother, had immigrated to Kitchener in the mid 1920s. Often referred to as "the great migration out of Russia," more than 20,000 Russian Mennonites arrived in Kitchener between 1923 and 1929. Some went on to Western Canada, but many stayed. With a population of 25,000, the city grew exponentially with the arrival of the Mennonites! Uncle David was comfortably established in Kitchener with his two sons, but his wife was more concerned about their economic situation than reaching out to this poor immigrant family with too many children.

We had reached Canada, but were still days away from our destination. Our sponsors were my grandmother's family, who lived in Vauxhall, a Mennonite farming community in southern Alberta.

We climbed onto the train in Kitchener. Once again, we heard whispers from the crowd who were obviously counting five little Mennonite towheaded boys speaking Plautdietsch. "Five boys?" was whispered time and time again as we travelled. In fact, we heard it so often that "five boys" were the first English words that Mom and Dad learned!

I was too young to remember the journey, but I'm sure we made quite a picture!

As we travelled, Mom kept an eye on her boys. Along the way, she noticed that we were scratching our heads. When she looked closer, she could see tiny creatures moving in our hair. Dad remembered those little critters from his weeks in the Chinese Monastery. How could this have happened? Mom was horrified. How could she present five boys infested with lice to her Canadian relatives?

As the train pulled into the station at Vauxhall, Alberta, five little noses were pressed tight to the window. Ten little eyes stretched wide in amazement. Why was the ground covered with feathers? We had never seen snow!

The ground had a light dusting of snow and we were intrigued. Mom's Uncle Abram (Friesen) welcomed us with laughter and warmth as did other members of the Friesen clan, our grandmother's siblings.

We stayed at the home of our relatives in Vauxhall overnight. They were not wealthy, by any means. Mom remembers her aunt scrounging through a drawer to dig up a few pennies with which to buy some meat. The food was generous and hot, the beds, clean and warm. It had been many days and nights since we all had had a good sleep.

The next day, Uncle Abram drove us to Coaldale. My great-uncle Heinrich (Friesen) offered his house as our temporary home in the promised land of Coaldale, Alberta, Canada. Poet Friesen was a self-made man. He had immigrated to Canada in 1912, so he was already well established. He was a farmer and a teacher. And, in his spare time, he wrote poetry. Most of it was written in High German, but occasionally he chose to write in Plautdietsch as well.

We were finally home! (Or so we thought.)

This is the poet Uncle Heinrich Friesen, one of Mom's Uncles who helped sponsor our family's immigration to Canada and who let us live in his house in Coaldale until we found a place of our own.

10: Settling in Alberta

Canada was booming. After the war, there was a high need for construction workers. My dad's first Canadian job paid $0.30/hour. These were the days long before minimum wage. He took what they paid him. He was resolute about stretching those $3.00 a day as far as possible to provide everything his growing family needed. My parents were bent on paying off their huge travelling debt as quickly as possible.

My mother was determined to help. She heard that the local strawberry farm nearby paid women to pick berries. With no money for child-care, she left us little ones in the care of our older brothers. Grandpa Jacob had stayed in Vauxhall with his Friesen in-laws. These were different days. It's hard for us now to imagine leaving five boys between the ages of one and eight at home alone!

She gave firm instructions to Ernie. He was the oldest. He was responsible for us. She left at sunrise, hoping to earn a dollar by the end of the day.

She rushed home for lunch. Still blocks away from our home, she heard shrill shrieking coming from our house. She broke into a run, terrified at what she would see when she arrived. There we were, five boys standing at the back door screaming at the top of our young lungs.

She counted, making sure we were all there. It was clear there was nothing lacking in our lung power. Our Ukrainian neighbour was shingling his roof. He looked over the chaos and couldn't help but chuckle.

It took a few minutes for Mom to calm us down enough so we could tell her what was wrong. My oldest brothers screamed in terrified unison, "Hartmut woat stoawe!" (Hartmut is going to die).

She looked over at her dear little "Harty klein" who was still screaming, and thought, "Well, his lungs are fine!" Bit by bit, the story unraveled. Too young to know better, I had swallowed a penny. Not just any penny. I had swallowed (by accident) a penny that had been set on the railroad tracks. A passing train had flattened it to almost twice its normal size.

My mother didn't know whether to laugh or yell at us! It's okay, she assured us all. I wouldn't die after all. The penny would follow nature's course. My brothers were intrigued. For the next few days, I, or rather my bowel movements, were the centre of attention. Everyone was enthralled with the thought that one day the penny would drop! That very same penny!

We arrived in Coaldale in April. In September, Ernie and Erv were set to go to school. We were dirt poor! We had no money for new clothes, shoes or even the required books. My mother scavenged what she could. She was grateful for the cast-offs given to our family by caring friends and neighbours. She scrounged through the boxes, looking for the perfect pair of shoes for her boys to wear to school.

She unearthed two matching pairs of faded red sandals. Mom had neither time nor money to bother with fashion. The sandals were in good shape. They were a perfect fit for her boys' feet. She sent them out of the door, off to school with a lick and a prayer. She had little time to worry about them as there were ample chores to keep her busy even in Canada.

My brothers were excited to go to school. Both were eager to learn, even though English was still a mystery to them. It's hard to imagine what it would have been like for them to walk into the school, the new boys in town. Dressed in hand-me-downs and shod in those red sandals, the boys really stood out. Everything was new to them.

At recess the children gathered around Ernie and Erv. They pointed at those red sandals, laughing and chanting, "You're wearing girls' shoes! You sissies! Those shoes are for girls!"

The young boys were horrified. How utterly embarrassing and confusing!

But they were quick learners.

Not wanting to bother Mom, they took care of the problem themselves. The next morning, just before arriving at school, they tossed the red sandals into a hedge. They were used to going barefoot. They had never worn shoes in Paraguay. Walking to school barefoot seemed like a much better idea than being ostracized by footwear. Poor Mrs. Emory. Teaching Grade One was hard enough, but dealing with two little barefoot boys who didn't speak or understand English was a new challenge. She was determined to instruct them in the proper etiquette for school and that coming barefoot wasn't appropriate. She tried to explain the rules to them, confusing them even more. In the end, she sent my bewildered brothers home.

We smile at the stories, our hearts warm for these innocent little boys. It was hard being the only children who couldn't communicate easily. It was even more challenging for our parents, who wanted the best for us and were as bewildered as we were in this new land.

But we were children, we learned quickly!

Canada was not quite the land of milk and honey we had anticipated. Perhaps, in the back of my father's mind, he saw the lush and fruitful community of his boyhood. The Mennonite colonies in Russia were at their height when he was a young boy. Yes, the war, revolution, Spanish flu and collectivism destroyed the villages, but each step of the way, the memory of the wealthy estate nagged him.

When I think back, it's hard for me to fathom the stubborn tenacity of my parents. They just didn't give up. They lived five different lives before they were 40 years old. Nothing was easy.

The early years in Coaldale were a mixture of hardship and hope.

In the fall, just after the opening of school, my mother and father made a big decision. It was their first investment in Canada!

They bought a tiny, older home on the far edge of town. The little house came with an acre of land. Long before spring, my mother was already imagining the lush garden she would plant. She hoped they could buy a cow. These growing boys needed milk and fresh vegetables.

We moved into the house that winter. All seven of us squeezed into the main floor of that little doll house, leaving the two bedrooms upstairs available to be rented to Bible School students. The rent they would pay was critical – we needed it to pay the mortgage.

We got a cow that spring. That meant we would have a daily supply of milk and butter. Mom planted a garden and a large bean patch. Mom was in charge of the house and the garden. Dad worked in Lethbridge, about 10 kilometers away. He had no car, so sometimes he walked and sometimes he hitchhiked to work. He did not have a permanent job, but took whatever was available.

A few weeks after my brothers' embarrassing introduction to Canadian school life, there was great excitement at home. Mom and Dad packed us all up and we headed for the Lethbridge train station. We had no idea what was going to happen! When we got there, we saw Uncle Isaac, Mom's older brother with his family. They had just arrived from Paraguay. Preparations for their travel had taken a little more time. Mom's sister, Tante Justine Siemens, and her family followed soon after.

My mother was thrilled to have more of her family arrive! Now we were home. The families had planned to come to Canada with us, but their plans were delayed. I still remember that day, the excitement! I had just turned three years old, but the memory of their arrival is very clear. It was so exciting to have our uncles, aunts and cousins in Canada with us now.

I loved going to Uncle Isaac's. His children were our age. Playing together was a special treat. We often begged to go there. Too often we were ignored. Our daily lives were busy. Dad worked six days a week and Mom was always busy – cooking, gardening, milking, caring for the cow and five growing boys claimed all her attention.

Then, miraculously, one day, my mom herded us all to Uncle Isaac's house. We had no idea what the hurry was – but we were too delighted to complain. Mom and Dad didn't stay, but we were too busy with our cousins to really notice.

Later that night, when Dad came to pick us up, he told us he had good news. We were five boys, consumed by our own schemes and play. It turns out that on that day, June 20, 1949, my sister Mary Ann was born! She had two names. The five of us born in Paraguay did not have middle names. The tradition in our culture had always been for boys to take the first initial of their dad's name as their middle initial.

After five boys, Mom finally gave birth to a little girl. We had a sister!

Maternity leave just wasn't a thing until the 1970s and paternity leave was not even a thought! So, the next day, as usual, Dad went off to work, leaving five little boys to fend for themselves. Mom was still in the hospital with Mary. We were independent little guys, with the quiet determination learned from our parents. Home alone, we decided we missed our mother. So, we set off to visit her at the hospital. It was a long walk. Henry was just two and I was four. But we did it. When we got there, we had no idea what to do or where our mother was. We walked around the hospital, peeking into window after window. We finally found her! Henry, never before separated from his mother, broke into an ear-numbing howl! It must have been a pathetic sight – five little boys standing on tiptoes to peer into the hospital window! One howling at the top of his lungs!

We didn't know what to do. We could see our mother, but there didn't seem to be any way to get to her. As Henry wailed, Ernie took action. Nine years old and clearly the leader, he turned us all around and shepherded us back home. He dragged the hysterical Henry behind him. My mother, not knowing what to do, wept from her hospital bed as she watched the five of us trudge home.

This is Mom with her five boys and our first sister, Mary in 1949. I am on the tricycle.

11: A Growing Family

With six children, our two parents and now Grandpa Jacob too living on one floor of our tiny home, things were getting too crowded. Our house was just too small. Mom and Dad knew we needed a bigger place to live, so they purchased a lot and began building a new house. Just to illustrate the tremendous work ethic so deeply ingrained in our parents, they built the house in the winter. Then in summer, Dad dug out the basement below the house by hand, carting excess dirt away with a wheel barrow.

It was a huge risk for them, requiring great effort and perseverance. Newly immigrated, dirt-poor, with Dad taking on jobs as they came up, they did what needed to be done.

Daily life was filled with stress. Dad, always on the lookout for a good construction job, struggled to find work. As Alberta temperatures plummeted, work in construction fell off. There was no employment insurance or social assistance in those days.

Fortunately, Canada had instigated the Family Allowance in 1945. Nicknamed the "baby bonus," all Canadian families were given an allowance per child. In the late 40s and early 50s, it amounted to a monthly payment of about $6.00/child. Throughout the winter, while trying to build a new house, we survived on little more than $36.00/month. Mom was a genius at cutting corners to save a penny. Generous by nature, she was also determined to survive. I'm not sure how she made it through these years, but her strength was in her love for her family, her promise to God, patience and prayer.

Even though our family lived in severe financial stress, Dad and Mom never neglected their sense of the stewardship of their resources. Everything they had (even if just a little), was from God. They lived in trust that God would provide. Each year, during the church's mission festival, Dad challenged each of us to memorize a Psalm. For each Psalm memorized, a dollar went into the offering plate on Mission Sunday.

"We are never too poor to give," Dad told us, as he showed us to our wide-eyed amazement the $100 bill which he was giving. That was more than he earned in a week at the time.

Brother Ernie remembers another Mission Sunday some years later. By this time, he had been taken out of school to work on construction with Dad. Mom and Dad discussed the mission offering with Ernie, as he was a contributor to our budget. They decided on $1,000. Ernie was so excited. The next Sunday when the result of the mission offering was announced he could hardly wait to hear the total. What a disappointment! After totaling all contributions, only $2,300 had been given by the entire church!?

Less than a year and a half after Mary's birth my mother went off to the hospital again. We five boys were not very observant. Why was she in the hospital again? What was the matter? We were terrified that Mom would not come back. "What is wrong with Mother?" we asked. No one answered. In those days, pregnancy was private. Mom went to the hospital, but we were never told why.

Our mom came home a few days later. Then, after a few more days, she went back to the hospital again. This time an old German granny came to stay with us. She brought with her the classic book, Swiss Family Robinson, in German. With these stories she took our troubled minds on flights of fancy to an exotic deserted island.

Finally, on November 21, Dad came home with the news that we had another sister. They called her Betty Helen. The joy of her birth became tempered with worry and anxiety six months later. Betty was brought to the Coaldale Hospital. After examining her, the doctor admitted her with the explanation that she was very ill and that he did not expect her to survive the night. She had contracted cerebral meningitis, a terrifying illness that would visit our family again some years later. These days are firmly implanted in my memory. I remember walking home with my weeping mother. Just a young boy, I didn't fully understand the situation. I asked what was wrong. She squeezed my hand and said, "We need to pray for Betty. She is very sick."

And so, we prayed. There was nothing more we could do. The medical staff was shocked that Betty survived the night. Our God was not at all surprised that Betty did not just survive the night, but lived to become a beautiful and competent woman. The doctor could not explain Betty's survival. God had answered a little boy's earnest prayers! Our family understood God's providence. God performed a miracle that night!

After five boys born in Paraguay, my parents were delighted at the birth of two girls in Coaldale. Here Dad is holding Betty after her miraculous recovery from meningitis. Mary is standing beside them.

It was time for me to start school. I can't remember much about my school experience in Coaldale. I know that I didn't speak any English when I started school. I had heard a few words from my older brothers, but at home we all spoke German – Plautdietsch for those of us born in Paraguay and High German for the girls.

Only one memory from school in Coaldale stands out for me.

There was a Halloween party at school which included food and drinks. Some of my classmates had brought bottles of pop. After school they carelessly left the empty bottles behind. I jumped at the opportunity to exercise my entrepreneurship. Together with a friend, we took the empty bottles to the store on our way home. We traded them for bubble gum.

I caught up with my brothers, chewing my gum and blowing bubbles like a sassy rich kid. When they asked where I got the gum, I proudly told them exactly what I had done. That night at supper the tale of my delinquent behaviour was a topic of conversation around the table. Dad was not amused. First, he lectured me severely about honesty and the evil of stealing. Then he took off his belt and applied it to my seat of learning. The next day he gave me two cents and told me sternly to take the money to my teacher, to apologize and to promise never to steal anything again.

My memories of our time living in Coaldale are few and far between, but I do have a couple of clear memories of our next-door neighbours, the Neuhof family.

They had come to Canada from Germany after the war devastated their homeland. Their daughter Ingrid was my age. One afternoon while we were all playing outside together, she and I decided to "play doctor," examining each other's bodies minus our clothing. One of my early Sunday school teachers had gone to Africa as a medical missionary and at the time I was telling people that I hoped to be a missionary doctor when I grew up. Somehow, we must have known that our behaviour would be frowned upon, so we chose the outhouse as our examination clinic. When my brothers realized what we were up to, they went and tattled. Mom came rushing out and demanded that we open the door. Then she lectured me very sternly with words that included involvement of the police in this kind of behaviour.

Herr Neuhof was a very stern German disciplinarian. Frequently when he was upset at our behaviour, he would shout, "Komm mal her, komm mal her, und bring auch gleich eine Rute mit" (Come here now and bring a rod with you).

One afternoon Jerry Roberts and his brother, two boys known for mischief in the neighbourhood, were at our house. The boys' mother was a German Mennonite who had married the "English" Mr. Roberts. As the Neuhof's cow was being brought in from the pasture, Jerry and my older brothers decided to create a little drama by kicking the cow in the udder, causing her to bolt off out of control. The boys knew they were in trouble, so they ran and hid in our root cellar.

Herr Neuhof was furious! He came running to our house. When he found the boys cowering in the root cellar, he was bent on revenge. He caught Jerry by the collar and was lecturing him in German. Jerry pretended he didn't understand a word. Herr Neuhof didn't believe a word of it (after all, the boy had a German mother), "Ja, ja, du kanst gut Deutsch verstehen! Deine Mutti hatst mir gesacht" (Oh yes, you can understand German perfectly well. Your mother told me).

I have a vivid memory of standing at our back door right beside Mom. She was trying her darndest to control her laughter. As her belly shook with laughter, we watched the boys being pulled out of the cellar one by one and tossed over our wash line.

Many years later, in Niagara District High I was surprised to see Ingrid, my Coaldale doctor play-mate, in my class. Their family had also moved to Niagara. Sadly, her Dad had taken his own life. We kept the stories of our childhood antics in Coaldale to ourselves!

Our father, struggling to keep five growing and active boys and two little girls busy, was convinced that constructive work was the antidote for delinquency. He struggled with living in a town where there were few chores to keep his children busy and away from delinquent behaviour. He couldn't control our lives when he was working miles away in Lethbridge. Boys like Jerry were a bad influence on his sons.

With farming in his blood, he looked into the possibility of buying a farm. But prices were much too high. At the time, Coaldale was a booming agricultural centre. Sugar beets were a high-yield crop with a good price, jacking up the cost of farmland.

I'm not sure if we were the real reason for my Dad to imagine greener grass, or if it was the "wandering Wiens" in Dad that drove him to think about relocating. Whatever it was, my Dad was constantly searching for the ideal world. His whole life had been marked by insecurity. As a child, he was forced to grow up quickly, given adult responsibility already at 12 years old as his family escaped to China. In Paraguay his family depended on him, but rarely rewarded him with a kind word.

Early in 1952 he scraped together enough money for a train fare to Ontario and headed east. His Uncle David and his cousins lived in Kitchener. They had good employment, but the urban context in which they lived was not what Dad had in mind for his family. From there, he traveled to the Niagara area, where there were many Mennonites involved in fruit farming, but again, these small farms were too expensive for his means. Undecided, he headed back to Alberta through the frigid February chill.

All seven of us kids – and mom – waited at the Coaldale train station to welcome Dad home. An elderly gentleman was watching us. He came to Mom and introduced himself as Peter Warkentin from Tofield, near Edmonton. Mom explained we were waiting for her husband, who had gone to scout out possibilities in Ontario. Warkentin's ears perked up. He was the lay leader of a dwindling congregation of Mennonite Brethren in the Tofield/Lindbrook area. A Mennonite Brethren family with seven children would certainly boost his congregation! He invited us to move north to his area.

The suggestion caught Dad's interest!

Two months later, Dad caught the train and went north to explore the possibilities. He didn't hesitate. He purchased a small farm, two miles north of the little Lindbrook general store on an unimproved dirt road. He bought the farm without Mom or the family having seen it.

This oversight in conjugal economy became a source of great stress and pain in our parents' relationship. As Mom's helper in the house, I was caught in the middle. She needed an outlet and I was there.

This is the last Christmas before our move from Coaldale to Lindbrook. Mom and Dad are top right holding Mary and Betty. Grandpa Jacob is beside Mom and next to him are Uncle Jasch and Tante Justin (Mom's sister). In front from left to right are Ernie, Erv, Hugo and me. I don't know why Henry is not on this photo.

12: Canadian pioneers in Lindbrook

When Dad came back from Lindbrook, he quickly got into action. He sold our house in Coaldale. Then purchased a 1938 Chevrolet stake truck. The truck, already old, had a wooden flatbed which would carry our belongings and all nine of us to Lindbrook.

We drove six hours north, excited to see the new farm my father had purchased. I don't know what my mother expected to see when we got there, but it was not anything like the old Robinson "farm"! Something like this had never appeared in her dreams of happy family life.

The land was covered in poplar scrub bush, not fertile enough for productive crops. The Robinsons had cleared about 80 acres on the 320-acre farm. The farm could not sustain a large family. But it did meet Dad's immediate concern about productive activity for his growing boys. Besides, it was really all our family could afford.

As we drove along the deserted and unfinished road, the farmyard came into sight. My mom went into momentary shock.

There was no neighbour in sight. My extroverted mother's heart sank. But it was worse. The farmyard was rudely constructed and minimal. There was no electricity and no telephone. Our water came from a deep well more than 100 meters from the house. Then, to get the water, we had to hoist it up about 30 meters on a rope and pulley.

The house?

Well, I'm sure our mom did not consider the shack on the farm anything that resembled a home. The Robinsons had built a tiny shack. We could see that they actually lived there from the filth they left behind. Mom refused to move into the house.

Fortunately, not too far from the shack, there was an old abandoned one-room schoolhouse. We had travelled more than six hours in a farm truck crowded with active children. She must have been exhausted. But before she put us to bed, she swept the old school house.

The next day she tackled the farm "house." With shovel and broom in hand, she threw out the human and animal excrement. She ripped out the filthy remnants of linoleum flooring and scrubbed the grimy soot-and-smoke-covered walls and windows. As she worked, she wept. Amidst the tears she sang: "Coaldale, mein Coaldale," a line from one of Uncle Heinrich's poems.[2]

"How could Abram be so insensitive?" she moaned. But once again she reminded herself of her marriage vows. She resolved not to nag her husband. This was the right time to grit her teeth and forge ahead. My father put his back into the task at hand – he had a lot of work to do!

We had nothing. Just the few possessions we brought with us on the truck. Dad began visiting auction sales. He bought an old Oliver tractor, a square, black 1932 Chevrolet car, and a few cows and pigs – the essentials to launch his foray into farming in northern Alberta.

Mom's extroverted nature pushed through. She did not hold her grief and disappointment inside. Her bitterness showed itself in her songs. There was little joy in the melancholic "Heimatslieder" she sang as she worked. But her frustrations boiled over into the kitchen where Erv and I worked alongside her (Mary took her place in the kitchen when she was old enough to help). We did our best to make and maintain peace at home, walking a fine line between my father's dream and my mother's bitterness. The determination to keep her vows were a weak buffer for the grief growing deep inside.

In May of 1952, Grandpa Jacob remarried. He chose Anna Penner as his new wife. This tiny, spritely widow had experienced much of the same grief my family had experienced: she had fled from Russia as a widow with two children, having lost her husband. But she did not live out of her pain. I can only remember her with a smiling face and a melodic laugh that seemed almost like a constant giggle. We called her "Kleine Oma" (Little Grandma). When they came to live with us in the summer of 1952, my father moved a small granary onto our yard. The little one-room shack became their home. Their gentle, quiet presence softened Mom's pain. The elderly couple encouraged our struggling family. Their presence gave us new hope.

---

[2] (https://mennonitehistory.org/heinrich-d-friesen-fonds-4-cm/)

This is Grandpa Jacob with Kleine Oma, taken in front of their house on our farm in Lindbrook.

The small Mennonite Brethren congregation in Lindbrook was a social and spiritual life-line for us, especially for Mom. Dad and Mom were still struggling with their English. German-speaking "brothers and sisters" in the church were regular Sunday visitors or hosts for us.

On the crisp winter evening of February 23, 1953, the Nachtigal family were guests and stayed late into the night. When they finally left, Mom hurriedly put us to bed and then she and Dad headed for the Tofield hospital, 16 kilometers away. Once again, it was time to give birth, and once again it was a girl. Five boys and now there were three girls in succession! When Dad shared the happy news with us the next morning, we all wanted to contribute to the naming of our latest sister. The choice was unanimous. She would be Margaret Frieda, named after the Warkentins' daughters who were our much-loved Sunday school teachers.

About this time, I made my personal decision to accept Jesus into my life. I remember very little about this experience except that I was very restless and unhappy after we had come home from an evening of evangelistic emphasis at the Lindbrook Church. I don't recall the content of the service, but it had to do with the need to be born again and have our sins forgiven if we wanted to go to heaven. I was sure I wanted to go to heaven and I was troubled to think that I might not be prepared.

The only gospel we understood was the "Gospel of Sin Management." We understood the Christian message as how we deal with our sin. Our ultimate goal was to sin as little as possible with the possibility of heaven at the other end.

When I think back, I'm sure this understanding of the Gospel had a lot to do with our mother's insecurity about her own salvation experience. On the night I remember, the night after the church service, I was so troubled I couldn't sleep. I got up and went to talk with my mother. She sensed that my dis-ease might be related to the service at church. She talked to me about my relationship with Jesus, then asked if I wanted to invite Jesus into my heart. When I nodded, she prayed with me.

The memory of that moment is very clear for me. Mom was sitting on the steps of the old farmhouse, and I was kneeling at her feet as we prayed together. This was not the first time Mom had prayed with me by any means. Since I was a small child, she taught me to recite German prayers before going to bed.

The prayer I remember best is:
Christi Blut und Gerechtigkeit, das ist mein Schmuck und Ehrenkleid, damit will ich vor Gott bestehn, wenn ich zum Himmel werd eingehen.

The prayer translates as: Christ's blood and righteousness, this is my adornment and my dress of honour; with this I want to stand before God when I enter heaven.

Mom used the German Luther Bible to teach me to read, even before I went to school. While my grandchildren think the gothic script is strange and exotic writing, that's really how I learned to read.

The lay minister at our little church in Lindbrook was Peter Warkentin. The Warkentins' daughters were my Sunday school teachers. The Warkentins also had a young son my age. Walter and I were in the same class at school and we became good friends. I loved going to the Warkentins' on Sunday after church. Their farm was much more productive than ours. They even had a young German immigrant serving as their hired man on the farm. In a gully at the back of the farm they had a collection of old discarded cars of various models. We pretended to drive these old Model A's and Model T's.

They had a large, new barn which gave us so many places to hide in our games of hide-and-seek. One day I was hiding up in the hay loft. When I realized that the "it" had seen me, I bolted for the door, forgetting I was in the loft. I flew out the open door, my legs continuing to flail in the air. I landed on the ground running and made it to home base first.

The tiny dilapidated house on our unproductive farm made the relationship between our mom and dad bristly. Dad knew Mom was not happy. Something needed to change.

During our first winter, Dad, along with Grandpa Jacob, foraged the 320 acres of poplar scrub for the largest trees. In the spring, a local entrepreneur brought his large portable sawmill to our yard and cut the logs into usable lumber. The first priority was food and income. So during the summer and fall of 1953 Dad and Mom worked together to build a modest barn.

Then they demolished the filthy old farm house and built a new one in its place. The new house was completed in stages, as time and money permitted. At first, we all lived in the basement. Eventually, rooms on the main floor were completed to the point that some of us older kids could sleep there. I recall during the first winter the rooms were so cold that water would freeze at night.

In good Mennonite fashion, other members of the church came to our farm to help out with the building project. I clearly recall fellow parishioners from the little Lindbrook church sitting around our yard straightening old rusty nails to be reused.

While building our house, we slept in one half of the new barn while the other half was occupied by the milk cows. Grandpa Jacob and Kleine Oma moved back to Coaldale, so the granary that had been their home became our kitchen.

There was plenty of work for us on the farm. The oldest three boys had a long list of daily chores. There were cows to milk, cream to separate (manually), pigs and chickens to feed, the large garden to weed in the summer and the younger children to keep an eye on.

We sold the cream from our cows to a creamery. Once a week the "cream" truck drove up to our farm to pick up the cream. We collected the separated cream in milk cans in our basement. There were few checks and balances from a sanitation perspective. I quickly learned the importance of keeping the can covered when we found a mouse floating in it one day.

Another clear memory of our church community at work from our early days on the farm were the times we spent together butchering animals in the fall for our meat supply. Friends from church would come over for the day to help with butchering (usually a pig) at least once a year. Since we had no refrigeration, most of the meat had to be made into smoked hams and long links of smoked sausage which could be kept in our cool basement. Some meat was preserved in jars.

But the best part of butchering was the cracklings. As the pig was butchered, the fat was tossed into a large vat to be rendered. It was impossible to remove all the meat from the fatty pieces. Little bits of pork were deep fried in the lard. My mother scooped this fatty meat into containers. These cracklings were delicious! There's nothing better than fried potatoes with cracklings and bread slathered in pig fat!

The farm was not highly profitable. Our family struggled financially. The heavy workload and tight finances were very stressful on Mom and Dad. But there were always hearty, healthy meals. Most of our food was grown in our garden. We stored enough potatoes and carrots for the entire winter in our cellar. We had plenty of milk – and, with no fridge to store it, we were encouraged to drink as much as possible. One of the few things we purchased was flour, which Mom turned into bread. She baked large quantities every other day in our wood-fired stove. I remember coming home from school and seeing a half dozen loaves of fresh white and brown bread on the kitchen table. We would polish off one loaf before going out to do our chores. The bread tasted delicious fresh from the oven at home, but in our lunch pails at school the thick homemade bread was an embarrassment. Our parents didn't have money for store-bought lunch boxes or the ever-so-popular Wonder bread. We carried our lunches to school in empty honey pails. We definitely stood out.

Dad was strict and determined to raise his family well. Following the traditions of Mom's family, meal times included lots of story-telling. Every day we had devotions together. We sang and we prayed. We always stood around the table while praying. As children, we were sensitive to the strange customs of our family. We knew that others could see us standing around the table and praying. We were different. It embarrassed us.

We were well disciplined. Dad used his belt on our bottoms with some regularity. Our infractions were many – we were active and mischievous boys. Even small things, like complaining about the food, were well disciplined.

One of Dad's motivations for moving our family out of Coaldale to our farm in Lindbrook was to protect us from delinquent behaviour. But boys would be boys. Left on our own, with a little imagination and free time, even in Lindbrook we managed to find trouble.

There was a family in the community that we thought was a bit odd. As kids we made fun of them, entertaining ourselves. This family lived quite a distance from us, but owned a second abandoned farm within walking distance of our place. One Sunday afternoon we were a little bored. Two of our friends from church were over, so we went for a walk to the abandoned farm. The abandoned house had lots of windows and our friends had a BB gun. We had a great time with the gun and broke all the windows. Then in the abandoned barn we discovered that pigeons had made this their nesting place. It was full of pigeon eggs and baby pigeons. We went on a tear, slaughtering baby pigeons and breaking the eggs.

Then we went home. We were, collectively, smart enough not to share our adventures with our family. But we were easy to find. The owner of the farm paid a little visit to our father, telling him about our adventures on his property.

My father was not amused. We were poor, but he dug deep and found enough money to cover the repairs of the windows. He gave us the cash and sent us to the farmer to apologize. It was a difficult lesson to learn. Not only did we have to live through the embarrassment of apologizing, but we knew our parents did not have extra money to spare. Our antics had cost them precious dollars they had not budgeted for.

The simple tradition of driving to church tested our family's faith! We lived two miles from Highway #14. Our road was really just a dirt trail between fields. It was not maintained and hardly passable after heavy rains, or in winter or during the spring thaw. This wasn't out of the norm for northern Alberta at the time. Most of our friends lived on dirt roads.

One Sunday afternoon we were visiting our friends, the John Warkentins. An afternoon thunderstorm churned the rural dirt road to an immense mud pie. As slippery as ice, my father carefully navigated the muddy ruts on the way home in our ancient '32 Chevy. As he drove, frantically trying to keep in the tracks, the mud sucked the wheels out of the ruts and over the steep embankment. Miraculously the door locks of the ancient car held as it tumbled over the wet grass and then came to rest on its wheels at the bottom of the ravine.

As the family emerged from the dust-filled car, Dad did a quick inspection and found that we were all accounted for. No one had been seriously injured. Hugo however, had a slight cut on his knee and was crying loudly. When asked if it hurt so much, he howled, "No, my knee doesn't hurt very much, but somebody is going to die now, because we've just had an accident!" Perhaps he had in his mind the story we had heard of Preacher Warkentin's young son who had been killed when a train hit their car.

The accident was never far from our memory. The whole family was tense whenever we drove in bad weather – from slippery ice and snow to heavy rains. There were many tears. Mom's personal way of dealing with stress and tension was passed on to the rest of us. When it looked tense and danger was approaching, she launched into song. One of her favourites was "Ein herrlicher Retter ist Jesus mein Herr" (A wonderful Saviour is Jesus my Lord).

Our new house was almost ready to move into. It wasn't nearly finished. The floor was rough used plywood. To save money Dad had acquired plywood that had been used for forming concrete walls. The plywood was covered with rough patches of cement that stuck to the surface.

One of my jobs as Mom's helper in the home was to wash the floors. She would inspect them after I was finished. She focused on the corners because in her mind if the corners were clean the rest would be clean too. My issue was more with the rest of the floor where I was constantly washing over dried crusts of concrete.

Although the house was not completely finished, my parents did not hesitate to extend hospitality to church families and even visitors from other communities. We almost always had guests over for dinner on Sundays. Our family regularly hosted missionaries on their "deputation" stops in Lindbrook. This had a powerful impact on all of us. I am sure it contributed to the choice of many of us to serve in foreign mission assignments.

Our home also became the very frequent destination of many of the other boys from church, especially in winter. The slough of our neighbours, the French Canadian Gobault family, became the community hockey rink. While we were at church, the Gobaults, who did not attend church, cleared the rink and got it ready. After a hearty lunch of such delicacies as fried potatoes with cracklings and "plume moos" at our house, we all headed across the road for an afternoon of hockey on the Gobault's slough. Elderly Mr. Gobault was the perennial goalie, minus skates. He kept the puck out as much with his shouting "Get it away from here" as with his homemade goalie stick.

Our hockey equipment was minimal. Our skates were $.25 Salvation Army issue. My first skates were size 8, the same as my age. I could practically get into them with my shoes on. Our hockey sticks were bent willow sticks cut from the bush on our yard. My older brothers, especially Erwin and Hugo, were superb athletes and often dominated the game. I learned very early that athletics was not my bent (maybe it was the skates!). Most afternoons I grew tired of lagging behind the play, and frustrated with my enormous and uncomfortable skates. I would duck out of the game and sit on the sidelines cuddling with our much-loved family dog, Corky.

As much as we loved Corky, he was never allowed in the house. A farm dog was a working dog. Their place was in the barn with the other animals. We had many cats – also residing in the barn. They were important to keep the mice population in check. They were well fed! When milking our cows by hand, our cats sat up on their hind legs, waiting for us to squirt milk into their mouths. Our aim was excellent!

Those of us who were school age were picked up by our bus driver, Mr. Bruce. His bus was basically a panel truck with benches on either side at the back. Between the six from our family, Gobaults' son Armand and another four from our neighbours, the Siemens family, we almost filled it to capacity. (Mrs. Siemens was our Tante Justine, Mom's older sister.) The bus would pass our house to go pick up Armand and the Siemens' children first. When we saw the bus pass by, we knew that we had about 10 minutes to get ready. If we were still in the middle of running the cream separator, we would crank it up and let it finish on its own – not recommended. The separator was meant to run at a steady speed.

The 16 kilometer bus ride to school and back was long enough for us to get sleepy. I recall often falling asleep on the bus, especially on the long ride home in the afternoon.

My older brothers were not just great athletes, they also did very well at school. I did not excel, either in athletics or academics. When the teacher at school assigned captains to choose baseball teams, I hung back with embarrassment because I knew I would be the last one selected. Even at home when we were tossing the ball around the yard, I was so awkward that my brothers would sometimes ask if I had a wooden leg. Academically, I believe I was more of a dreamer than a student. I dreamed of inventing things, and when I was asked what I hoped to be when I grew up, I always answered, "A missionary." Where did that come from? Was our mother's prayer at work in my life? I do remember comparing the words of songs in our German hymnal with the words to the same hymns in English. I found the comparisons fascinating. Was this a harbinger to my future career in linguistics and Bible translation?

In Grade 2, around the coronation of Queen Elizabeth, each student in the classroom was given a "gold" commemorative coin to celebrate this historic event. The coin had no monetary value, but to me, a coin meant the power to buy and sell. When a classmate offered to trade my coin for some bubble gum, I eagerly accepted the offer. This was at least something I could enjoy and this time it was not purchased with stolen property, so that Dad would not discipline me at home.

Like most young boys, I also had mischief in me. I recall one year when our school was adding a new wing to our building. Watching the workers during recess was fascinating, especially for us boys. Our teacher, Mrs. Torrey, came to tell us we were not allowed to be so close to the workers. When I thought she had gone, I insolently turned around and stuck out my tongue.

She scolded me and let it go. But on further reflection, I knew that what I had done was very wrong. My "sin" weighed heavy on my conscience. Even during our next summer holiday, I was so troubled by what I had done that when I saw a car just like Mrs. Torrey's '53 Chevy driving onto our yard, I ran to the barn out of shame. Finally, the next year when I was already in another grade, I had the courage to walk across the hall and apologize to Mrs. Torrey.

During all the work and worry in our new life on the farm, and in spite of the tensions provoked by our move to this miserable farm, Dad and Mom still found time for intimacy in their marriage. The fruit of their ongoing love emerged on March 11, 1954, in the birth of their ninth child, another son.

Of course, the rest of us wanted a hand in naming this new brother! My Dad brought up his youngest brother, David. In all the pain surrounding his family of origin, he still carried a deep love for this brother. He suggested we consider the name David in honour of his brother. The family readily agreed.

We welcomed David John into our family! He quickly became the joy and delight of the entire family, especially Dad. The standing joke in the family was that David should have been called Joseph, because he certainly had been given the "colourful coat." Dad loved him dearly! In fact, he had a special place in all of our hearts. David knew how to tell stories and crack jokes, to the delight of our whole family. A German hymn we often sang included the line "er ist mein Bruder mein Freund" (he is my brother and friend), referring of course to Jesus, but David would snuggle up in his brother Erwin's lap singing, "du bist mein Bruder mein Freund."

In 1955, in an effort to improve our economic prospects on the farm and to build our tiny herd of cattle, Dad agreed to manage a large herd of prize Aberdeen Angus cattle owned by a young Mennonite man who lived in Edmonton and did not have property on which to run his herd. We had enough pasture land for the summer and would work hard to make hay to feed them for the winter. In exchange we would be given a percentage of the offspring that would be added to the herd while in our care. That summer, making hay in preparation for the winter became a top priority. It was not the best summer for crops. So Dad and my older brothers cut hay grass in all the dried-up sloughs they could find.

One August evening, after an exhausting day of making hay, they came home to find our household in chaos. I was trying to calm our younger siblings, who were in a panic of fear and worry. Elderly Mrs. Gobault was in the basement, cleaning up a bloody mess.

I was at the center of this story and it was a defining moment in my relationship with our mother. Just nine years old, I had gone to the pasture with her to bring in the cows. I can still see the time perfectly. As we went in search of the cows, she told me stories from her childhood, especially about how much she had loved to run. She commented about how the weight she had gained around her middle from the birth of nine children made it harder to run like she used to. Later, when she had finished the milking, I took the cows back out to the pasture.

On my way home, I dawdled, picking ripe saskatoon berries and raspberries along the way. Suddenly I heard my sisters yelling at the top of their lungs for me to hurry home. When I got to the house, I found Mom down in the basement, sitting in a pool of blood. She instructed me to hurry and get help. Of course, there were no telephones. Gobaults, our closest neighbours, were about a half kilometer away. I ran there to see if anyone was there who could help.

Elderly and overweight Mrs. Gobault was home alone with her grandson and she was in the outhouse. I told her what I knew and asked if she could come and help. She came as quickly as she could, but her walk was little more than a slow waddle. I ran on ahead to inform Mom that Mrs. Gobault was on her way. She responded, "I don't know if I can live long enough."

That injected a terrifying urgency into the situation for me. I ran as fast as I could to the next closest neighbours', our Tante Justine Siemens, Mom's sister. Not athletic, I was a fantastic distance runner. I covered the two kilometers to Tante Justine's in record time. I ran cross country to save time. I don't remember how I hurdled over the two fences along the way, but I was determined to get to help as fast as possible.

Tante Justine and her family were eating supper when I burst into their kitchen, shouting, "Mama woat stoawe" (Mom is dying). Tante Justine responded calmly, "Neh, so schwind stoawe de Mensche nich" (No, people don't die that easily). In spite of her calm demeanor, she quickly sprang into action. Fortunately, her son, my cousin Rudy, had just arrived home from work in his truck. We all jumped into the 1950 Chevy pickup and roared down the dusty dirt road at top speed. (Rudy had a reputation for speed)!

When we got to our house, Tante Justine and Rudy worked fast. Everything was "schwind, schwind." They lifted Mom, carried her up the stairs and put her into the truck. Then they rushed off to the Tofield hospital, 16 kilometers away. I was left in charge of my younger brothers and sisters.

When Mrs. Gobault finally arrived in response to my appeal for help, she had brought along her young grandson. I remember standing in the yard with him, telling him earnestly that we needed to pray for my mother. I don't know if he understood anything I was saying, because their family was not involved in church. But for me this was the time to pray harder than I had ever prayed in my life and that is what I did.

Dad finally got home with my older brothers. He rushed to the hospital.

The news was not good. The doctor explained that Mom had been hemorrhaging for hours and had lost a lot of blood. He did not expect her to survive the night. With a heavy heart, Dad drove home to report the situation to us. He did his best to care for us in our needs. All of us were terrified. Mom was the heart of our family. With unspeakable sorrow and fear, we prayed and wept. We did our best to comfort each other.

Late that night, as Dad struggled to find sleep in the midst of his anxiety and sorrow, a group of young adults from our little congregation in Lindbrook gathered at his window and sang hymns of comfort and hope. Miraculously, beyond all of our expectations, God granted our mother an extension to her life. Of all the experiences of my life, often working closely at her side in the home, there is none that bound me more closely to her and her to me. We were bound together in life by our kindred spirits and now in this near-death experience.

The strong bond between us was always evident to me and I expect it was to others in our family as well. While she didn't tell me the prayer she had prayed during her pregnancy with me until much later, she instilled in me a deep devotion to Christ and a passion for service to others.

Her knowledge of Scripture profoundly impacted me. Her source for all things was God. My life and the direction I chose were highly influenced by a couple of specific biblical texts. One is Ezekiel 22:30 where God says, "I looked for someone among them who would build up the wall and stand before me in the gap on behalf of the land so I would not have to destroy it, but I found no one." Then she showed me Isaiah 6:8: "Then I heard the voice of the Lord saying, 'Whom shall I send? And who will go for us?'"

Even as a young boy I clearly determined that when God called, I would answer. I would stand in the gap, serving in God's Kingdom. No one would say that when God called, he found no one. This clearly impacted my decision to commit my life to missionary service.

As we worked, my mom sang. She had a huge collection of songs, not all from the hymnbook! She used to add my name to a little folk ditty: "Harty klein Ging allein in die weite Welt hinein. Stock und Hut Steht ihm gut, er ist wohlgemut. Aber Mama weint so sehr, Hat ja nun keinen Harty mehr!" (Little Harty went out alone into the world at large. His cane and his hat suit him well. He is very pleasant and good-natured. But mother cries and cries. She no longer has her Harty!) She personalized it for me because the actual German lyrics have "Hänschen" instead of "Harty." I often feel that her playfulness and imagination, even in our harsh circumstances, birthed my penchant to dream!

Sometime after Mom's near-death experience, we attended the funeral of Mrs. Goerz, the wife of one of the lay ministers in the Lindbrook Church. Our cousin Rudy had married their daughter, so there was an affinal kinship connection. We mourned with the family at their loss. Their tears touched us deeply. After the burial, I remember Mom squeezing my hand and saying, "See what it's like when people lose their mother." I'm sure she was thinking about the premature loss of her mother in Paraguay, but to me it was a powerful statement encouraging me to thank God again for saving my mother's life.

After my mother's brush with death, my own duties as her helper were extended. Just nine years old, I took on her share of the "milk-maid" duties. Everyday Erwin and I milked the cows and hand-cranked the milk through the cream separator.

With my older brothers busy in the field, I had to step up. One day they told me to cook borscht and have it ready when the haymakers came home that night. The only meat available for this borscht was a hunk of old very fatty mutton, a meat we had rarely, if ever, used at home. That afternoon I put the meat on to cook and then got the vegetables ready. The potatoes were new and fairly clean, so I thought, why spend my precious playtime washing them? They would be boiled anyway.

By the time Dad and my brothers got home, the borscht was on a steady boil. When Erv lifted the cover, he was horrified. There in the pot was a boiling mass of dirt-blackened fat. After skimming off the black mess and adding a few spices, the borscht was declared edible – barely! I have never lived this down. My infamous "Schoaps Borscht" is a prized entry in the family lore. My brothers and sisters still love to tell the story of Hart's borscht. It was my first attempt! I have learned a lot about cooking and baking since then.

The fall and winter of 1955-56, following Mom's near-death experience, were the most difficult and trying days in the life of our family. Canada had not yet introduced universal health care. With no health insurance, the surgery Mom had was costly. After the hysterectomy, she needed to stay in the hospital for a long time.

Mom had brought nine children into the world. Little David would be the last one. Life was very difficult. We were nine children under 15 years old. There were three preschoolers; two of them still in diapers. Daily life was overwhelming. When we asked my Mom years later how she managed with so many children, she said that the older kids were always there to help with the younger. I was in the middle.

The commitment to the prize herd of cattle brought tremendous pressure. Not only was the hay crop poor, the winter was one of the coldest winters in history. The cattle suffered extensive casualties. So much for building up our own herd. The financial stresses were severe. Reluctantly, Dad asked fifteen-year-old brother Ernie to quit school to help with chores. More than that, Dad asked him to go with him to find work on construction in Edmonton. We could not survive on the farm alone. Our family needed a regular and dependable income to survive.

Christmas was bleak that year. Much to Dad's chagrin and embarrassment, food hampers from local women's groups were delivered and awkwardly received at our door.

Mom was overwhelmed. With Dad working away from home most of the time, the hard work of managing the day-to-day chores and caring for the children were too much for her as she continued to recover from her major surgery. We all felt the heavy weight of her sadness. Resourceful Hugo thought of a way to bring a ray of sunshine into Mom's depressed mind. Just before Christmas, he cut small trees from our substantial stand of spruce. He bundled them on our truck and went to Edmonton with Dad. He went from door-to-door to sell them.

He earned a handsome sum. Selfless, he bought a fancy bedspread for our mother. She was still not well. Loving to give gifts, the financial stress of daily life was hard on her. She frequently tried to inspire us to unselfish service with the words, "Others Lord yes others, let this my motto be." We tried to live by that motto.

But she shocked us that Christmas. Hugo proudly presented his generous and loving gift. We all expected joy from Mom!

But she burst out with uncharacteristic anger. "How could you spend that much money on such a lavish gift when there is hardly enough money to feed the family?"

Mom was better at giving than receiving gifts. The hurt of this story grew dim as our family survived the Lindbrook farm. Today we can laugh about it, understanding the incredible pressure on our parents.

The stand of spruce trees where Hugo cut his trees was good for more than harvesting Christmas trees. The wood lot was full of squirrels and birds, especially the hated magpies. Hunting these critters was one of the things we loved to do, especially when Uncle Isaac's family would come from Coaldale to visit, with their two young boys our age, also named Ernie and Erwin.

We loved spending time with our cousins Ernie and Erwin.

I remember a trip to Coaldale to visit Grandpa Jacob and Kleine Oma. Uncle Isaac and his family lived there as well. Our whole family crowded into our new Fargo pickup truck. Dad and Mom and the little kids sat in the front. We sat in the back! Dad built a plywood cab on the back and where we boys sat on wooden benches on either side.

This particular visit was special. Ernie and Erwin (our Coaldale cousins) were coming back to Lindbrook with us.

We had a great time! They taught us how to make arrow guns using tongue and groove siding boards. We cut the siding to look like guns, with the groove on top to form the trajectory for our arrows. The arrows were fashioned from wooden shingles. We used inner tube rubbers to provide impetus. Cousin Ernie was especially good at shooting with these arrow guns. Quite a number of squirrels and magpies met their demise under our fire power.

Even though life was filled with stress and our days with hard work, Dad and Mom attempted to make time for fun and play with us. On Sunday afternoons Dad would come out in the yard to play ball. One Easter they worked together out in the woods behind our yard to make a very special swing, called a "pogge schockle" (frog swing), hanging from a branch jutting out high up in one of the taller trees. It had a long board on which several of us could sit and swing together.

As I grew older, I was assigned more work, given more responsibility. On one cold winter day, it was my turn to take the cattle to drink at our slough. It was about a half kilometer away. In the Alberta winters, the sloughs always froze over. To water the cattle, we chopped a trough right in the ice. Then we chopped a hole through the ice in the middle to fill the trough. It took a bit of work for a young lad.

As I flexed my 10-year-old muscles to chop at the ice, the thirsty cows crowded in, eager to be the first to get at the water. I hauled off and brought the axe down. Just then one of the cows stuck her nose under the falling blow. The axe head stuck deep into her nose. I ran home crying! I was afraid I had killed the cow. She survived! (Until it was time to take her to the slaughter house.)

I carried my full share of the load in the milking barn. But my father and brothers kept me from the machinery. They didn't consider me adept at anything mechanical.

One summer while making hay, I begged to drive the tractor pulling the sled-type hay rack. We piled hay high on the rack as the tractor traveled from one clump of hay to another. When I finally got my turn to drive, I jerked the clutch so hard that the entire rack came apart. The almost-completed load of hay dropped out. We not only had to restack the hay, we had to fix the rack! You can imagine that story was also added to the family story book.

Another time I begged my father to let me stay home from school and work the summer fallow. When I got out to the tractor, it refused to start. When things like that happened on the farm, I had seen others tow the machine that would not start. So, I hooked the truck up to the tractor and began to pull it around the yard. Of course, there was no one on the tractor and I didn't think about what I would do IF the tractor actually started while I was pulling it.

To add to the family's pain and stress that bitter winter of 1955-56, the slipped disc Dad had in his back from those childhood experiences of carrying more than his share of heavy loads, flared up. In January, he spent several weeks in the hospital as the doctors applied traction to his injured back with very little improvement. Again, with no health insurance, another great financial burden was added to the family. Depression and gloom descended on our household and threatened to overwhelm us. The pain from his slipped disc was something Dad carried throughout his life. He rarely complained about it, but he walked with a pronounced limp. When anyone asked him about his limp, he would say, "Daut es bloss enne domme Aunjewahnheit" (That's just a silly habit of mine).

The recovery of family health, renewal of hope and restoration to financial equilibrium, was slow but sure. As Dad and Ernie commuted to Edmonton to earn money in the construction industry, the rest of us worked hard to run the farm. All of us had chores to do. There was not a lot of time for play.

Gradually some hospital debts were paid off and the financial stress began to ease. For Mom, the stress was never conquered entirely. I still hear her lament ringing in my ears, "Die Schult, die Schult!" (the debt, oh the debt). Those of us who worked closely by her side were most deeply affected by this anxiety over our finances.

Her worry over finances impacted me, even as a young child. I didn't understand the dynamics of the family and specific financial information, but I had heard my Mom moan about the debt. And I knew the debt was a result of Mom and Dad going to the hospital.

Yet, as you already ascertained, accidents were bound to happen.

One afternoon, we were playing with our cousins on the haystacks piled up near our barn. We were having a great time climbing up and then sliding down. To show off, I decided to slide down backwards. At the bottom was a large log used as a weight to keep the hay from blowing away. I hit the log hard with my forehead. The blood gushed out.

I needed stitches. When my parents told me that I needed to go to the doctor, I became unreasonably distraught. Crying loudly, they asked me if the pain was very bad. "No," I told them, "but it will cost so much to go to the doctor." I didn't want to be the reason for more debt.

They took me anyway. The doctor did a good job stitching the gash, but I still have a dent and a scar in my forehead to remind me of that experience.

Besides managing the work on our own farm, people from our church community often asked if we would care for their farm chores while they went on vacation. After all, we were a family of nine children and needed the extra income. They left "exotic" canned food for us to eat while we managed their farm animals. I loved these side jobs. We never had canned pork and beans at our house!

Except for the Christmas that terrible winter of 1955, our parents always did their very best to come up with gifts for all of us. We had so little, so we appreciated the effort they made.

Dad would usually buy a huge bulk bag of assorted nuts, sweets and a generous tin of halva. On Christmas Eve we all went to church. Every year the Sunday school put on a special Christmas program. As we left the church, every child received a "tute" (bag). Each bag was stuffed with unshelled nuts, candy and fruits. We savoured the orange or apple. We rarely had that kind of fresh fruit at home.

While the Christmas Eve Sunday school programs, with the much awaited "tute" to follow, were always a highlight, there could also be some embarrassment. As the Sunday school children were presenting the program, we were all up in the choir loft in front of the church. With my penchant for falling asleep at any time and anywhere, I fell asleep during one of our programs. There I was in front of everyone, fast asleep, with my head back and my mouth wide open. Mom was mortified and let me know it. I was embarrassed too, but it would not be the last time I would fall asleep in public.

After the church program on Christmas Eve, we would come home and lay our plates out at our place around the large kitchen table. This is where the "Wienachtsmaun" was to deposit a gift for us.

One Christmas, a few of us woke up shortly after midnight. Curious to see if "Wienachtsmaun" had already arrived, we snuck out to the kitchen to check. There, lying across three plates – Hugo's, Henry's and mine – was a brand-new toboggan. You can't expect little boys to go back to bed! No, we took it outside and tested it right away.

We had few toys, but vast amounts of imagination. In the summer, when our chores were done or we had a little free time, we made elaborate roads and towns in the loose soil near the pig pen. We improvised in many different ways to do the excavating and landscaping work required.

My gift for our last Christmas in Lindbrook was a beautiful dump truck. It had a lever which I could activate to actually make the dump box go up. I was thrilled. But I never got a chance to test it out in our miniature town.

This was our last Christmas in Lindbrook.

These are my parents with five of us in 1957, two years before our move from Lindbrook to Ontario. I am at the top left and Hugo is beside me. In the front row from left to right are Muggs, Dave and Mary.

13: On to Ontario

The farm was neither large enough nor fruitful enough to make a living for a large family like ours. We were not afraid of hard work and we all pitched in to give our best, but the real limitation was Dad's fear of making choices and taking financial risks.

My mother and father were active and caring members of the Lindbrook Mennonite Brethren congregation. Their spiritual life and commitment to Christ did not go unnoticed. In time, they were called to the diaconal ministry.

Serving and supporting their faith community was a given for them. However, their increased responsibility and involvement in the leadership of the congregation was stressful. My father was especially affected by the stress of conflict and resolution. Risk-averse, he avoided getting involved in conflict as much as possible. As a deacon, he became entangled in a power struggle between the two ordained lay ministers in the congregation. When he felt he was being forced to choose between two senior leaders in the church, he felt trapped.

He began to look for an exit strategy.

Whether it was Dad's need to run from the tension, or his restless spirit, is up for debate. Whatever the reason, in January of 1959, he once again boarded the train and headed east. He was looking for greener pastures and more opportunities.

We had lived on our farm in Lindbrook for more than six years. It was by far the longest stretch our family ever stayed put in one place.

During his visit to Ontario, the Niagara area caught his attention. His sister, Tante Lena Sawatzky, and her family had immigrated to Niagara from Paraguay a few years earlier. Unlike Dad, Tante Lena's husband, Onkel Jasch, was not risk-averse. He had only been in Canada for a few years and he was already well employed. He had started his own construction business.

Dad was really impressed with the region. He saw many churches, large and active. He took note of the active youth programs. He had nine active children – a good church environment was important.

Many immigrants from Paraguay had left the Mennonite colonies since our parents had emigrated and many were settling in the Niagara region. There appeared to be plenty of work available in the construction industry. And the work was close by. Eliminating an hour-long commute appealed to Dad.

He also noted that the fruit farms allowed mothers to take the younger children as they picked fruit. This would give Mom a chance to earn some extra money during the summer.

Dad returned to Lindbrook with renewed energy and enthusiasm. In almost no time, the farm was sold, an auction sale scheduled and a trailer built to accommodate our household goods and our personal belongings.

On Good Friday morning in 1959, Dad, Mom and eight of their nine children piled into our almost-new 1958 six-cylinder Chevrolet Belair. With a trailer in tow, we headed east for the 3,500-kilometer drive across the country and through parts of the USA. Our brother Erwin stayed behind in Lindbrook with our friends Dick and Netty Thiessen to finish his Grade 11 school year. Staying also allowed him to play on the school baseball team for a final season, something he loved with a passion.

I was in eighth grade when we left Lindbrook and moved to Niagara-on-the-Lake. This close to the end of the school year seemed like a most inconvenient time for us to make such a major move, not just to a new school, but a new province altogether.

I'm sure it was disruptive to our education for all of us. However, it hit me especially hard. For one thing, I had not been at the head of my class in Alberta. Also, there was a huge difference between the eighth grade curricula in the two provinces. The Alberta curriculum did not focus a lot on teaching grammar. Apparently, it was assumed that children would learn the grammar intuitively through reading and writing. In Ontario, elementary school was actually called "Grammar School." By the end of eighth grade, students were expected to have mastered English grammar.

When I arrived at Colonel John Butler School, I was totally lost and confused by what I encountered. Every day, students were up at the blackboard diagramming sentences – underlining subjects and predicates, nouns and verbs, etc. I felt like I had just come from another planet. I could not recall ever hearing of nouns or verbs before, much less subjects, predicates, infinitives and gerunds. I didn't have a clue what was going on.

Miss Alice Howe, our principal and home room teacher, called my parents to a meeting. With great apology, she informed Mom and Dad that she would not be able to promote me to the next grade. With my very limited academic preparation, she was sure that I would not be able to manage in high school. Since money was tight for our family, and I already knew I would have to do Grade 8 over again, I stayed home for the month of June and earned some money, helping my mom pick strawberries. The money I earned went straight to the family budget. Our family continued to struggle financially. Every dollar we earned (collectively) went into the family "bank."

Our financial struggles frustrated me. I was embarrassed by it. While my friends had money to spend, I didn't have a dime.

One night, at Boys' Brigade club at church, the leaders announced a Brigade campout. I eagerly looked forward to participating. Each camper was to bring money for the small registration fee required for this weekend. When I went to register, I put down the exact amount which Dad had given me to cover the cost. The Brigade leader, in voice crystal clear for everyone in the room to hear, told me my cost had already been covered.

I was mortified. Apparently, the church had a budget for children from families with tight budgets. My parents had gone to the church to see if the church could help out. I was humiliated in front of all my friends. When I got home, I was furious. How could they do this to me?! I made sure my parents knew how upset I was.

Not long after we moved to Niagara, I was sitting up on the balcony of the Virgil MB Church. Most of the kids sat there. As I looked at the crowd of people all around us, my eye caught a cute girl sitting with her friends in the girls' section off to my left. Her mother took delight in dressing Ginny Wichert in the latest fashions. She looked like she was far above my status, but I took that as a challenge.

I went home and told my brothers that I intended to marry Ginny Wichert someday. I tried my best through my early years of high school to get her to respond to my overtures. Our neighbour in Virgil was Mrs. Hamm. She couldn't drive, so she used to ask me to drive her in to work at Lincoln Upholstering in Virgil each morning in her VW Bug. This gave me the perfect opportunity to swing by the Wichert residence and see if I might catch sight of Ginny.

She went to Eden Christian College, the Mennonite high school in Niagara which Grandpa Wichert had helped establish and where three of her uncles were teachers. Eden had a tuition fee, which made it out of reach for our family at the time. So, we went to different schools. I knew the bus she took home after school, so one afternoon I waited casually at the bus stop near her home, hoping to be able to at least walk her the few steps to her house. She was very shy and not ready for a relationship with this strange fellow approaching her out of the blue. She walked home as close to the fence as she could. My clumsy approach was not working. Besides, I was a Paraguayan immigrant. Some of the people in our Virgil MB Church considered us below them. That did not help.

However, Ginny's best friend at the time was Heidi, who lived just a few houses down from her. While Ginny was an introvert, Heidi was an extreme extrovert. Since we knew each other in the youth group, I began to share with her my pain about not being able to get a positive response from Ginny. Heidi was also a postwar immigrant from Germany, so she understood my pain and the insecurities of an immigrant. Before we knew it, we were more than just casual friends.

When that relationship ended, I went back to the Wichert clan. Ginny had a cousin her age who lived in St. Catharines and also went to Eden. I began to wonder if in my youth I had fixed my eyes on the wrong Wichert family. I made an attempt to get Ginny's cousin to notice me. That didn't work either. In the end, Ginny was the one for me, but it took quite a few years and some false starts before we both recognized our shared destiny.

While I did not exactly ace my second go-around in Grade 8, I did well enough to be streamed with the top bracket of students entering Grade 9 at Niagara District Secondary School in 1960. In those times, educators found it useful to stream students according to their academic achievements or potential. Some students were considered capable of going on to college and university, while others were being prepared for technical trades and less academic employment. I was assigned to Grade 9A. Students entering Grade 9F were deemed less able to excel academically. This is where I would have been assigned if Miss Howe had not given me another try at Grade 8.

Students in the top academic streams were allowed to include French in their timetables and then Latin in Grade 10 and German in Grade 11. I had hit the jackpot. Unlike many other students, I discovered that I enjoyed languages. By my last year of high school, the only subject other than languages on my timetable was biology.

I finally understood why Miss Howe had considered it so important for me to learn about grammar in elementary school. Since I enjoyed what I was learning, I actually began to do well academically. In fact, I did so well that at graduation I was granted a monetary incentive to go on to university.

At the beginning of high school, I was still harbouring the dream of becoming a missionary doctor. That was one of my reasons for selecting Latin in Grade 10. Also, since I was not very athletic in team sports, I volunteered to be the "trainer" on the football and basketball teams. This allowed me to travel to other schools with the teams. I also learned skills I thought might be useful for my future medical training. I bandaged ankles using specially prescribed techniques to protect them from injury on the field. I felt proud to be there with the team, carrying the medical kit, along with the water.

While I did not excel at team sports, I did rediscover my running legs. Remembering my epic run at nine years of age to help save our mother's life, I went out for cross country. I ended up winning the bronze medal in that sport, just a step behind my classmate Art Wiens, the high school jock and my idol.

As I entered my third year of high school, I turned 16. This was the age at which most of my friends who took their faith commitment seriously were considering baptism. This is a church ordinance practiced by immersion in the Mennonite Brethren Church.

Our Baptismal group in 1962. I am 2nd from right in back and Ginny is 4th from right in front.

That summer there was quite a large baptismal class, which included two of my best friends, Ernie Wiens and George Reimer. Ginny, her friend Heidi and Susan Klassen were also in this group. Heidi would later marry George, and Ernie would choose Susan as his life mate. Later, during our courtship, Ginny and I discovered that on our applications for baptism, both of us had written that we felt called to become missionaries. We were baptized together in the waters of Lake Ontario at Niagara-on-the-Lake.

As I began to realize that my academic competence lay more in the languages than in science, it became clear to me that my career would not be in the medical field. I would not be a medical missionary after all. So, I entered university to study languages. I graduated from Brock University with a BA degree in modern languages, majoring in German and French.

I still did not know just how this might fit into my plan for missionary service, so I decided to take a year of biblical studies at the Mennonite Brethren Bible College in Winnipeg. In addition to digging deeper into the Bible, I also studied Greek and Hebrew, in order to be able to access Scripture in the original languages.

While at MBBC, I came across the monthly magazine put out by Wycliffe Bible Translators. In the magazine was information on summer linguistic studies required to qualify a person for engagement with Wycliffe's Bible translation ministry. This looked interesting to me, so I sent in my application for the summer program.

But I had second thoughts. I had been a student for most of my life, and I felt pressed financially. So, I decided to spend the summer working on construction instead of pursuing the Wycliffe course. Then, in the fall, I entered the Ontario Institute for Secondary Education in Toronto for the one-year BEd course to qualify as a high school teacher in French and German.

When the relationship with Ginny finally came together for us, it was at Ginny's initiative. She was finishing nurses training and needed an escort to graduation. It had been at least five years since we had seen each other. I had been away at Bible College. Meanwhile Ginny's cousin Carrie had married my good friend Henry Dyck. Ginny asked them if I was seeing anyone. I wasn't, so she wrote me a letter asking if I would be her escort for graduation. I agreed, but I thought we should at least go on a date before the graduation. She agreed! We went out on a lovely double date with my sister Mary and Peter Warkentin who were already planning to get married in the summer of 1970. This time we clicked. The rest is history. I am writing this in the 50th year of our marriage.

I am not suggesting that our 50 years have gone by without some relational challenges. Although we are both descendants of solid Mennonite families, there are a lot of differences in our upbringing, our childhood experiences and our personalities. Ginny essentially lived in the same house on Penner Road in Virgil her entire life, until we got married. I, on the other hand, had been raised as a "wandering Wiens," having lived in more than a dozen different places by the time we were married. This difference would greatly impact the way we would experience our frequent moves as a missionary family.

Our personalities too were about as different as could be. On the Myers-Briggs personality type indicators I come out as ENFP, while Ginny is ISTJ. The Myers-Briggs type compatibility chart rates a match between people with these "opposite" types in the red zone. So, we had to learn a lot about ourselves and each other in order to be able to build a solid and healthy marriage.

One of the areas in which we struggled was in our different ways of telling stories. I carry the "chatter" gene inherited from my mother and her father, Grandpa Jacob. I tend to be ebullient and outgoing. Sometimes I have a tendency to just spill what is on my mind, including personal information and family lore. Ginny is more careful in her expression. Often, I felt like I needed to add detail and context to her stories. Both of us had to work at understanding that we did not need to try to change the other.

When Dad moved our family to Niagara-on-the-Lake, he purchased a small, three-bedroom house on Hunter Road from the Harder family. Mr. Harder was one of our Math teachers at Niagara District Secondary School. My five brothers and I were packed, wall to wall, into one of the bedrooms upstairs. In spite of the crowded conditions, we felt like we were living in the lap of luxury. We had inside facilities, including a flush toilet and a bathtub.

In Lindbrook we had had an outhouse, frigid in the winter. Our toilet paper in Lindbrook was stiff pages from the Eaton's catalogue. We took our weekly baths in a small wash tub that was set over the warm air coming up from the furnace. In winter, it was less laborious to fill the tub with snow and let it melt rather than hauling water from the well. We took our baths in the same water, beginning from the youngest to the oldest. Now, in Niagara, we had a tub and plenty of water, both cold and hot, at the turn of a tap. We even had a telephone and electricity. That changed everything in the kitchen; we had an electric stove and a fridge. Washing the floor was so easy – no more blotches of cement to wash over.

The oldest boys joined Dad on his construction jobs in the summer, framing houses for Bill Arbeck. There was plenty of work on local fruit farms for the rest of us. By the time I was 16, I too joined Dad on construction, learning skills which helped me find jobs throughout my years of high school and university. Thanks to these jobs I graduated from university debt free, with enough left over to buy Ginny's engagement ring.

As our family finances became more manageable with the extra work opportunities for all of us, Dad decided it was time for a larger house, so he bought a two-acre lot on Line #1. There Dad built a 4-bedroom house with a full basement. With the two acres, we now had room for a larger garden and even a cow. It was my job again to milk the cow before and after school each day.

The improved financial situation of the family allowed Dad and Mom to follow through on their commitment to give us each a thousand dollars and the freedom to keep our earnings when we reached 21. Dad remembered his pain at not being allowed to study, so all of us were encouraged to follow our dreams and pursue higher education.

Mom was true to the promise she made to God when she was pregnant with me. She had a powerful impact on my spiritual development throughout my life. Although she did not tell me about her bargain with God until much later, she helped shape the course of my spiritual commitments by drawing my attention to verses of Scripture such as the verses already cited from Isaiah and Ezekiel. She treasured a little metal box containing a collection of Bible verses which she knew by heart. Each day she would draw one of these verses for each of us nine children and make that the context of her prayer for us for the day.

As I entered university, I began to learn things that raised questions for me about some of the lessons I had learned from the Bible at her knees and through attendance at church. I was being presented with other perspectives and ways of exploring truth. Mom and I did not talk much about this, but she knew I was experiencing some doubts and she was concerned for me.

We were members of Scott Street MB Church at the time and she asked Pastor Henry Penner to arrange a pastoral chat with me to enquire about how it was going in my spiritual life. I could tell right away that Pastor Penner had not walked the road I was travelling himself, so I did not find much satisfaction in our conversation. The summary of his counsel that day was, "Have faith, brother." Through this experience, I knew how much Mom cared about my spiritual journey and how much she was praying for me. I did not want to disappoint her.

At the end of my first year of university, our family experienced a life-changing crisis. We all were impacted, but my parents felt it the most. Our younger brother Henry had just begun his apprenticeship as an electrician. Saturday, March 27, 1966, was a day off for him, so he spent the morning working with Dad on construction. He went home for lunch, and while at the table with Mom he told her he had a severe headache and was going to lie down for a rest. As Mom continued her work in the kitchen, she suddenly heard a banging noise coming from Henry's bedroom. When she went to see what was going on, she found him in convulsions, thrashing about violently.

She called the ambulance and he was rushed to the hospital where he spent a week lying motionless in a deep coma, breathing through a respirator. The doctor diagnosed cerebral meningitis, the same condition that had almost taken the life of our sister Betty so many years ago in Coaldale. Dad took time off from work to sit and pray at his son's side. We all prayed that God would grant another miracle, as we had experienced during Betty's illness. This time the divine intervention we were praying for did not come in the way we were hoping. On April 3, Dad's 48th birthday, Henry took one final breath.

For Dad, whose most precious life dream had been of a happy and healthy family, the death of one of his children was devastating. "It should have been me! it should have been me!" he kept insisting.

But this was also a liberating experience for our father. For the first time in his life, he gave up control over his grief. We had never seen him weep, but now he wept and sobbed unashamedly. Years of pent-up emotions poured out through the dark nights of grief. We began to experience a side of our father we had not known before. Words of love and tenderness had always come easily from Mom, but we had rarely heard those from Dad. After Henry's passing, he became more tender and patient in his interactions with us. Now he would rarely say goodbye without adding, "I love you." Mom grieved too, but she had always been open and free with her emotions. Her tears were familiar to us. Always the tender comforter at heart, I remember how it seemed to fall to me to sit next to Mom at the funeral, holding her hand and trying to soften her grief.

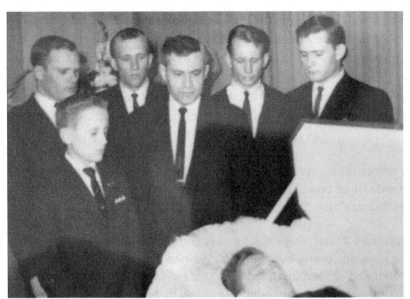

Standing at the head of Henry's coffin are Dave and Dad. Behind them from left to right are: Erv, Hugo, me and Ernie.

14: Missions and Marriage

The birth of their first two grandchildren later that summer was a special gift from God and a token that family life would continue to expand and grow. This was also a season where the vision and example that our parents had instilled in us for service to our Lord and to the world were coming to fruition. Erv and his wife Marian went with Mennonite Central Committee to serve in Kenya.

Finally, there was an opportunity for our family to give back in gratitude for what MCC had done to help resettle our parents after their escape from Russia. Four of my siblings would follow in some type of foreign missionary service. All of us found meaningful avenues of leadership and service in the church and the world.

In addition to service overseas, my siblings and I all served in a variety of Christian service assignments, including pastoral ministry, church leadership, Habitat for Humanity projects, Mennonite Disaster Service, boards of senior homes and other service organizations.

Our family grew as in-laws and grandchildren were added. My three older brothers were already married, and in 1970 we had two more weddings. My sister Mary and brother Henry's best friend Peter Warkentin were married on June 27, 1970. My reacquaintance with Ginny the previous year, as her escort for graduation from nurses training, had blossomed into romance and we were married on August 29, 1970.

Our courtship had progressed through the winter as I studied for my teacher certification in Toronto. Initially, we planned to marry in May, a month before my sister Mary and Peter. However, there was a nagging sense in my mind that I may have been too quick the previous year when I opted to work on construction instead of attending the Summer Institute of Linguistics (SIL) training offered by Wycliffe for Bible translation. If God was calling me to the ministry of Bible translation, I should at least take the opportunity to learn as much as possible about this ministry and whether I could even handle the rigorous academic requirements.

Before Ginny and I sent out our wedding invitations I asked, "Could we postpone the wedding to August so that I could go to SIL?" Of course, she was surprised. "What is SIL?" she asked. We had discussed our common calling to missionary service and she had heard about Wycliffe Bible Translators, but SIL was new. I explained that SIL (Summer Institute of Linguistics) was the academic arm of Wycliffe. She graciously agreed to the change of plans. It meant that she would be doing all the preparations for our wedding on her own that summer.

I would spend two months, right up to August 25, away at Gordon Conwell Seminary in Boston to begin my graduate studies in linguistics. The school also had to extend some grace, as they allowed me to write all my exams in one day so that I could at least spend two days with Ginny before the wedding.

With the help of her mother, Ginny planned a fabulous wedding celebration. The ladies of Virgil Mennonite Brethren Church, the church where we had been baptized together, prepared a sumptuous dinner for 250 guests. Both of us came from large families, but I'm sure more of the guests were from one of the Wiens sides of my family, as by now many of our relatives had followed my parents' immigration to Canada. Mom's brother Jacob's family accounted for at least 20 guests! He had 13 children and most were married!

Our wedding photo on August 29, 1970.

With the completion of my first summer of linguistic training, we began the process of applying to serve abroad with Wycliffe Bible Translators. Our marriage was the next step on this joint journey. We wanted the Lord to guide us in this endeavour, so we chose "Saviour Like a Shepherd Lead Us" as the theme song for our wedding. Our joint commitment to missionary service was clearly an answer to Mom's prayer for me. Many of our guests were aware of our plans and sent appropriate gifts accordingly. However, there were a number of beautiful gifts which remained safely stored in Ginny's parents' attic until our return to Canada 20 years later.

As we reflect back over 50 years, we can certainly see evidence of the Lord's leading and also God's protecting hand over us during our participation in the Bible translation ministry. At the time of our wedding, we still had a couple of summers remaining in our initial linguistic training. We were grateful that I had been offered a teaching job in Newmarket, Ontario to help carry us through the winters between the remaining summer courses.

After our wedding, we had exactly a week until I had to report for duty to Newmarket High where I had been hired as a French teacher. There was not time for a long honeymoon. But we did have a little time for a quick trip to Eastern Ontario.

Before leaving on our trip, we had to devise a way to get away without being pursued and harassed by some of our young "friends" in Virgil. It was customary at the time for young lads to make the get-away as challenging as possible for the newly married couple. We needed some help to execute our plan. When we were ready to leave, Ginny's mother turned out all the lights in the house and yard. My brother Erv and my sister Mary dashed out the front, hopped into a waiting car and roared off through Virgil. Ginny and I went out the back where our friends George and Heidi had hidden our car in George's orchard which bordered Ginny's parents' house. We drove calmly to Niagara Falls while our rambunctious "friends" soon discovered that they were chasing after the wrong car.

We spent our first night in Niagara Falls at the Carin Croft Inn, and then spent the week touring through Kingston, the Thousand Islands and Ottawa, ending in Keswick, just north of Newmarket, where we rented a suite in a motel on Cook's Bay, a part of Lake Simcoe. The motel had suites that could be rented by the day or week in the summer and by the month in the winter. It was a beautiful setting and gave us a chance to look for more suitable accommodation closer to Newmarket once we got started in our new jobs – mine at Newmarket High and Ginny's at North York General Hospital.

The move to Newmarket marked the beginning of our move into a little more ecumenical expression of our faith. There were no MB or even Mennonite churches in the area. We tried a variety of churches that we thought might be similar to the faith community in which we had been raised. Each Sunday we were recognized as visitors, but no one reached out in friendship to welcome us into their community. At school, I was coaching the volleyball team, and at one of our meets I met Harold Minor, a fellow coach from a neighbouring school. Harold and I had been at university together and Ginny had been in nurses training with his wife, Mary Ella. Harold invited us to visit Parkside Tabernacle, the small Pentecostal Church in Newmarket that they were attending. We had never considered that church. The Pentecostal expression just seemed too wild for us – too far from the conservative Mennonite denomination in which we had been raised. But we decided one visit couldn't hurt.

Before the first service we attended was over, we had been invited out to dinner, and then we had another invite after the evening service. Before that day was over we had joined the choir, had agreed to be youth sponsors and Ginny had agreed to help with the Pioneer Girls club. Some of the friends we made in our two years there have stuck with us. A few became faithful and valuable partners with us throughout our missionary career with Wycliffe with their prayers and financial contributions.

Our parents took an open-hearted and loving posture to the world and other people. Ginny and the other in-laws felt and appreciated their loving acceptance. At one family gathering after our parents had passed away, a number of the in-law siblings were in debate, insisting they had been the favourites of our parents. But my parents' loving hearts extended beyond the family to the wider world of human need. I don't know if there was a Christmas gathering in my adult years where there was not a widow or other needy person from outside the family at our table.

One family from Nigeria felt so cared for by my family that they called our parents Dad and Mom. Chi Waboso came to Canada from Nigeria for doctoral studies. Brother Erv, now back in Canada from service in Kenya, was taking an evening course at Brock University. Homesick for Africa, he noticed this African student and engaged him in conversation. This was the kind of thing we learned to do from Mom. A number of us share the genetic predisposition inherited through Mom from Grandpa Jacob to reach out and chat with strangers as if they are our friends. Before long Chi was invited to a family gathering, where he was warmly received by our parents and siblings. When Chi wanted to bring his family to join him in Canada, immigration would not recognize their Nigerian marriage, so they needed to confirm their marriage in Canada. Mom and Dad sponsored their wedding, and from then until now they were Mom and Dad to Chi and Boma, and Grandma and Grandpa to their children. It was as if a new child had been added to bring us back to our original complement of nine siblings.

In the summer of 1972, our family celebrated Betty's marriage to Peter Loewen. And, at the same time, we said good-bye to Ernie and his wife

Marie and their three children as they left for an MCC assignment in Zambia.

While growing older, Dad and Mom were not done with their restless wanderings.

Tensions in leadership that Dad experienced as a deacon and member of the board in the Virgil Church, had led to a move from Virgil to St. Catharines during my last year of high school. After three different homes in St. Catharines, farming was tugging at them once more.

Together with our youngest brother David, they bought a farm on 9th Street Louth, west of St. Catharines, where they planted French hybrid grapes. Mom could sing to her heart's content as she tended to her chickens. She planted a garden large enough for her own family and many in the church!

The large farmyard, with adjoining pond, provided endless hiding places for Easter egg hunts which she eagerly organized for their growing number of grandchildren. Dad also experienced the joy of frolicking with their grandchildren. When a December snowfall covered the valley behind their farmhouse, he eagerly went out tobogganing with the grandchildren. As his toboggan sailed over a sharp bump, he came down hard and immediately doubled over in pain. X-rays revealed a cracked vertebra to add to his perennial slipped disc. When the family came together at his hospital bed for a Christmas celebration, Dad minimized his pain, as he had done all his life, and he challenged the grandchildren to another toboggan ride upon his release.

15: Wycliffe Bible Translators

Ginny and I spent that Christmas in Mexico. We were in "jungle camp" training as part of our preparation for service with Wycliffe Bible Translators. During the first two years of marriage, we had worked in Newmarket, while building a support base of Christian friends and relatives who would invest in this ministry with us through their financial offerings and prayers.

During the summers, we had continued our training with additional graduate courses in Linguistics at the University of Washington in Seattle and the University of Oklahoma in Norman. Although Ginny was not as much in love with languages as I was, Wycliffe required both husband and wife to complete the essential basic training in linguistics. With her analytical mind, Ginny actually did better than I did at some of the skills we had to learn.

One of the aspects of our jungle training was learning the local Tzeltal Indian language. I was held up by our instructors as a champion in language learning. As a young couple, without children, we both enjoyed our Jungle Camp experience. It was like an endless camping adventure. We were challenged to go beyond what we thought we could do in physical exertion, new foods, cultural adaptation and relationships.

Wycliffe's theme song included the lines, "Faith, mighty faith, the promise sees and looks to God alone; Laughs at impossibilities and shouts: It shall be done!" The group motto for our Jungle Camp session of 25 campers was "Calmness in uncertainty and change."

One of the important training aspects of Jungle Camp was in the area of building relationship skills. Because of experiences in my childhood such as my lack of athleticism and my poor academic performance through elementary school, I was carrying a bit of an inferiority complex. I tended to notice and envy the gifts and skills I saw in others. But I struggled to see God's unique gifting in me.

God had a lot to teach me in Jungle Camp. I was working closely with a fellow camper when he turned to me and said, "I really appreciate you." That was like the balm of Gilead to my soul. It not only helped me to appreciate my own unique gifting, but it also helped me see how important it was to acknowledge and express appreciation for the gifting I saw in others around me. This would be a great help for me in later years when I was given leadership responsibilities in our work in the Philippines, which involved direction and supervision of colleagues.

In addition to language learning and building relational skills, we had to learn practical things like first aid, butchering animals, cooking over a homemade mud stove, swimming, canoeing, hiking on jungle trails, building our own "champa" and surviving alone (individually) in the jungle for at least one night. We were mentored in devotional practices to keep us in tune spiritually, away from our faith communities and churches.

While I excelled in language learning, Ginny did better at things like first aid. We could see that her training and experience as a nurse would open great doors for ministry in remote tribal communities. During the last eight weeks of our jungle training, we lived alone as a couple in one of the Tzeltal villages. There we participated in community activities, worked on our language skills and engaged in some literacy and other educational activities with the children.

Ginny is cooking at our mud stove at Jungle Camp in Chiapas, Mexico.

Earlier, after our summer of linguistic training in Seattle, Ginny had discovered she was pregnant, but in a near-death crisis a few months later, we learned that it was an ectopic pregnancy. It was a weekend when we had gone to visit our families in Niagara. Ginny was increasingly uncomfortable. Mom prescribed her home remedies to relieve the pain. We left to go back home late in the afternoon.

By the time we got to Newmarket, Ginny was experiencing intense pain. I wanted to take her to the hospital immediately. She wanted to wait. I persisted. That decision saved her life.

When the doctor did his examination, he found that her fallopian tube had burst and she was bleeding internally. She would not have made it through the night. Now our chances of another pregnancy were reduced by 50% because she only had one tube. So, we were thrilled to learn shortly after our return from Jungle Camp that Ginny was expecting again.

We still needed to build our support base and I needed surgery on my knee for an old football injury. But we were eager to get to the mission field to practice all that we had been learning.

Pat and Joanne Cochran, instructors at Jungle Camp, had spent a term in the Philippines. They were actively recruiting members to join the Philippine team. Wycliffe had also identified the Philippines as a priority for new recruits. That helped us make our decision about where to serve.

Because of my French competency, we had contemplated assignment to French West Africa, but Ginny thought that would put me at an unfair advantage in language learning. During her nurses training, Ginny had worked with nurses from other countries. She found the Filipino nurses the most congenial. So we decided to join the Philippine team. We would learn which language community when we got there.

Thanks to positive responses from friends and family, as well as active intervention and assistance from some of Ginny's uncles who were respected in our family and faith community, promises of financial support began to grow. Wycliffe wanted us to demonstrate a certain level of committed support before we were cleared to leave for the field. The level of financial support required was about half of what one of us had been making the previous year in our professional jobs.

We were finally cleared to leave in September 1973. Until that time most missionaries had been travelling to the Philippines across the Pacific by ship. Some of our colleagues were still doing that, partially to accommodate the shipment of their personal goods. We were among the first who chose to travel by air and then ship a few essentials in two 55-gallon steel drums.

Wycliffe's ministry in the Philippines was administered under the auspices of the Summer Institute of Linguistics (SIL). SIL negotiated an agreement with the Philippine Department of Education. Under this arrangement SIL members would conduct linguistic research in the indigenous communities of the country, documenting their languages and conducting literacy campaigns to expand their educational opportunities. In exchange, we were cleared to assist churches and Christian missionaries with the translation of the Bible into the indigenous languages.

This photo was taken at the time of our departure for the Philippines

When we arrived in the Philippines and our colleagues there saw that Ginny was very pregnant, they urged us to spend some time at SIL's translation base on the island of Mindanao. The base there at Nasuli was quite close to a mission hospital of the Association of Baptists for World Evangelization (ABWE). The chief physician at the hospital, Dr. Linc Nelson, said it stood for Association of Baptists for Wycliffe Expansion, based on the number of Wycliffe babies he had delivered at the Bethel Baptist hospital in Malaybalay.

Because of Ginny's extended belly, some of our colleagues recommended that we go to the ABWE hospital for our delivery. They believed many Filipino doctors would consider our baby too large for natural delivery and be too quick to do a C-section.

So, our SIL director assigned me to some research work in the Nasuli base library. During this period at Nasuli, Morrie Cottle, the Branch Director of SIL's work in the country, visited the Nasuli translation centre. He made a point of meeting personally with each of us under his direction and care. In a remark that came as a complete shock, he turned to me at one point and said, "You may find yourself in my position one day." I had never imagined myself in a leadership position at that level. But his comment turned out to be prophetic.

After a very pleasant Christmas and New Year's celebration with our new SIL colleagues at Nasuli, we made our way to the ABWE clinic where our first child, Jason Douglas, was born just after midnight on January 2, 1974. He was delivered by Dr. Nelson and his Filipino associate, Dr. Rene Sison, along with the medical assistance of a pitocin drip to speed up the labour. We were over the moon with excitement and joy at the privilege of raising a child of our own here in this land of our new mission assignment. I like to say that Jason was made in Canada and assembled in the Philippines.

Now it was time to give some serious thought to where our ministry in the Philippines would be focused. As we met with our directors, we came to understand that there was an urgent need for new field workers among the tribal communities in the Cordillera mountains of northern Luzon island.

The tribes in this region represent a proud warrior culture. They are referred to by some anthropologists as "head hunters" because of their practice of taking heads to prove their success in warfare with enemy tribes. The 300 years of Spanish colonial domination in the Philippines left these tribes essentially untouched. They prided themselves of being "genuine Filipinos" because they had never been colonized.

After the Spanish American War, Spain ceded the Philippines to the United States at the Treaty of Paris in 1898. This prompted a fierce guerilla war in the Philippines, because nationalist forces claimed they had already defeated the Spanish colonizers and did not need the Americans. About 20,000 Philippine troops and as many as 200,000 civilians died in this conflict. The result was a persistent love-hate relationship between the Philippines and their American colonizers.

When peace was restored, the US sent boat loads of teachers to establish a new education system, using English instead of Spanish in their instruction. The tribes in the Cordillera came to appreciate education as well as the economic and infrastructure development instituted by the US in the Cordillera. Rough roads were carved out through the rugged mountains and Christian missionaries, many coming from the US, established new mission frontiers. While the areas under Spanish colonial rule had been brought into the Catholic faith, the Cordillera tribes were considered unevangelized by Catholic and Protestant missions alike. The American Episcopal Church came into the Philippines with a policy of not putting an altar against another altar. They determined not to open new work where the Catholic Church was already established and instead concentrated on the Western Cordillera as their new frontier. The United Methodists also established mission outreaches in the Cordillera, with most of their missionaries coming from the US. New Catholic missions were established, with missionaries coming mostly from Belgium, Holland and Germany.

The Wycliffe field operations were conducted under the auspices of the Summer Institute of Linguistics (SIL), which had established an agreement with the Department of Education. SIL agreed to conduct a thorough scientific research into the indigenous languages, and publish the results for the benefit of Philippine education. In exchange the Department of Education sponsored visas for expatriate missionaries. They gave their approval to our assistance provided to church and mission organizations in translating the Bible into these previously unwritten languages.

149

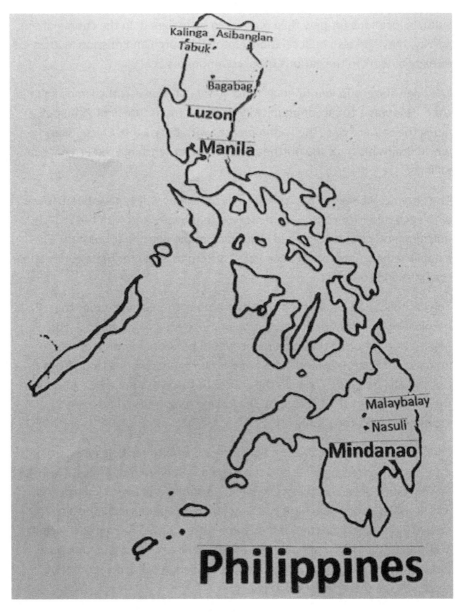

This map of the Philippines shows Nasuli and Malaybalay on the southern island of Mindanao. This is where Jason was born. North of Manila on the island of Luzon is Bagabag, our northern Translation centre and further north still is Asibanglan where we began our work among the Kalinga tribe.

Our SIL colleagues had already conducted a thorough linguistic survey of the Cordillera, identifying language boundaries and recommending the most suitable locations for new field recruits to be assigned. In the course of this survey, they had also built relationships with church and mission leaders already at work in the various tribal communities.

The linguistic group identified as most suitable for us was the Limos Kalinga tribe. This was a tribal community living in the municipality of Pinukpuk, along the Saltan River. The Saltan merges with the mighty Chico River, which drains much of the northeastern Cordillera through the Province of Kalinga.

The Province of Kalinga has at least a dozen tribes which have been at war with each other for centuries. In more recent years, and with the encouragement of mission and civic leaders, the warring tribes had established an elaborate "Peace Pact" system to allow for better inter-tribal relations and commerce.

The Catholics had established churches among the Kalinga under the auspices of the CICM or "*Congregatio Immaculati Cordis Mariae.*" The English translation of this Latin name would be "Congregation of the Immaculate Heart of Mary." Most of the CICM missionaries came from Holland and Belgium. Through the course of the years since SIL's entry into the Philippines in 1953, a charitable working relationship had been established with the CICM.

Their priests regularly called on SIL's aviation service for help with transportation and supplies into the rugged Cordillera mountains. The priest serving much of the northern Cordillera, including the Limos Kalinga tribe, was Fr. Mike Halterman, a rugged Dutchman. His parish included a wide area of at least 50 churches and mission outreaches. Covering such a wide area meant that he would only be able to reach each church or mission three or four times a year. Added to this challenge was the fact that he could not speak the tribal language.

The CICM had calculated that, given the wide scope of their outreach, they would focus the language learning of their missionaries on Ilocano, the language of wider communication across northern Luzon. Fr. Mike was keenly aware of the disadvantage at which this put him among the Kalinga people. As much as he wanted them to understand the gospel, he could only be there to teach them a few times a year, and then in a language many hardly understood. To compensate for this, at least in part, the CICM had trained catechists in each community to help carry on the work of the Church while the priest was away. The catechists spoke the language, but the written materials and the Scriptures provided by the CICM to support their ministry were still in a language foreign to the people. Fr. Mike had previously served an area in the Cordillera where SIL already had an established work. He saw the advantage of having Scriptures in the language of the people, so he requested assistance with the translation of the Bible in the language of the Limos Kalinga people as well.

I remember the first time one of our pilots took me with him on a flight crossing over the Limos Kalinga area. I looked down and wondered, "Where do the people live?" I saw very few houses. The Limos Kalinga live in little hamlets, scattered in the jungle covering the mountains along the Saltan River. They live by subsistence farming on rice terraces carved out of the mountain slopes, supplemented by slash and burn gardening. Their houses are small and often built in the shade of trees, so that they blend in with the topography.

About a third of the languages in which SIL was working in the Philippines were on the island of Luzon. Many were located in the northern Cordillera, a range of mountains forming a sort of spine up the middle of Luzon. The northern projects were administered out of a translation centre located near the town of Bagabag, Nueva Vizcaya. This translation centre provided a library and study facilities where translation teams could meet for workshops and concentrated research work. The centre also provided other facilities to support the work of the northern teams, such as a school, an aviation program, a guest house and buyer services. The Field Director for the northern program at this time was our colleague, Dick Roe.

To get a better look at the region of our assignment, I accompanied our Dick, on a visit to the area. We borrowed a colleague's Willys Jeep for this trip. The trip took two full days. We went from the centre in Bagabag to the Kalinga capital of Tabuk over rough gravel roads. From there, the road got even rougher, going north along the Chico River and then inland to the Pinukpuk municipal centre in the village of Taga.

The road ended there. The CICM mission had extended the road up the Saltan River to their mission clinic in Allaguia. But this "road" was merely a dirt path and our director decided it would be better to park our Jeep in

Taga and walk the 20 kilometers to the village of Asibanglan, about six kilometers up the mountain from the Catholic mission station at Allaguia.

The hike took us four hours. We arrived in Asibanglan around noon. Benito Aggueban, the local catechist, whom Fr. Mike had asked to show us hospitality, was there to greet us.

Anthropologist Edward Dozier had written about the tribe, referring to them as "headhunters." But the people of Kalinga are famous for their hospitality. Benito gave us a little tour of the central part of Asibanglan around the school and church. Then he took us to his home, where his wife had gone all-out to provide a delicious lunch for us. Benito's six children joined us.

Many years later, his eldest daughter Noemi, who is now the head teacher in the Asibanglan school, told me how she remembered our first lunch. When we were seated around the table getting ready to eat, I noticed that my director and I were the only ones with an eating utensil. Kalinga people usually provide a spoon for "foreigners." Noemi remembers that I asked, "What are the rest of you using?" They showed me their fingers. As the Kalinga like to say, "We use the utensils God gave us."

She watched for my response. When I said, "If that is how you eat, then that is what I will do too," she decided right then and there that this missionary would do well in Asibanglan. I don't remember that detail myself, but when I think about it now in retrospect, I am so grateful that God gave me the wisdom to respond in this way. I am grateful to Mom who taught me the posture of loving and gracious openness to the wider world.

On that first visit to Asibanglan, the weather forecast was threatening a typhoon with heavy rain the next day. We knew that if the rains came, we would be stranded by landslides along the road for days. So after lunch with Benito's family, we said our farewells and started the four hour hike back to Taga and our waiting Jeep.

About half way to Taga it started to rain. Soon we were up to our ankles in muck. We were so glad we had not come with the Jeep over this barren dirt road. When we got to Taga, the postmaster at whose house we had parked the Jeep advised us to get going as soon as possible to avoid the landslide which regularly cut off the road out to Tabuk during heavy rains. Just a few kilometers out of Taga, we came to the dreaded place. The shale on the side of the cliff was already sliding into the road.

Our first run at the accumulated treacherous morass brought us to a dead stop with muddy shale up to the floor boards. We didn't have a shovel. The only thing to do was to drag away as much of the muck as possible with our bare hands. We worked for more than an hour to free the Jeep. When we were finally through, I was so exhausted that I began to vomit. When we reached the town of Pinukpuk, Fr. Mike welcomed us warmly to his parish house and even pulled out a bottle of communion wine to settle my grumpy stomach. What a blessing it was to join Fr. Mike around the table for a good meal and then be given a clean, dry bed for the night. I slept well that night and was grateful for the friendships our colleagues had built with ministry partners like Fr. Mike.

We lived with Lucille and Col. Mars Primero during our national language study in 1974.

Before we could actually begin our life with the Limos Kalinga people in Asibanglan, our director decided that we ought to spend at least six months in national language study, learning Tagalog in Manila. We hadn't been in the Philippines six months and we needed to move! Finding a suitable home in Manila, a metropolis of about the same population as the entire country of Canada, seemed like finding a needle in a haystack. Perhaps it would have been different if it was just the two of us. But we had a little baby to think about.

We had no idea where to find a fitting temporary residence while studying the language. But God opened the way.

During our summer session at the University of Oklahoma in 1972 I was assigned to teach a course for people who were joining Wycliffe as "support staff." This included pilots, teachers and administrators. A Filipino couple, Col. Mars and Lucille Primero, were in my class. Mars was a retired Colonel from the Philippine army. Mars and Lucille had become friends with some of our colleagues in the Philippines. It became clear to them that they could be a great help in a public relations role to assist us in our many interactions with Philippine officials. Thanks to the kind of assistance that people like them provided to the Philippine Branch of SIL, the work was highly regarded around the country. A year before our arrival, SIL had been awarded the Magsaysay Award for International Relations, the Asian equivalent of the Nobel prize.

Since I had been their teacher in Oklahoma, Mars and Lucille felt a parental obligation toward us. They invited us to move in with them and their children for our six months of Tagalog language study. That way we would not only have Tagalog classes during the day, but we would have actual in-home practice outside of school.

I am so grateful for the hospitality of the Primero family in that introduction to our ministry in the Philippines. To this day I still practice my Tagalog every chance I get and Filipinos who hear me often say, "You sound like a Filipino." I know, of course, that they are being generous. I know there is still a lot I don't know about Filipino vocabulary and grammar, but the language immersion experience that the Primero family gave us certainly was invaluable in helping me imitate their speech patterns and accent.

In the final years of our ministry in the Philippines I was elected by our colleagues as Branch Director. Our Tagalog learning experience was a great help to build smooth interpersonal relationships, a primary value for Filipinos. The position of Branch Director meant we were to live in Manila again. We had considerable interaction with national leaders in the Department of Education and in other government offices.

Travel in crowded Manila was a big challenge for us. Initially we rode the bus from Primero's house to the language school. Buses were so crowded it took courage and significant aggression to get on the bus, much less find a seat. Then there was always the fear of being pickpocketed in the crush of bodies.

One day Ginny felt a hand reach into her purse as we pushed forward to board the bus. That did it for us. We bought a little 100cc motorcycle and that became our transportation to and from language school and then around town, with our little baby snuggled between us. No one used helmets or other protective gear in those days. I shudder now when I think of how little caution we took for our safety then.

We are standing on the porch of our house in Asibanglan shortly after our arrival there in 1974. This is where we regularly entertained Kalinga visitors. The main path was in front of our house.

In September of 1974, we were finally ready to move to Asibanglan and begin our first ministry assignment. The leaders in the community selected a house they thought would be suited to our needs. It was the oldest house in the village, owned by Binuloc, one of the old "pangats" (elders). He lived in another house across the river and had given this house to his only daughter Aning. Aning and her husband had moved to Tabuk, the provincial capital, where her husband was an elected leader in the provincial government.

The house had a dubious history.

It was considered "haunted." Apparently, someone had been murdered there. The Kalinga people are very sensitive to the spirit world and proper care of the departed souls. They believed that the soul of the person murdered in the house would trouble its inhabitants. The house had also been the village headquarters of the occupying Japanese invaders during the Second World War.

While no one in the village would dare to live in the house, they didn't think "foreigners" would be troubled by the spirits that bothered their people. The house had been vacant for quite some time. The flooring inside was badly rotted. With the help of local carpenters, we had a new floor put in, using locally harvested mahogany lumber. We also installed some partitions to turn the 6x6 meter inside room into a 6x3 meter front room and two 3x3 meter bedrooms in the back. Across the front we added a covered 6x3 meter porch.

Our Field Director, Dick Roe, was a great helper, counsellor, guide and companion to help us make arrangements and get settled into village life. Dick was an experienced field worker who had chosen to enter missionary life as a single man. He was about the closest we had seen to a genuine Filipino among our SIL colleagues. He spoke at least three Philippine languages fluently. The only area where I found that he chafed a little was when we, as married couples, didn't want to be away from our families for more than a few days.

In retrospect, the location and design of the house the community chose for us could not have been more perfect. It was a few meters away from one of the main water sources in the village – a spring which had been tapped with a pipe that provided fresh, cold water continuously. People from a number of surrounding houses came by our house regularly to fetch water from the spring. This provided regular interaction with members of the community. We used that water as well.

The village was a collection of more than a dozen hamlets scattered across several kilometers in this valley. Our house was on the main trail, so people passing through the village or children going to school passed by our house. The family across the path from us consisted of a single mother, Umek, and her two daughters, Dominga and Doleng. They became as close and dear to us as our birth family.

Dominga, a key member of their family, had been afflicted with polio as a child. Now a young woman, she was physically handicapped, but she had a joyful spirit. She exhibited a winning smile and always had a pot of coffee ready. People were constantly stopping by for coffee and a chat. She was like the "Starbucks" of Asibanglan. The many people who stopped by at their house became a source of constant language practice for us. In the early days, I set up a table on our front porch and used it as my office, documenting what I was learning in the language. Dominga's younger sister, Doleng, was still attending high school outside the village when we moved there.

Our early days in Asibanglan were very lonely. We couldn't speak the language, so our relationships tended to be limited to the few people who had been to school outside the village and could speak a little English. We were so very lonely for our friends and family back home in Canada, or at least our SIL colleagues back at the translation centre in Bagabag. As Christmas 1974 approached, we were eager to take a break from village life and celebrate Christmas with our colleagues in Bagabag.

As the day came for the plane to pick us up, it was raining. The rain and the thick cloud cover made flying unsafe for our missionary aviation service. We begged the pilots to stay on the radio so we could alert them as soon as the weather cleared. My family laughs at how I kept the pilots on the radio with the optimistic weather report, "There is a definite clearing trend," which all around there was a steady rain. Those are the words I choose as my epitaph. Deep down in my soul there has been an eternal sense of optimism that behind the clouds there is a silver lining.

Getting ready to leave for Christmas break was a huge undertaking. Even our bedding had to be stored and sealed in metal drums to keep the rats from destroying them. As the rain continued day after day, we had to pack up each day and then unpack everything again for another night. Finally, on the fourth day, Christmas Eve, there was enough of a break in the clouds for the pilot to swoop in and land. What a relief to be back with friends who understood us and with whom we could communicate freely.

Letters from our family and friends in Canada were a lifeline. Mail came with the supply plane, once or twice a month. We waited for letters from my mom. She understood the loneliness of a new home in a strange land. Our new home in Asibanglan brought back memories for her of her childhood in Paraguay. Her romantic personality put aside snakes, poverty, sickness and hard work and remembered walks in the village under the light of the brilliant tropical moon. She would often write, "Der selbe Mond der scheint auch da bei euch" (the same moon is shining on you too). We still chuckle about this whenever we see a bright full moon.

One of our first projects after the renovations to our Asibanglan house was to build an airstrip so planes would have easy access to the village. Almost all our essentials, including food, came via air. At the time, there was not even a little store in Asibanglan where one could buy a coke or essential supplies like sugar and salt. These staples were carried in by travelling merchants from other Kalinga villages along the road, who bartered the supplies for rice, of which Asibanglan had a plentiful supply.

As we scouted for a site that was long enough and could be smoothed out enough to accommodate one of SIL's Helio Courier airplanes – short take-off and landing craft – we located an area just above the school. The land was being used as pasture for water buffalo, Asibanglan's farm tractors. We needed a landing pad at least 100 meters long and preferably 120. When I walked the length of the land we were looking at, I thought we could just make it with the excavation of a hill in the middle and the removal of a couple of betel nut trees on the approach. With some excavation, we could bring the slope within the tolerances given to us by the pilots.

We consulted with the village leadership and they threw in their support, asking people to contribute volunteer labour. The village saw the benefit in having access to aviation for better access to the outside world and especially for medivac in emergency situations. With the help of several water buffalo pulling excavator sleds, and a crowd of people cutting down guava bushes and moving soil with shovels, we were soon ready to call in the pilots for an inspection.

The Catholic mission clinic six kilometers away had a strip which we had used in the meantime. We had landed there when we first came in as a family. The pilots landed there again for the inspection of our new strip. After a brisk hike up the mountain from Allaguia to Asibanglan, the pilots walked up and down our newly built strip, measured the distance and the slope and declared it ready for use.

What they did not know is that the soil from the hill was soaking wet when we moved it. The sun had dried a thick crust over it. When the Helio landed, the weight on its wheels was too much. The plane sank slowly into the ground, up to the middle of its wheels. With some help from the crowd of people that had gathered to watch this historic sight, we were able to maneuver the plane back onto solid ground and the strip was approved. There was just one restriction. The plane would not be able to land after 2:00 pm, as the strip only allowed a one-directional approach. That approach faced the western sun, which would create too much glare for a safe landing later in the afternoon.

The airstrip was a lifeline for us and for the community – especially in times of emergency. One day the brother of our friend and Kalinga coworker Pedro fell from a coconut tree. He had severe injuries and needed emergency surgery in a hospital better equipped than the nearby Catholic clinic. We were able to fly him out and he recovered completely.

Near the end of our first term in the Philippines, I was hiking through a large area around our village, distributing some of our first printed books. The immense heat and physical activity dehydrated me. I had intense pain.

What I didn't know is that I had a kidney stone.

Our friends, the doctors at the Allaguia clinic, did their best to help me, but the pain was so intense that I vomited all night. By the morning, I was so weak that I could not even walk. Our friends in Asibanglan created a blanket sling over a bamboo pole to carry me up to the airstrip and the plane flew me out.

Our work depended on our ability to learn Kalinga. There was no written record of the language. We knew we needed the help of the community to succeed in our mission of learning and documenting the language, and then translating the Scriptures.

But we wanted to do more than translate words, we wanted to incarnate the gospel in life. How could we do that? What would Jesus do?

We knew that one of the things Jesus did was to choose a collection of disciples into whose lives he invested himself and his wisdom, and who in turn assisted him in various ways. We began to pray that God would send people we could invest in. We prayed for people to help us learn the language. We needed native speakers to help us with translating God's Word.

Benito, the first person I met in the community, was eager to help us. He was a godsend. Although a Roman Catholic catechist, he had attended a Protestant high school in another community. He understood much of the gospel from both a Catholic and a Protestant perspective. At school he had learned quite a lot of English. Also, as I came to learn, he was one of the most intelligent people I have had the privilege of knowing. He would read anything he could get his hands on, including many books and magazines we left lying around.

Benito introduced us to Contes, another leading man in the community who was a little older. He was old enough to be my father. Contes had volunteered as a guerilla with the American forces fighting Japan during the Second World War. Because of that, he had learned quite a bit of English. At the end of the war, he was shot in the leg, which left him with a limp as well as a disability pension. His pension made him independently wealthy. He had plenty of land and people to work his land, so he was free and willing to help us. His wife had gone to the same Protestant high school as Benito.

Contes was considered a "pangat" (chief) in the community. He was frequently called on to help negotiate peace pacts across a wide Kalinga area. He was also a gifted orator, frequently called on to serve as the master of ceremonies at public events. His skill as an orator and gift with words made him an outstanding gift from God as a key helper in our mission.

I am working at the translation desk in Asibanglan with Pedro.

The third key "disciple" God sent us was Pedro. The youngest of the three, Pedro was unmarried when we first met him. He was about five years younger than me. He made a special effort to apply himself to his studies, travelling to places outside of Asibanglan for high school and then a college secretarial course where he learned to type. He also learned a lot of English at school. One of his favourite games was Scrabble; he could beat us any day. He often used his spare time to read the dictionary, where he would find words that we hadn't even heard of and use them to defeat us.

We first met Pedro when he came to our house to ask for medicine for someone in his family. As Ginny is a nurse, we carried a small supply of primary care medications that we made available to people in the community. For most medical needs, we encouraged them to visit our friends at the Catholic clinic in Allaguia, Doctors Jaime and Ruth Morales. Pedro had been treated at the clinic for rheumatic heart disease when he was younger. This had left him with an enlarged heart, which hampered him in some of the difficult farm labour. He was delighted to work with us and earn a little money, which he could then use to pay people to do some of the more strenuous field work.

Our relationship with Pedro was a very important to us. We didn't even realize just how important until the night Pedro literally gave his life to protect our team from bandits. But I am getting ahead of the story here.

When Doleng, our neighbour across the path, finished high school and returned home to Asibanglan, we discovered that Pedro was courting her. The first hint was seeing him chopping firewood for Doleng's family. This is how a serious courtship begins in Kalinga culture. As the courtship progressed and they got married, Pedro came to live in the house across the path, also in line with their culture. He was now not just our language teacher and translation helper, but also our neighbour.

As we progressed in the language and began to translate the Gospels into Kalinga, Pedro shared how difficult it was for his people to accept some of Jesus' teachings such as love for those who act as enemies toward us. He said, "This teaching that we should love our enemies does not work for us. In our culture, when someone injures my brother, I am obligated to take revenge." I acknowledged this reality, but responded that we should just continue the work and see what God would teach us.

As the beauty of Jesus' teaching began to penetrate his heart, Pedro paused again one day and said, "Maybe I could follow Jesus." We stopped and prayed together, asking God to help him do just that. As close neighbours, we had a front row seat as we watched Pedro and his family from our front porch. We saw how God was truly helping them to live out this commitment to discipleship in the way of Jesus.

In most Kalinga homes, there was a stark division of labour between men's work and women's work. For example, when I would carry water from our spring, people would frequently say to me, "Kalinga men don't carry water." We began to see how Pedro bucked the cultural norms by working alongside Doleng in their chores at home and in the field.

The ultimate test of the faith commitment of these dear, dear friends came some years later when Pedro gave his life to protect our team from bandits who were terrorizing Asibanglan. The morning after his brutal murder, when I went to the spot about 100 meters from his house where the assassins opened fire, I picked up 21 empty shells from the 303 rifle they had used. His face and body were so disfigured that I could barely recognize my dear friend and co-worker.

Now, the test of their commitment to discipleship in the way of Jesus was on his family. The community pressured his widow and family to take revenge on Pedro's killers. Doleng responded, "No, that is not the life my husband chose. We will not take revenge."

By this time Doleng had been appointed as the village catechist and one of her responsibilities was to meet with families bringing their children to the Church for baptism. When she recognized one of the families as being among those implicated in Pedro's murder, she faced a difficult choice. How would she respond to their request to have their child baptized?

She chose forgiveness over revenge. All of the three daughters Pedro left behind faced similar decisions among their peers. His youngest daughter, Syrine, discovered years later that one of her good friends at school had been related to her father's killers. Her mom kept this knowledge from her so that their friendship would not be hindered.

One of the most heart-wrenching experiences of our life came with a letter we received from Pedro's eldest daughter, nine-year-old Christy, on December 8, 1985. She wrote in Kalinga: "Apay si Apudyus ngata ud nangipalubus un patoyun da si Daddy?" (Why did God allow them to kill my Daddy?)

This and a long list of seven "why" questions came bursting out from her broken heart. Why did God allow this when the work of translation is not finished? Why did God allow this when we are still so young? Why did God allow this when he was teaching others about God? She said that her Daddy had just prayed that nothing bad would happen to them and he had also prayed for us, and then his killers were at the door. Could God give me words to help bring healing to this broken heart?

The only words that came to me were the words of Jesus as he hung on the cross and cried, "My God, my God, why did you abandon me?" We all felt that pain when Pedro was murdered. Had God abandoned us?

We would discover years later that God was there in this family's grief and in our grief. As we see so often in life, what those killers intended for evil, God turned into a blessing for the Kalinga community. Pedro's family lived out their discipleship. They chose forgiveness over revenge.

When we first went to live in Asibanglan, we were young and naïve. There was so much we didn't know.

The understanding of the Gospel we carried with us was still essentially the "gospel of sin management" in which we had been immersed. That's how we were raised. We were colonial and paternalistic in understanding our role in the building of the Kingdom where Jesus is Lord. How many slideshows and mission reports had we witnessed in our childhood picturing missionaries going out to evangelize the "benighted" peoples in order to dispel the darkness?

An image that lingered in my mind was of a little child peering out of the doorway of a darkened hut, with the light of faith coming to him from the approaching missionary. Little by little, as we came to know the Kalinga people, we found our preconceptions being challenged. The book we had read by the anthropologist, Dr. Edward Dozier, describing them as "headhunters," had fed our naïve misapprehensions. The people we got to know were among the most generous and hospitable people we had ever met. Yes, they lived and died by the maxim, "an eye for an eye and a tooth for a tooth," but how did that make them less civilized than nations that fly over cities and incinerate them with bombs?

As we came to know more people in Asibanglan and were able to communicate more, we began to appreciate the hospitality and generosity with which they welcomed us and the ministry of Bible translation among them. We realized that God had been with the Kalinga people long before our arrival and had prepared the way for us and the ministry to which God had called us.

The occasion that really forced us to seriously rethink our naïve preconceptions happened one night, about a year into our life in Asibanglan. By this time, we were beginning to understand the language and customs a little. We had discovered that the Kalinga people like to party. Usually, a party begins in the evening, after the field work is done. Then it would go through the night with lots of singing and dancing to the music of their brass gongs. People would tell stories and make up songs on the fly. The "pangats" would sit in a circle and pass around a bamboo cup of sugar cane wine – a kind of communion among the elders.

I was beginning to really enjoy the dancing and regretted the part of my Mennonite Brethren heritage which had prohibited this practice. On this night, we were urged to come to the feast and we did, along with our young son. At some point during the festivities, we were called out and placed in the spotlight, where a formal ceremony was conducted to officially adopt us into their tribe. Now we were Kalinga people, like them, complete with our family and the rights and obligations that go with this privilege. We were given our place in the family of Binuloc, the "pangat" who owned our house. His relatives were now our family as well. This included Doleng, the family into which Pedro had married.

To this day, we consider the family from which Pedro was taken so prematurely as our family. His daughters call me their father and have accorded me the privilege of walking them down the aisle at their weddings. His grandchildren consider Ginny and me their grandparents, and his youngest daughter, Syrine, even came to live with us in Canada. Pedro's eldest daughter Christy even named her only son Hart.

During our early years in Asibanglan we learned how the publicity generated in the homeland to support overseas missionary work can have its drawbacks. One of the Philippine projects that was being profiled in Wycliffe as a real success was a project about 30 minutes south of Asibanglan by Helio plane. At the time that project began, Fr. Mike Halterman was the parish priest there. Wycliffe sent a publicity writer to research the project they wanted to profile. Fr. Mike considered himself a very good friend of SIL, especially of our pilot, with whom he often flew to visit his flock. As the publicity writer toured the area, Fr. Mike extended him his gracious hospitality and assistance in many ways.

It took a few years for the book to be completed. By that time, we were living in Asibanglan and Fr. Mike was the priest in our area. The publicity writer sent us a copy of the book and asked if we would deliver it to Fr. Mike as a gift in gratitude for his help and hospitality to the writer. We delivered the book, not having read it.

The next time I saw Fr. Mike, he was livid with anger. "How could SIL betray my friendship like that?" he asked. What was troubling Fr. Mike was how the book opened with the implication that neither he nor his parishioners were Christians. The book opened with the statement: "When Wycliffe members A and B came to this village there was just one believer, a woman...." Of course, the author was writing for an evangelical audience for whom the term "believer" would have a particular significance.

"I thought SIL people were my friends," fumed Fr. Mike. "Do they think I am a pagan?" That encounter was one of the most painful I had to endure during our time in Kalinga. Until that time, Fr. Mike had always been very open with his hospitality when I would be travelling through his parish and needed lodging for the night. After this event there was never room in his home for me.

This experience angered me and made me realize how important it is to vet the publicity materials we produce. Later when I became the Director of SIL's work in the Philippines I took this as a cautionary tale as I scrutinized the way our members wrote and spoke about our ministry.

I am carrying Andrea near our house in Asibanglan in 1976.

During our second year in the Kalinga project, we had begun producing the first books in the Limos Kalinga language and it was time for another translation workshop. This was an opportunity for us to meet with some of our colleagues at the Bagabag translation centre, to learn from more experienced colleagues and to discuss translation problems.

Ginny was expecting our second child, so after the workshop, we decided she should stay at the centre, while I went back to Asibanglan to tour some of the other villages in the area that spoke the same language, in order to share our new booklets. When I returned to Bagabag, we knew that Ginny's delivery was imminent. Our doctor there had a little clinic just 6 kilometers from our Bagabag centre. The weather was getting hot and Ginny was feeling more and more uncomfortable and ready to deliver. According to our calculations, she was already well past her due date. So, we decided to take a little ride out to the river on our motorcycle. The road was rough. When we got back to the Bagabag centre, some friends came by for a visit. As they were leaving, Ginny said she had a backache. Was her labour setting in? The pains became more intense and regular, so we borrowed a colleague's vehicle and headed to the clinic.

When we arrived, there was not even enough time to complete the intake form, Ginny had to be rushed right into the delivery room and within minutes our new daughter, Andrea Mae was born. Within a couple of hours, we were back at Bagabag. We opted not to have Ginny stay at the clinic, where there were no screens on the windows to keep out the mosquitoes and we would have had to bring in meals for her. At our Bagabag centre we had screens on our windows to keep out the mosquitoes and we had a young woman to help with meals and housework.

At least we got to the clinic in time. Not long after this experience, our colleagues Bruce and Judith Grayden were also expecting and chose to use the same clinic near our Bagabag centre. They made arrangements to borrow the same vehicle we had used. Judith's labour intensified during the night, so Bruce went and got the vehicle and they headed off to the clinic. Half way there, the vehicle just stopped and Bruce could not get it started again. It was pitch dark and Judith was in the final stages of labour. Bruce needed to go back to the Bagabag centre to get help. He could barely see where he was going, but finally got back to the centre and woke up Winston Churchill, the owner of the vehicle. Winston didn't even take time to put on a shirt, he just hopped onto his motorcycle with Bruce behind him and roared out to where Bruce had left the vehicle and his labouring wife. Fortunately, Judith was a nurse, because when they got back to the vehicle, she was already in the process of delivering their baby. Winston knew that the vehicle had a spare gas tank. He flipped the lever to the spare tank and they were off again, Winston racing ahead, shirtless on his motorcycle, with Bruce and Judith and their new baby following close behind. They had to pass a military checkpoint on the way but they just proceeded through without stopping. When they got to the clinic, the medical staff cut the cord and they were ready to return home. Our colleagues on the field were like family to us.

The support of our families at home in Canada was also a great encouragement to us. During our first term in Asibanglan, we had visits from Ginny's parents, her sister Pat and her aunt Louise, as well as my parents and my sister Mary, her husband Peter, their son Kris and Peter's recently widowed mother. Ginny's parents made a second visit in 1982 while I was the Field Director at our centre in Nasuli, supervising our southern Philippine projects.

Later in our ministry when I was the Philippine Branch Director and we were already living in Manila, my parents visited again, together with my brother Hugo and his wife Lydia. On that trip they also spent some time in China and revisited the house at 53 Ji Lin Street (had been 53 Grenskaya) in Harbin, where they had spent a year as refugees so many years before. That was quite an emotional experience for them. They even met an old man who said he remembered the refugees living there.

We appreciated the full-fledged support we experienced from our parents and many of our siblings. With their open-hearted posture toward the wider world, Mom and Dad Wiens especially demonstrated that they were not just supporting us, but the wider ministry we were a part of. Over the years they hosted, prayed for and supported many of our friends and colleagues as well as our Filipino friends and co-workers.

On their first visit, Andrea was just learning to crawl. After spending about a week in Asibanglan with them, we spent some days at our translation centre in Bagabag. There, all our houses had bare concrete floors. It bothered them to see Andrea crawling on these cement floors. I found this surprising, given the conditions under which they had brought us into the world in Paraguay, where the floors of our homes were regularly freshened up with a mixture of mud and cow manure. Nevertheless, they insisted that we needed some carpeting on the floor, at least in our living room. So, they sent a special order to Manila for a piece of carpeting to cover a section of our living room floor.

At the time, we also had a young lady from the community named Nori helping with some of the household chores, so that Ginny could be free to contribute to the ministry in other ways. Mom and Nori hit it off right away. It bothered Mom to see Nori washing the dishes alone, so she insisted on coming alongside to help, something our house-helpers found hard to accept. But Mom did it in such a loving manner that she and Nori were soon chatting and laughing together as friends. Mom talked with Nori about her eternal destiny. Later when they embraced as Mom and dad were leaving, Mom asked Nori, "Will I see you in heaven?" Nori struggled in her response, but it got her thinking. Not long after that she made a firm commitment to follow Jesus and joined Campus Crusade for Christ. Her ministry team even made a foray into Kalinga country, visiting us in Asibanglan. Later still, Nori immigrated to Canada and settled in the Toronto area. When she married a man whom she met here in Canada, Mom and Dad were part of her wedding.

During our time in Asibanglan, on my parents' first visit, we decided to follow the Kalinga custom and sponsored a feast for the village in their honour. We bought a cow to be butchered for the feast. As is their custom, the people spent all day working in their fields and then came out in full force to visit, sing and dance with us and to honour our parents. Mom and Dad were getting on in years by now and as the night grew late, I asked if they didn't want to lie down for a bit. My dad responded, "No! If they are coming out for us after a full day of work, we can certainly stay awake with them." And stay awake they did. For the first time in her life, Mom got to fulfill her dream of dancing. She danced and laughed with the people in uninhibited joy. Our doctor friends from Allaguia even made the trek up the mountain to Asibanglan to show their respect for our parents as well. How we loved our friends in Kalinga for the honour and respect they showed to us and our families.

Before we went to the Philippines, Ginny's older brother had questioned our wisdom to abandon our good jobs for a career in mission. He also wondered if it would be safe to raise our children among tribal people living in the jungle. We never felt that we were putting our children at risk any more than they would have been at risk in Canada. Filipinos love children and we always felt our children were safe among them, even among the tribal community in the mountains. There are health and safety risks anywhere in the world and we did encounter a few with our children.

When Jason was two years old, he came down with a high fever. Fevers are common in young children, but his persisted even with medication. The local doctor diagnosed malaria. This was surprising to us, as the altitude in our mountain village of Asibanglan is above the level where malarial mosquitos thrive. Somewhere in our travels he had obviously encountered this disease. The doctor prescribed a common anti-malarial drug. But Jason's condition continued to worsen. One night, as Ginny was nursing Andrea and praying for Jason's health, a thought came to her, as if by revelation from God. Were we administering the right dosage? I had brought the medication home with instructions to give him a tablespoon three times a day. I should have said teaspoon. When we adjusted the dosage, Jason soon recovered and never had a bout of malaria again.

Although snakes were not top of mind for us, we knew of at least two people in Asibanglan who had died of snake bites. So when Jason showed us his hand one day and we saw that it was badly swollen, we were worried. I quickly scooped Jason up in my arms and asked a young Kalinga friend to go with me to the Catholic mission clinic, six kilometers away in Allaguia. We ran as fast as we could. When we arrived at the clinic, Dr. Morales examined him calmly. She assured us that it was not a snake bite. "If it was a snake, he would not be alive," she said.

Another time Jason came back from playing in a flooded rice field, complaining about something uncomfortable in his pants. When we looked, we saw a giant leech that had sucked almost half a cup of blood from his leg.

The Kalinga people often felt more threatened by the harm they believed they could suffer from evil spirits than physical dangers in their world. One day Ginny took Jason to play in the stream near our house. The water flowed in a bit of a whirlpool there, which made it fun to play in. Later that night Jason had a high fever. Our Kalinga friends were sure that this was because he had been bathing in the haunted pool. In their cosmology, things that seem unnatural, like water flowing in circles, may be caused by malevolent spirits.

Our front porch was the most comfortable place for us to entertain people. Many would regularly stop by to visit, or to consult with Ginny about illnesses or injuries and to get some of the first aid medicines that we carried to spare them the long hike to Allaguia. One day after such a visit, we noticed that Jason had white powder around his mouth. He was just a toddler. Apparently, he had gotten into the medication we had given to one of our friends. What medication was it? How much had he consumed? Those were our questions as we tried our best to get him to vomit up whatever it was. Our Kalinga friends were mostly concerned that we were making him cry by trying to get him to do something he did not want to do.

Andrea was born at a little clinic near our translation centre in Bagabag. A few weeks after her birth, we went back to Asibanglan. We began to get concerned, when after eight days, she had not had a bowel movement. What could be the problem? I hurried to Allaguia to consult our friends at the clinic there. Graciously the doctor accompanied me back up the mountain to Asibanglan. After examining Andrea, he assured us that she was just fine. He observed that sometimes nursing babies can go for a week or more without moving their bowels because breast milk is so pure.

The terrain all around our home in Asibanglan was uneven. There was no level ground. In some places, the people had laid stones on the trail, like paving stones, to keep from walking in the mud when it rained. I had suffered an injury in my right knee, playing football in high school. I had had surgery on the knee before we went to the Philippines, but I still found it to be unstable at times over rough terrain. One day, I was carrying Andrea near our house. When I stepped down from one stone to another, my knee gave out and I dropped Andrea on the rocky ground. I was terrified! Could she have been badly injured in such a fall? She cried a little, but we did not find any serious injuries. How thankful we were.

One of the things we soon noticed about our Kalinga friends, was that almost all of them had nicknames. We would meet or be introduced to new people and they would give us their name. That might be the last time we ever heard them referred to by that name. It was their formal "baptismal" name, but almost everyone had another name by which they were known in the village. For example, one of our Kalinga co-workers was Luis Balutoc. That was his legal name, but not the name by which he was known. There was a big contest of some kind when he was born and so he became known as "Contes." The Kalinga people also showed their pride in and love for our kids by giving them Kalinga names. Jason was named "Danason," after a renowned Kalinga warrior, and Andrea was "Gamelayan," the acclaimed Kalinga princess of old.

By 1978, the Limos Kalinga project was in full swing. We had completed the preliminary grammatical analysis of the language and established a practical orthography suitable for writing in Kalinga. Imagine me documenting the grammar of a language after my first disastrous pass through Grade 8! With excellent help from Benito, Contes, Pedro and others we produced a book of Old and New Testament Bible stories drawn from a collection of similar stories in English. The story book became a real hit with the religion teachers in the Kalinga schools. For the first time they had something in the children's first language to help them understand the core stories from the Bible.

We also translated and published the Gospels of Mark and John, and recorded Gospel selections on cassette tape which people could listen to in their own homes. Pedro was the narrator on many of the recordings. So, for years after his death he continued to share the gospel with his people through the recorded Scriptures. Many years later, after we had returned to Canada, we had a library built in Asibanglan as our gift to the community and in commemoration of our departed co-translators. By then all of them except Contes had died. As the cornerstone in the library, we laid a stone plaque with the names of our departed co-workers and the text from Hebrews 11:4: "Because of faith they speak, even though they are dead."

This is the memorial plaque on the Asibanglan library to commemorate those who worked on the translation of the Scriptures in Limos Kalinga.

With the help of two SIL colleagues, Kathy and Carol, there was a thriving literacy outreach in several Kalinga villages, teaching people to read in their own language. As part of this program, we produced several slim volumes of Kalinga folk stories.

Together with Ginny and our doctor friends in Allaguia, the team produced a health booklet to assist with the training of village health workers. We felt we had had a productive first term and we were ready for a return home to share our work and strengthen our support base again. Our financial needs had increased with the addition of two children and our ministry budget too was growing as we employed Kalinga co-workers to work alongside us.

In consultation with our directors in the Philippines, we decided to devote a good part of our time back in North America to further graduate studies in linguistics. SIL had established a year-round graduate program in linguistics in partnership with the University of Texas at Arlington.

I applied and was accepted into their Master's program. We returned to Canada in April of 1978 and then moved to Dallas to begin the study program. Given my early experience in elementary school, I was a reluctant scholar. I still lacked confidence in my capacity to thrive in this rigorous atmosphere of academia. With our two young children we found a subsidized rental apartment in Duncanville, a suburb of Dallas. At 45 celsius, it was the hottest place we had ever lived, so we were delighted to find that the apartment had an air conditioner. It also had a dishwasher. But we were not so thrilled by the multitude of cockroaches that came out to visit at night.

We had a good laugh one day when Rudy Barlaan, a Filipino colleague, came to Dallas, also to work on his graduate studies. He arrived one night and I went to pick him up from the airport. Since it was late, we made a bed for him on our living room couch instead of taking him to his dorm room. When three-year-old Andrea got up in the morning and saw him sleeping on the couch, she came running into our room and exclaimed, "There is an Englishman sleeping on the couch."

As we moved from place to place, it was sometimes hard for our kids to keep up with where we were and which language they needed to be speaking. Once when we were out shopping and ready to go home, we said, "Let's go home." Jason replied, "Where is home?"

I applied myself with all I had to the study of linguistics and even served as a teaching assistant in the translation studies program. When all was said and done and my final grades were released in December of 1979, I had graduated with a Master of Arts in Linguistics with a grade point average of 4.0. In Canada, that means I earned straight "A's" throughout this 16-month program. Other colleagues who had completed this program had gone right on to the doctoral program. I still did not have the confidence to tackle that. I was afraid that if I got the PhD, I would not be able to meet the expectations that went with it. Besides, we were eager to get back to the Philippines and reignite the translation project we had left behind in Asibanglan.

16: From Translation to Administration

Then, on New Year's Eve 1979, we got a surprise phone call from the Philippines. The SIL Philippines Branch Director, Len Newell, was calling to ask if we would consider putting the Limos Kalinga project on hold for some time in order to serve the wider ministry. He asked if I would accept a new position as Field Director at Nasuli. The Philippine Branch was supporting linguistic research, literacy work and Bible translation in 75 Philippine languages at the time. They were administered by three Field Directors – one for about 25 projects in the south, another for about 25 projects in the central region and a third for the remaining projects in the north.

We had to think and pray about this for a bit. Were we ready to put the Limos Kalinga project on hold just as things were picking up steam? After some thought and prayer, we returned the call and agreed to serve, but we had some caveats. First, we wanted to be granted another six months back in Asibanglan to bring a decent closure to what we had started there. Second, we asked that a replacement team be assigned to keep the project going, stipulating that the replacement should be selected from among the young Philippine recruits who SIL was training to work alongside us.

We specifically requested that Bel Labaro, a young lady we knew well, be assigned to continue the work in Asibanglan. Bel had been a house helper in the home of one of our pilots at Bagabag. Through her relationships there, she had come to make a personal commitment of discipleship to Christ. We and other colleagues had helped her complete a course in biblical studies at a seminary in Manila, and now she had completed the linguistic training the Philippine Branch had established to train co-workers from among the Philippine Christian community.

Our Director accepted these conditions and we agreed to move our family to the southern translation centre at Nasuli, where Jason had been born. During the six months back in Asibanglan, we shared these plans with our Kalinga "family" there. They were heart broken. They initiated a petition which they circulated around the village. They asked our Director to reconsider this plan and to let us remain in Asibanglan. They desperately wanted the translation project to go forward. It was painful to leave them

176

for our new assignment in Nasuli, but we placed it all in God's hands. We would visit, and we would intercede for them and for Bel as they continued the work.

As we moved to SIL's southern translation centre in Nasuli, my brother Hugo and his wife Lydia wound down their construction operation in St. Catharines and joined Wycliffe as well. With their four children, they went to Papua New Guinea to assist the world's largest SIL branch in training New Guineans in construction skills. Mom and Dad's oldest four sons going overseas on mission assignments may have had something to do with the "wandering Wiens" spirit our Dad had modeled, but it also demonstrated the fruit of our parents' prayers and their example of service in the church and the wider community.

While my younger siblings did not go out on long term mission assignments, they were all active in leadership and service in their churches and communities. Our large families, both on the Wichert and the Wiens side, made up a substantial part of our financial and prayer support.

This is our family at SIL's southern centre in Nasuli, about 1980.

When we began our new assignment at Nasuli, we recognized immediately one great benefit for our family. We lived on the translation centre where Jason and Andrea attended school. Many of our colleagues living in remote village locations had to send their children to the boarding homes on the centre, where they lived under the care of boarding home parents. Our children sometimes thought that it would be fun to live in a boarding home, but overall, we decided that it was God's gift to us that we were able to all be together as a family.

The project in Asibanglan continued to go forward under the leadership of our newly assigned Philippine colleague, Bel Labaro. Since she was a native speaker of Ilocano, the language of wider communication in the northern Philippines and a language closely related to Kalinga, it was not long before she was fluent in the Limos Kalinga language – more fluent than we who had not been immersed in related languages from our birth would ever be. We were grateful that the project was in good hands and our colleagues were making good strides.

I had to adjust to a whole new rhythm in my new role as an administrator. I was responsible to oversee 25 language projects across Mindanao and surrounding islands. I felt a little insecure about my place at first, because a number of the colleagues under my supervision had PhD degrees and many more years of experience in the Philippines and in Bible translation. Over time, I came to realize that what had prompted the Branch to call me to this position had more to do with the outgoing and pastoral nature they saw in me, than with my education or years of experience.

My new position required frequent trips to visit teams in their language allocations. When we tallied up my absences from home after our first year in this position, it came to 40% of the time. This required a great deal of adjustment for Ginny, and Jason and Andrea as well.

It seemed that family crises tended to strike while I was away. After one trip, I came home to find Jason in a cast. He had broken his arm. Another time when I got home, Ginny had a great snake story for me. Our house helper had come running in to announce that there was a cobra in our storage room. Ginny went out with her to see. There was a giant cobra, standing on one of our packing drums, its hood fully flared out, ready to strike if challenged. Our neighbour, Sue Forman, came over to lend a hand and Ginny went out to see if there were any men available to help as well. Along the path, she encountered Sue's husband and asked if he wouldn't like to come assist her with the cobra. He declined until she added, "Your wife is there, wouldn't you like to help her?" By the time some of the Filipino staff came around, the snake had crawled back among the things in our storage shed, never to be seen again.

After another trip, as our plane was approaching the airstrip, Jason turned his head to look up and his collarbone popped out of place. The day before, he had climbed one of the tall pine trees on the centre to get a closer look at a bird's nest, when the branch he was on broke and he came crashing down. The initial examination by the doctor didn't uncover any serious injury, but apparently the collarbone had been cracked, and had broken when he turned his head to look up at our plane coming in.

On another one of my frequent trips, the children were out playing when Andrea and one of her friends collided face to face. She had a broken tooth and severe cuts to her mouth, which required an air trip to the doctor in Manila for stitches and dental repair work. This was all in Ginny's hands. I was grateful for the strong and capable partner God had given me.

Other colleagues sometimes marveled at Ginny's calm faith and courage in her role as the wife and mother in our family when I was away so much. Sometimes my travel took me to areas which were known to be infiltrated by armed insurgents opposed to the government.

On one trip, Dr. Lynip and I were going out to visit a team of Filipino associates engaged in literacy and community health outreach in a remote mountain village. The team reported insurgents had been seen in their area. The government required that we report our travel to military commanders responsible for security over the area, and to get their permission for our trip. The military commander wanted to send an escort to ensure our safety. We declined, saying that a military escort would make us less safe. The commander insisted and so our negotiation went on for four hours. Finally, he relented.

We hiked up to the remote village. As we came near, a young boy came running out to meet us. "Do you have an escort?" he asked. We said "No" and he expressed relief because the insurgents were in the village. Sure enough, as we came around the final bend in the trail, there they were, seated under a house with their armalites in hand. Traveling with a military escort, we would have been in grave danger.

It felt a bit strange that night when we went to sleep, knowing who was in the village "protecting" us. Aware of the kinds of dangers we faced on this trip, colleagues back at Nasuli asked Ginny if she had slept at all. She had. She was able to put our safety in God's hands. I was grateful for her "calmness in uncertainty and change."

While SIL had an aviation service which helped a great deal with access to some very remote and rugged locations, there were some destinations that were too difficult for even our missionary planes. They were uniquely designed for short take-off and landing strips. Before we moved to our translation assignment in Asibanglan, we were sent to visit one of the remote mountain villages where experienced translators were working, who could teach us some things from the benefit of their experience.

This village was in the mountains, accessible only by bus over very rugged roads. Ginny and I were travelling with Jason, who was less than a year old. The bus was entirely open on one side. From there, passengers would slide in on rough wooden benches across the width of the bus. As the bus wound its way over the one-lane mountain roads, we could look out the open side, down hundreds of feet into deep gullies.

On another trip in the same mountain region, I was travelling with a colleague in a borrowed Willys Jeep. Suddenly, as we got to the top of a steep rise and rounded a curve, we lost the steering entirely. When we got out and opened the hood, we saw that the bracket holding the steering column to the frame had broken. We had no steering at all. We were high in the mountains and it was cold and dark. Finally, a passing motorist stopped and offered to help. He was carrying a rope with which he towed us to the next wayside vehicle repair shop.

Most of the problems people encountered along these roads were flat tires, so the vehicle repair stations were mostly simple vulcanizing stands with very little capacity for more serious repair. But one thing we discovered is that Filipinos are resourceful. The bracket that was broken on our vehicle was cast iron, which cannot be welded, so we wondered what the local "mechanic" would come up with. He brazed the broken piece and it held for many miles to come.

After I became the Field Director, I was responsible for visiting teams in their language locations. I did this using any travel means available.

Sometimes when the location was accessible by road, I was able to use the group-owned four-wheel drive Toyota HiLux on such trips. Since the travel conditions were so very rough, it was not unusual to have problems along the way – if nothing else, at least a flat tire.

On one trip we were nearly back at our translation centre. We were tired and hot, but otherwise in good spirits. We commented that this had been such a good trip. We had not had any emergencies. Just then there was a hard bump at the front of the vehicle and a tire rolled down the road ahead of us. We had lost one front wheel completely.

On another trip in the same area, we were coming home after dark. As we bumped along the road, it felt like something was bouncing around in the back of the vehicle, but we were too tired to stop and check. The next morning, when it was light, one of our colleagues called me over to look at the vehicle where I had parked it. It was sitting there looking like a sway-belly horse. The entire frame had come apart in the middle. The only thing holding the back and front of the vehicle together was the drive shaft.

One of the defining features of our Nasuli translation centre was the spring-fed swimming pool. Its chilly water, fed by an underground stream coming down from the highest mountain in the area, provided a great source of refreshment for all of us, and it became a place where we experienced great fellowship and fun. Both Jason and Andrea were baptized in the Nasuli pool. The water from the pool drained into a river which flowed through the surrounding countryside of Bukidnon province. Some of the older children at the centre enjoyed rafting trips down the river on inner tubes.

One Saturday, a couple of teachers gathered a group of eager young people to go down river together. They paired up in a buddy system to ensure the safety of each participant. Sadly, at a point of very swift flowing rapids, Tammy Cochran, the youngest daughter of Pat and Joanne, who had recruited us at Jungle Camp, got her flowing hair entangled in some roots underwater and drowned.

We were all devastated. As the Field Director in charge of the centre, it was my responsibility not just to comfort the grieving family, but to conduct the funeral of one of our dear children. The pastoral gifts passed on to me from my parents and given to me by God were surfacing in this time of great grief.

During the 1980s, while we were living at Nasuli, the opposition to the dictatorial regime of President Ferdinand Marcos was growing. While life seemed to be very peaceful at Nasuli, we were beginning to see evidence of turmoil around us.

We heard stories of bodies floating down the river, the result of counter-insurgency operations the Filipinos referred to as "salvaging." One day as I walked on our airstrip, I noticed a body lying in the corn field nearby. When I got closer, I saw that it was the body of a man with his hands tied behind his back and his throat slit.

We had heard that the communist "New People's Army" (NPA) was becoming active in our area. This seemed to be evidence of their activity. We also learned that most of the Filipino staff at our translation centre had been forced to participate in "indoctrination" sessions conducted by the radical elements.

The Catholic Bishop in this part of the Philippines, Bishop Francisco Claver, was born and raised in one of the tribal communities in the Cordillera where the Kalinga lived. He was viewed in the Marcos regime as a radical. They accused him of communist sympathies because of his firm opposition to the excesses of the Marcos dictatorship. He came very close to being imprisoned.

He began to think about how he might adjust his pastoral responses in order to be more effective. As he contemplated what to do, he realized that the activism he encouraged needed to be grounded in a deep spirituality. Through contacts in the USA, he came across a Catholic family who were products of the charismatic renewal in the Catholic Church at the time. Frank Summers came from a political family in Louisiana. He was raised in a long line of District Attorneys and was himself an assistant DA. He was struggling in his marriage with Genie and went to his priest for council. His priest heard his confession and instructed him to go home and read the Gospel of John. As he did this, Jesus became real to him and his life was transformed, as was their marriage.

Frank and Genie committed themselves to active missionary service in the Catholic Church. This was something new for Catholics, as ministries were generally the work of ordained clergy or nuns. They were among the first lay people approved to serve as missionaries abroad. Bishop Claver invited them to come to Malaybalay, Bukidnon, the town where SIL missionaries at Nasuli did their shopping.

Frank and Genie helped establish "Couples for Christ," a lay renewal movement in the Catholic Church. The movement has gone all around the world and helped many families to live out their faith in Christ in a more vibrant way. Frank and Genie became very good friends of ours and since then we have continued to have many warm interactions with Couples for Christ.

This experience, as well as the support we experienced in our translation ministry from Catholics in the Philippines, gave us a new and positive perspective on the Church and helped expand our understanding of the gospel and of the reach of God's Kingdom in this world. We could see that any boxes we create through our denominational emphases are too small for God.

We built many warm friendships among our SIL colleagues at Nasuli. Among our dearest friends were the Lynip family. Dr. Steve and Karin Lynip had begun their mission exposure in the Philippines at an orphanage not far from Nasuli, which Steve's aunt, Louise Lynip, had founded. After a term of service as medical staff at the orphanage, Steve and Karin joined SIL to help build our primary health care and literacy outreach among the tribal communities.

We had many great adventures with the Lynip family. Their children were also good friends with Jason and Andrea. The Lynips introduced us to Camiguin Island off the north coast of Mindanao, where we enjoyed many excellent vacations together. Ginny and I also joined Steve and Karin on a motorcycle trip across Mindanao to Davao on the southern coast, where we enjoyed a great vacation in a first-rate hotel. When we drove up to the hotel in our 100cc cross-country motorbikes, the bellhops responsible for parking guests' vehicles were dumbfounded. What should they do with our muddy, filthy bikes?

My job as Director for SIL's southern programs came with many surprises. Not all of my travel was by air. On a trip to assist with book distribution in one of the tribal communities, I joined four Filipino men riding together on one 100cc motorbike. We travelled on logging roads from village to village.

We were five men on one bike, and a couple of us were carrying a box of books in each hand.

The bridges we had to cross consisted of two big logs felled across a gully. When we got to the bridge, all of us passengers would get off and the driver would gently maneuver the bike across on one of the logs, while we followed on foot.

On another trip I joined 12 other people riding on a motorcycle with a sidecar. The motto in the Philippines is, "There's always room for one more."

One day we were surprised when one of our single ladies flew out to Nasuli from her remote tribal location with a set of twins in her arms. The tribe where she worked had a taboo about twins. They were considered abnormal and one would be left to die. The parents of this set of twins were also very ill with TB. As a single woman, fully occupied with her translation work, Shirley could not care for the twins. "Would someone at Nasuli be able to take them?" she asked. We felt we could care of one, and another friend at Nasuli, who was also a nurse, agreed to take the other twin.

We loved little James, and as a family we began to talk about possibly adopting him. To help us know what to do, we went with Steve and Karin Lynip to visit Steve's aunt at Bethany Home, the orphanage she had established. Her counsel was extremely helpful. She strongly urged that whatever we do, we should not separate the twins. They should remain together. Her other strong advice was that the twins be returned to their parents, if at all possible.

This set us on a new course of action. Now we put extra effort into restoring the twins' parents back to health, with the view to uniting the twins with their parents. That was what happened. However, the time we spent caring for James and the conversations we had about adoption planted a seed in our minds and hearts.

Our initial assignment to the administrative position in Nasuli had been intended for two years, after which we would return to the Kalinga project. However, as I got into this new role, I began to realize that I actually enjoyed it and my colleagues seemed to appreciate my leadership. I liked the variety. I enjoyed visiting the many and varied tribal locations, and seeing the many different and creative ways in which my colleagues were pursuing their missions. I relished the opportunities to partner with leaders of other missions and denominations as we worked together to build the Kingdom where Jesus is Lord. I began to sense that perhaps this was the kind of service for which God had been preparing me all my life.

As we came to the end of our second term in the Philippines, we were due for another home assignment and we needed to plan for that, and for what the Branch might have for us on our return. In consultation with our Director, we decided that I should enroll in a study program to build on my pastoral gifting.

I enrolled in the Interfaith Pastoral Counselling program in Kitchener, Ontario. Jason was in Grade 4 and Andrea was in Grade 2. It was encouraging for us to discover that our children's education in the Philippines was well up to the standard of schools in Canada. In fact, after about a week in Grade 2, Andrea's teacher called and asked if they could put her into Grade 3. They thought she was advanced well beyond her grade. We declined, because we did not know how this would work out for her reentry into our schools in the Philippines and we wanted to keep her with her age cohort. In the end, the school put her in the combined 2/3 class. Jason also thrived in this year at A. R. Kaufman Public School. As an extreme extrovert like his dad, Jason had often struggled to stay focused on his work at the Nasuli mission school. In Grade 4 at A. R. Kaufman, he was blessed with the teacher that seemed to know just how to keep him focused and motivated. When we attended the first parent-teacher interview and heard the teacher extol this child of ours, we asked, "Are you sure you are talking about our Jason?"

Our year in Kitchener gave us lots of time to reconnect with brother Erv and his family. They were living in Waterloo and pastoring the Mennonite church in Breslau. I was delighted for the opportunity to build on my pastoral skills through the Interfaith Pastoral Counselling program with a view to returning to the Philippines for another administrative assignment.

When we returned to the Philippines, we were asked to assume a temporary assignment in Manila. During that time, I filled the role of Acting Director, while the Branch Director went on a return assignment to the USA to build his support base.

After this temporary assignment, we were asked to go back to Bagabag, where I was to serve as the Field Director for the northern third of our language projects in the Philippines. Most of the remote tribal locations did not have telephones, and cell phones had not yet been invented. So, the way that we were able to stay in touch with our translation personnel out in the field was through a single side-band radio system. Each team was required to come on for "roll call" each morning to report and help ensure that all was well.

Through this roll call, on July 30, 1985, Bel shared the horrific news of Pedro's murder. I immediately asked the pilot to fly me in to Asibanglan to be with our Kalinga family there, and to evacuate Bel and her partner from the village.

We were aware of the growing threat of a gang of bandits, and had wondered how safe it was for them to live in Asibanglan. The bandits had barged into their house previously, tied them up, threatening their life, and then robbed them. When that happened, I had gone in to meet with the village leaders to assess whether it was safe for them to live there. The village was unanimous in their call for the translation team to remain in Asibanglan. To help ensure their safety, Pedro volunteered to set up a battery-operated alarm system from their house to his. It was nearby.

The alarm worked, because the next time the bandits came, Pedro was able to warn the village and drive them off. Sadly, this made him their next target. When they came back again, they were dressed in fatigues, pretending to be with the military.

For safety, the village had established a curfew. People were not to go out after dark. Since the bandits looked like military personnel, Pedro opened the door. They pretended to be lost and asked his help to guide them through the village. Pedro agreed and began walking ahead of them in the direction they needed to go. Just 100 meters from his house, they opened fire with their high-powered rifles.

It was now obvious that our team would not be safe and that their presence was endangering others. We needed to evacuate our translators from the village. When we flew into Asibanglan, we were met by a group of about 25 "New People's Army" rebels who had come into the village to rally the people. They challenged the people saying, "See the government is not protecting you. You should join us." The NPA was becoming more brazen as the writing seemed to be on the wall for the Marcos dictatorship.

I arranged for the evacuation of Bel and her partner, and then went to meet with Pedro's family. The NPA rebels were meeting with the community leaders at the school and sent a message down to warn me that if the military should arrive while I was there, that would be the end of my life. They were concerned that I might send out a message to the military about their presence in the village.

From that day on, for a decade, the NPA would not allow anyone from SIL to return to the village. Bel brought some of her co-translators from Asibanglan to Bagabag to continue the translation, but no one from SIL was to go to the village. The NPA believed an outside presence would be risky to their program. We learned that the NPA now made Asibanglan one of their bases of operation, and that they recruited many young people from the village to join their cause.

For the young people, it felt "macho" to be out with the rebels, carrying guns. We were sad to learn that one of Jason's best friends in Asibanglan was killed in one of their skirmishes with the military. Because of her close association with us and her unwillingness to participate in revenge against the killers, Pedro's widow was put on house arrest to ensure that she would not inform on the rebels.

That was a particularly dark period for us, our Kalinga family, and for the country. Had God abandoned us and the people he sent us to serve? That was how we felt at times. But still the work continued. Bel was able to bring people out to our translation centre in Bagabag and God was at work in the lives of many of our dear friends through the translated Scriptures. Thank God for the perseverance of the translators. Finally, in 2004, 30 years after we had first set foot in Kalinga territory, we were able to go back to the community for the dedication of the completed New Testament. What a celebration it was! Our pastor and his family, along with Jason and Andrea, and a dozen friends from WMB Church joined us for that celebration. No, God had not abandoned us, the Kalinga people or the work God had commissioned among them. God had been there before us and God was still at work. When we had first arrived in Asibanglan, Benito was fortunate if he could gather a half dozen people for worship on a Sunday morning. When we returned in 2004, the Catholic church was full and another community of believers gathered regularly in a newly established Alliance church. We saw and felt God's Spirit at work in the love and joy of the people who had embraced us and adopted us into their tribe, just as God had embraced them.

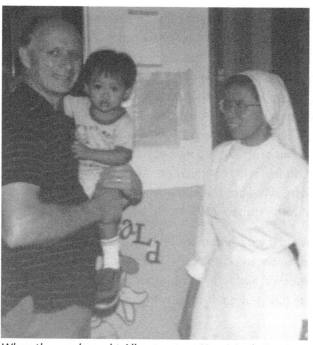

When the nun brought Allan to me at Hospicio de San Jose on October 15, 1984 he put his arm around me and the nun commented "It looks like he has found his family."

In the latter half of 1984, while we were living in Manila where I was covering for the Branch Director, Ginny and our two kids were finding great joy spending time at a nearby orphanage, playing with the little ones so hungry for love and attention. Frequently this became a topic of our conversation at dinner, and Jason and Andrea would plead, "Can't we bring one of the kids home?" Andrea was especially tender-hearted. Whenever it was raining hard, she asked if we couldn't bring some of the squatters, whom she saw living in cardboard shelters nearby, into our yard where they would be safe from flooding. The family's time spent at the orphanage in Manila added to our earlier experience fostering the twins at Nasuli. The orphanage experience in Manila got us thinking seriously about adoption again. We knew that Ginny would not be able to give birth again, but we felt that we still had love to give in our family. Cautiously we reached out to a friend, who was a social worker in Manila, to ask if adopting a child there was even an option for us. Before long she had completed our home study and we were approved for adoption.

The next step was to match us with the right child. One day she called. She began, "I am going to see a little boy that might be a suitable match for you. Are you still interested?" We just heard, "Are you interested?" We assumed she was inviting us to go along. Yes, we were interested. She graciously took us with her to Hospicio de San Jose, a Catholic orphanage on an island in the middle of the Pasig River, which flows through Manila. At the orphanage, one of the sisters brought out a very cute little boy who was just waking up from his nap. He wrapped his arms around my neck and a lifelong relationship of love was kindled with our new son. At the orphanage, he was "Allan Melchor de San Jose." We kept the name Allan, but changed the middle name to John, with the surname Wiens.

After a little while, we asked if we could take him home. "Oh no," they said. "There is still a lot of paperwork to complete." We continued to chat with the nuns and our social worker. Suddenly the Mother Superior came and said, "We can let you take him, but don't tell anyone until we complete the paperwork."

We made a quick call to my secretary in our Manila office to ask her to take some money out of our account for us, so that we could buy a few supplies. He was 15 months old. He came with the clothes he was wearing and a bottle of antibiotic he was taking. We had to go out and buy milk and diapers for the night.

For the first 12 hours he seemed catatonic. He didn't say anything or even cry. But he did sleep. The next morning, he seemed a little more relaxed. When he started to respond, we discovered a most delightful child and our whole family fell in love with him.

The Marcos dictatorship had been in trouble since 1983. In 1972, Marcos had declared Martial Law to prevent Benigno Aquino, who had defeated him in the polls, from taking power. Since then, he had been ruling as a dictator, with support from the USA. Aquino had initially been put in prison, but in the early '80s he had been permitted to go to the USA for heart surgery. On August 21, 1983, he flew home to Manila and was assassinated coming down the steps of his plane at the airport.

I have a vivid memory of that day. I had a clear sense then that this was going too far for Marcos. I was convinced that this marked the beginning of the end for his dictatorship. More than two very turbulent years ensued, with rigged elections and increasing public protests. Aquino's widow assumed a prominent role in the opposition. In an attempt to quell the protests, Marcos declared a snap election in November 1985, assuming he could rig another win.

Cardinal Jaime Sin persuaded Cory Aquino to throw her candidacy into the race. She won the election in a landslide, but Marcos again refused to turn over the reins. This sparked several months of growing unrest and protest, with millions of people marching in the streets. Finally, in February of 1986, two members of Marcos' cabinet, Juan Ponce Enrile and Marcos' cousin and Defense Minister General Fidel Ramos, broke ranks with the dictator, barricading themselves at Camp Aguinaldo, a key military base in Manila.

They called on the people to stand up in support for them and the people came out en masse. Marcos sent out the military loyal to him with tanks, but the people blocked their path at a key intersection. Finally, President Reagan and the US government had had enough and they arranged for Marcos to be flown to Hawaii. The People Power Revolution had succeeded and Cory Aquino assumed the presidency. People loyal to Marcos continued to foment turmoil for much of Aquino's presidency. During all this turmoil, we were working on completing Allan's adoption. For a time, our lawyer had to go underground. The whole process took more than two years.

The People Power Revolution happened while we were living in Manila, where I was covering the position of the Branch Director for six months. It was a chaotic time. As the chief executive for our organization, I was responsible to look after the security and well-being of our missionaries.

I remember one call to a young mom whose husband was out of town. I wanted to check on her safety. As we were talking on the phone, she suddenly let out a scream. What could be the matter?

Apparently, a US military jet had just swooped down over Manila and, looking out of her window, it looked like it was coming right at her. On another occasion, I stood in our front yard and watched a military helicopter hovering overhead, shooting rockets into the military camp just a kilometer away, where General Ramos and Senator Enrile had taken cover in defiance of Marcos.

Another time I received a frantic call from one of our colleagues who lived in an apartment near the office. She had been entering the gate to her apartment, when a "purse snatcher" came running by and grabbed her purse. I rushed over to see how I could be of help. When I arrived, I saw the guilty man kneeling in front of our colleague. Beside her stood a man with a gun asking, "Shall I shoot him?" To curb criminal behaviour, the government had deputized bands of secret marshals in Manila. Some of them felt they had liberty to take justice into their own hands. Of course, we did not want to see the poor man shot on the spot, and the likelihood of getting anywhere with legal action was slim. When the under-cover officer realized I was the SIL Director, he left the situation to me. I realized that the poor fellow was acting more out of poverty than criminal intent, so I gave him a Bible I had with me, and drove him to where he asked me to drop him off.

These prominent Filipinos advised us in our work. The chair of our Advisory Council here is the Minister of Education, Dr. Lourdes Quisumbing (lower left, front). I am at the top right.

Allan's adoption was finalized! And a semblance of calm was restored in the Philippines with Cory Acquino as the first woman president in its history.

As an expatriate organization, we had been very careful to avoid getting embroiled in the political turmoil. We had a committee of prominent Filipinos to advise us on how best to conduct ourselves in order to make our work of maximum benefit to the nation.

Since the Department of Education was our visa sponsor, it was customary for the Minister of Education to chair this advisory board. A driving force on the advisory board was our in-country legal advisor, Attorney Sedfrey Ordonez. He was influential in the nomination of new board members. Throughout the Marcos years and the ensuing turmoil that brought down his regime, we didn't know where our advisors stood politically. It never came up in our meetings. When Cory Aquino swore in her new cabinet, we were surprised and delighted to find more than half of our advisors were either in the cabinet or appointed to top ambassadorial posts.

Attorny Ordonez became Minister of Justice, and Manuel Pelaez, another key advisor and former Philippine Vice President, was named Ambassador to the United States. Ambassador Pelaez had been the target of an assassination attempt during the Marcos years. While recovering in the hospital, his daughter, who was active in the Charismatic renewal, came and read Scripture to him. Through his daughter's testimony and his reading of Scripture, he experienced a profound spiritual renewal in his own life. In addition to his service on our advisory board, he also chaired the board of the Philippine Bible Society. At his departure for his ambassadorial post in Washington, he declared that he was going to the US as a missionary, disguised as the Ambassador.

This is our family at the end of our third term in the Philippines in 1987.

By 1987, we were beginning to discuss with other leaders in the Philippine Branch what the future might hold for us. Some close friends and confidants encouraged me to stand for Branch Director at our biennial Branch conference scheduled for 1988. The policy was that the Branch Director was elected by their peers. The Director would then appoint Associate Directors to manage the various academic portfolios and the three regional centers.

We were advised to take a brief home leave before the 1988 conference so that we would be fresh, should I be elected. During the brief period that we were back in Manila before the Branch conference in 1988, I served in the public relations office and got acquainted with our advisory council and other prominent Philippine leaders with whom we regularly interacted. At the Branch conference, I was indeed elected to the Branch Director position. This meant a term of at least two years in Manila – and four, should I be re-elected in 1990.

The timing of this move was a blessing for our family again, as Jason was beginning high school and Andrea would follow soon after. The SIL children went to Faith Academy in Manila for high school. For many of our colleagues, this meant putting their teenagers into boarding homes. Our children got to live at home. Due to the distance of our home from the school and the extreme traffic congestion, they boarded the bus daily at 6:30 AM.

Our children did very well at Faith Academy. Jason joined the cross-country team and was their lead runner for four years, travelling with the team to other Asian countries such as Korea. He was also inducted into the National Honor Society.

Again, the academic rigor of this missionary school prepared our children well for our return to Canada later. When we made our longer term move back to Canada in 1992, Andrea entered Grade 10 at Eden Christian High School, where Ginny had studied. Andrea graduated two years later at the top of her class, being awarded the Governor General's award for her academic achievement.

As Branch Director, I was responsible for overseeing the overall work of more than 300 expatriate missionaries and more than 100 national staff in the Philippines. In this responsibility, I was assisted by three Regional Directors, as well as the Director of Academic Affairs, responsible for overseeing the work being done in translation, linguistics, anthropology and literacy.

I also appointed a Director of Support Affairs, who supervised the work of our pilots, teachers, and maintenance staff. The Director of Human Resources was in charge of the overall care of our missionaries and national staff. As Branch Director, I was also responsible for overseeing plans for the longer-term future of our work.

Given the rich Christian history of the Philippines, it seemed obvious to us early in our work that Filipinos should be trained to work alongside of us in the ministry of Bible translation. Already before we arrived in the Philippines, our colleagues were engaged in a program to train young Filipino recruits, to share the load in every aspect of our ministry. One of the early Filipino recruits, was Bel Labaro Caress who followed us in the Limos Kalinga project in 1980.

When I became the Philippine Director of SIL in 1988, our investment in training young Filipino colleagues in the academic disciplines required for Bible translation was paying dividends. They were beginning to coalesce around a national organization, the Translators Association of the

Philippines (TAP), which we hoped would eventually replace us. A key part of our long-range planning was what we called "completion of task." We were beginning to lay down markers which would signal readiness for the turn-over of responsibilities to the national organization and winding down some of the facilities SIL occupied. Part of the "completion of task" plan involved making good on promises to cede some of our properties to the Department of Education who had been our sponsor for all of our years in the country.

I considered it a privilege to work in partnership with the leadership of TAP to assist this national organization in their growth. I soon realized however, that even with good motives and the best of intentions, I could be hampered in this partnership endeavor by my own ethnocentrism. The organizational ethos of Wycliffe and SIL were deeply engrained in us. I began to realize that we were following a thoroughly western leadership and organizational style. It took time, and some friction, to teach me to appreciate and accept the style that was more suited to our Filipino colleagues.

By this time, one or more New Testament translations were being completed and published every year. It was my privilege to represent our organization at church and community celebrations of these milestones in the work. It was a delight to experience the various indigenous cultures and to celebrate with them the coming of God's Word in their own languages. It was always encouraging to see people from a wide variety of denominations and missions coming together around these celebrations of the Scriptures in indigenous languages. I had the privilege of visiting and interacting with people, from the most northern island of the archipelago of 7,000 islands, to the most southern.

I recall a memorable trip to the island of Batanes. It is a small island located in the South China Sea, at the most northern fringe of the Philippines. I was joining the President of the Philippine Bible Society, some Bishops and other dignitaries, for the dedication of the Ivatan New Testament. The weather was blustery, and our flight kept being delayed. When we finally got going, our pilot struggled to locate the island. He was flying by visual flight rules, and the island was just a tiny dot in the Sea. "If we miss it, we will end up in Taiwan," he remarked. When we finally landed, the pilot asked, "Who would ever want to live in such a God-forsaken place?" My Public Affairs assistant quipped, "It won't be God-forsaken when we leave." Our cargo consisted mostly of Ivatan New Testaments.

In my role as Director of the work in the Philippines, it was my privilege to represent our organization at many celebrations of completed Scripture in various tribal communities. I recall one memorable experience. As usual, I had been asked to address the community. I read Colossians 3:16. "Let the word of Christ dwell in you richly." Then I was asked to offer the dedication prayer. Something happened that I can't explain. There was a hush over the gathering and I felt something like a soft wind blow over me and the entire gathering. I'm sure my words were not particularly profound, but I felt like the presence of God's Spirit come over the gathering in a powerful way. I was not the only one who felt it, as others commented on it later. Even in our imperfections, we can be channels of God's Spirit and blessing.

It was also my responsibility and privilege to regularly meet with, and report on our progress to, church and mission leaders and partner agencies such as the Philippine Bible Society. One of my great joys was seeing the Bible at work in the Catholic Church, especially through Episcopal Commission on the Biblical Apostolate. Through our warm cooperative relationship, we were able to obtain the Churches official "Imprimatur" on many of our Scripture publications. It was a great privilege for me to get to know the avuncular and cheerful Cardinal Jaime Sin. His typical greeting when I arrived at his residence was "Welcome to the house of Sin!"

On my last visit with him we talked about the diversity in God's Kingdom and the church. As our meeting came to a close, he leaned back in his chair and began to sing, "Father make us one. That the world may know that you sent your Son. Father make us one." My own understanding of the nature and beauty, diversity and magnificent reach of God's Kingdom was growing.

In October of 1988, our family in Canada helped fund a brief trip back to Ontario for us, so that the whole family could be together to celebrate Mom and Dad's 50th wedding anniversary. The difference in the demeanor of our dad in the picture taken for the 50th anniversary from the photo taken on their wedding day is striking. Our mom brought much love and joy into his life. It was a great privilege to be with the entire family to celebrate their 50 years together.

Mom and Dad celebrated their 50th anniversary on October 1, 1988. When I compare this photo to their wedding photo, I marvel at how Dad's demeanor has brightened since their wedding photo. Marriage and family brought much joy to both Mom and Dad.

Aside from all the blessings and privileges I experienced in my two terms as Branch Director of SIL's work in the Philippines, the greatest blessing was to be able to sit under the ministry and teaching of Darrell Johnson, the pastor of Union Church of Manila. Union Church was our home church during our time living in Manila. Jason and Andrea participated in youth activities there and together with us they helped to teach a Sunday School class. But the powerful teaching ministry of our pastor, Darrell Johnson, was transformative, especially for me.

Darrell is a profound biblical expositor who would later serve as the professor of preaching at Regent College in Vancouver. When he opened the Gospel of Mark for us at Union Church, in a series entitled "The Gospel of the Kingdom," it felt like scales were falling from my spiritual eyes every week. I felt like I was walking on tiptoes, eagerly awaiting the next week's sermon.

How could I have missed this glorious understanding of the Kingdom where Jesus is Lord? I was no longer satisfied with the narrow and self-centered confines of "the gospel of sin management" I had heard all my life. The gospel of the Kingdom was so much greater than anything I had imagined until then. Darrell's teaching began to put meaning to the inklings that had been growing in me as I rubbed shoulders with brothers and sisters from the Catholic faith and realized that God was always at work beyond the boundaries and boxes that my earlier understanding of the faith had built for God.

In my readings in missiology, I also came across new ideas that helped to open my eyes, such as Dr. Paul Hiebert's exposition comparing bounded-set thinking and centered-set thinking. I saw that God cannot be confined to any boundaries we create and that our focus must always be on the center, our Lord Jesus Christ.

There is so much out of Darrell Johnson's preaching that has stayed with me. His sermon on "The Friend at Midnight" parable in Luke 11 showed me how our understanding of Scripture is often determined by our cultural presuppositions. It is impossible to understand the parable in Luke 11 without a deep understanding of, and appreciation for, eastern hospitality, something we were beginning to understand, and experience, through our relationships in the Philippines. Through this and other sermons, Darrell pointed me to the writings of Kenneth E. Bailey, especially "Poet and Peasant and Through Peasant Eyes: A Literary-Cultural Approach to the Parables in Luke." This helped me a great deal to better understand the Scriptures for my own edification as well as for my calling as a Bible translator.

One of Darrell's messages affected me so profoundly that the text on which it is based has become a defining text for me in my life. The text is Philippians 2, where Paul encourages us to have the same attitude that Jesus had. Then he quotes an early Christian hymn in verses 5-11. Jesus' journey to greatness by the downward path to become like us, and then further down to obedience and servanthood, and then down further yet to death on the cross, has inspired me to try to emulate this path of servanthood over a life of privilege.

While in general we found the Filipino people to be among the most generous and hospitable people in the world, it was also uncomfortable at times to stand out as the only "Americanos" in a crowd. To our chagrin, the Filipino people saw all of us non-Filipinos as "Americanos." This harkened back to the years of US colonial administration in the country. It was impossible to get anyone to understand that among our SIL members there were as many non-Americans as there were Americans. Australia, New Zealand, Germany or Canada meant nothing to most of them. In their minds we were "Americano" and as such we were rolling in money.

Children on the streets of Manila would shout out, "Hey, Joe!" The name Joe was reminiscent of GI Joe. So, in their minds we were not just rich Americanos, but also somehow associated with their understanding of the American military. This also had to do with the fact that the USA still had a number of prominent military bases in the Philippines out of which much of the war in Indochina was launched. The importance of these forward military bases in Asia was one of the reasons why the US backed the Marcos dictatorship for so long. Their foreign policy needed these bases. It was often uncomfortable, especially for those of us who were not Americans and not in favour of the militarism of the USA, to be associated with all this. But it gave us a little window on what it is like to be a visible minority in our country or anywhere else in the world.

The care and safety of all the missionaries and staff under my supervision were always top of mind. Of course, there were associates to assist with this, but the buck stops at the Branch Director's office. All of our leaders were given a "contingency preparedness" course by specialists sent by Wycliffe. I tried to keep abreast of where our people were and what they were doing.

One morning, I arrived at my office to find an urgent message from two of our ladies serving on one of the smaller islands in the Sulu Sea. The ladies reported that they had been out on the sea with some of their national colleagues on a book distribution trip. Their boat had capsized. Miraculously the two ladies had made it back to their home island. Now as the new day dawned, they were concerned for their co-workers, whom they had left hanging onto the overturned boat. What should I do? I was contemplating a call to the coast guard when the ladies came back with another message. Their co-workers were safe.

On another occasion, our family was on vacation on another island, completely out of touch with what was happening in our work. I had left an associate in charge. When we got back to the mainland and caught the bus heading back to Manila, I picked up a newspaper. Suddenly my eye caught the names of some people whom I recognized as our members. There had been a kidnapping and one of our members was being held for ransom along with another missionary.

This was the kind of contingency we had been prepared to navigate. The protocol was to assign a point person to handle all communications and negotiations related to this event, leaving me free to care for the ongoing management of the entire Branch. Again, God was gracious and the missionaries were ultimately released without harm.

This was just one of three kidnappings involving members of our SIL Branch. All were attempts by militant elements to raise awareness of their cause and put pressure on the government. Our members were released unharmed and we did not pay ransom.

Another mission organization in the Philippines, experienced the kidnapping of one of their couples. Tragically, the husband died in the incident.

One night, at Faith Academy in Manila, there was a break-in at one of the high school's children's homes. Some of the girls housed there were girls we knew well. The residents were terrorized. The young daughter of one of our families was sexually assaulted. That experience, so close to our own family, was terrifying.

As the lead administrator in a very large missionary community, I also experienced the reality that even missionaries are not free from sin. As one of my fellow administrators commented, we had to deal with every sin in the book, except for murder, as far as we knew. Having to confront unethical or immoral behaviour was definitely my least favourite part of the job. It was stressful and demoralizing at times.

But the job wasn't all serious or even difficult. Many times, the situation was so funny we couldn't help but laugh.

Most of our members did not have their own cars. There were a few group-owned vehicles and a few individually-owned cars others could borrow. One of our members had just returned to Manila from the US. He was on jet lag but needed to go get a few things at the mall. He borrowed an older model Toyota from a colleague who lived in Manila. When he got back to our guest house, he was feeling sleepy. So, he parked the car and went to bed. Soon the police were at the guest house looking for him. It turns out that after some time the keys on these older model Toyotas get worn and become interchangeable. Our member thought he was driving home with the same car he had borrowed. It was the same colour, but he had accidentally brought home a car belonging to someone else. I was away on a trip, so it fell to Ginny again to help sort things out with the police.

There were times when we met up with lawless elements. Some people looked at us and saw us as wealthy "Americanos." These incidents made us uncomfortable and were disconcerting. However, as a general observation about the Filipino people, we would have to say that we found them to be among the most generous and hospitable people we had ever encountered.

I have often said (and I stand by this statement) that it is impossible to outgive a true Filipino. Embedded in this culture is a value they call "utang na loob." A common translation is "debt of gratitude." The essence of *utang na loob* is an obligation to appropriately repay a person who has done one a favour. Filipinos' sense of *utang na loob* is typically inspired by acts that are hard to value or quantify.

The internal dimension, *"loob"* differentiates *utang na loob* from an ordinary *utang* (debt); being an internal phenomenon, *utang na loob* thus goes much deeper than ordinary debt or even the Western concept of owing a favour. Filipino psychology explains that this is a reflection of the *kapwa* orientation of shared personhood or shared self, which is at the core of the Filipino values system. What "utang na loob" means to them is that whenever they experience an act of kindness or generosity, it triggers a response of gratitude in them that will prompt them to return the kindness at an appropriate opportunity in the future.

We discovered early on that there is no indigenous word for "thank you." To accommodate the sense that saying thank you is considered good manners by people from other cultures, they have integrated the word "salamat" into their national language. It is essentially a borrowed word.

Among the Kalinga people, we were puzzled at first when we would give people a gift or do something kind for them and they would respond, "I won't say thank you." What they were trying to communicate was that they would carry their internal debt of gratitude until an opportunity presented itself to return the favour. For many of them, saying thank you right away was like discharging their debt of gratitude with a word and without the appropriate action.

Our insistence on saying "thank you" might communicate to some that we were too quick to expunge any debt of gratitude with a word. They might have wondered if we truly shared their deep internal sense of gratitude. We discovered the depth of the Filipino sense of gratitude when our best friend Pedro literally gave his life to protect our team from bandits. We know that we owe his family a debt that we will never repay in this life.

17: Service with the Canadian Bible Society

As our fourth field term in the Philippines came to an end in 1992, we were exhausted. In addition to the heavy weight of my leadership responsibilities, we had also discovered, with the help of a psychologist who came to serve on our staff, that Ginny had some painful childhood issues that needed our attention. With all of my travels, leaving Ginny home alone with the children and other stresses, she was battling serious mental health concerns. These needed additional counselling and medical care. We knew that Mom Wichert had suffered severe mental health crises during Ginny's childhood and beyond. In fact, our counsellor helped us to see that depression ran deep in her family of origin.

We needed to take time to establish a more stable home life. It was important to have access to good health care to help Ginny through this period of her life. Jason and Andrea would be off to higher education soon. We wanted to be nearby to see how they would adjust to life in North America after high school. So it seemed an ideal time to return to Canada.

The big question was: what would I do in Canada?

Wycliffe Bible Translators of Canada had some suggestions of assignments for me in Canada. But none of them really appealed to me. More than that, we felt that many among our support base were investing in our work because we were engaged in overseas missions. We didn't think there was much motivation to support our ministry if we were to take an assignment with Wycliffe in Canada. That was quickly confirmed when the month after we landed back in Canada the financial support we had been receiving from our home church simply did not appear in our account. They didn't contact us. The support just stopped.

Overall, in practical ways, we experienced exceptional generosity and support from many in our family and from many friends. Some of my siblings initiated a project to build a house for us in St. Catharines. When other relatives and friends learned of the project, they stepped in with all kinds of support. When we arrived back home in August 1992, a new house was waiting for us with a very affordable mortgage. What a blessing!

To clear my mind and to devote my energies to something completely different, I agreed to help my brother on construction for a few months. This helped us pay the bills, but I also soon realized that I simply was not made for this kind of work. I would not be able to spend the rest of my life as a carpenter. My gifting was different from my brothers'.

Then I remembered a conversation I had had with Dr. Harold Fehderau many years ago while we were still preparing for service overseas. At the time, Harold was serving as a Bible translation consultant in the Congo with MB Missions. While on home leave, he heard about my interest in Bible translation and took me out for lunch. He followed up that conversation by sending me several books by Dr. Eugene Nida, the father of the modern Bible translation movement and the prime mover behind the global network of translation consultants in the United Bible Societies (UBS).

By the time I was thinking about our future in 1992, I learned that Dr. Fehderau was now the Director of Scripture Translations for the Canadian Bible Society (CBS). I took a chance and wrote to Harold. I asked if he might have a position for me at CBS. Harold responded warmly. In addition to his responsibilities at CBS, he was also serving as a UBS consultant and in particular he was leading the Translation Computer Resource Group (TCRG) in the broader UBS fellowship.

He asked about my interest in, and experience with, computers. I had to confess that, while I had used the computer in my administrative work for word processing, I did not know much more than that. I was aware that SIL was deeply involved in a massive research effort on how to harness computers for linguistic research and Bible translation. A hub for some of the research into computers for SIL was the JAARS centre in Waxhaw, North Carolina. After some further correspondence, Harold offered me a part time role as a translation consultant for CBS if I would spend a month or so at Waxhaw to learn more about the computer as it applied to our work. The offer from CBS included a financial contribution to our Wycliffe account to assist with our living expenses. Essentially, I would be on loan from Wycliffe to CBS.

The first assignment Harold had for me was one that I am sure he would have done with great joy, but it was not enjoyable at all for me. It involved a lot of detailed research into translation issues in the biblical text. He asked me to identify the nature of the issues and then organize them into categories and tag them in ways that would make them accessible by computer. I worked at the computer all day and every day.

Since we were living in St. Catharines and the CBS Translations office was in Kitchener, I worked alone at home. However, the space we had available for my office was down in the unfinished basement of our new house. For an extrovert, working alone, day in and day out, sitting at the computer, confined in the basement is deadly. At the time Ginny was still battling mental health issues that had come out during our time in Manila and I began to realize I had not fully recovered from the stress of our last four years in the Philippines.

Before long I also found myself plunged into a deep pit of depression. I realized that I had not recovered well from our last stressful years in Manila and on top of that I had accepted the position of board chair at our Church which was going through some rough waters financially. With prayer, medical help, counselling and moving my office to a brighter room upstairs, I slowly climbed out of this pit. Also, Harold began to give me assignments that were more fitting and enjoyable for me.

He sent me to Schefferville in northern Quebec, to assist SIL translators Bill and Norma Jean Jancewicz with the training of indigenous translators in the Naskapi language project. I was also assigned to translation checking of some of the indigenous language translations that CBS was helping to support. This got me out of the house and gave me the opportunity to visit and get to know some of our indigenous communities in Canada. I enjoyed this immensely. As a consultant, I was assigned to check the quality of translations being produced in various indigenous languages of Canada. Most of the projects for which CBS was providing support were projects being managed by SIL translation personnel. The agreement was that CBS would manage the typesetting and publishing of the finished work. To do that, CBS needed to ensure the quality and integrity of what was being produced. Harold assigned me to meet with translation teams to review and check the quality of the work being done.

In 1982, the Canadian Bible Society had authorized Harold to purchase "computer equipment for translation manuscript processing." The cost of $10,000 was a major investment at the time. Harold defended this very expensive investment with the promise that this equipment "would put Canada and the UBS Americas Area at the forefront of applying computer technology to the task of providing Scriptures for the world."

This was just the beginning of a powerful team that changed the trajectory of the Bible translation ministry. Ten years later, in 1994, Dr. Fehderau, at the request of the United Bible Societies (UBS) and under a mandate by the Canadian Bible Society, began to coordinate the formation of a "Global Computer Training Resource Group for Bible Translation."

This group was working closely with Dr. Kees de Blois, a UBS colleague from the Netherlands. The request in 1994 was for the CBS Translations office, under Harold's direction, to function as a "service center" supporting the activities of the Global Computer Training Resource Group (eventually named TCRG - the Translation Computer Resource Group). The mandate given to this working group was:

- Advise UBS translation leadership on computer technology and training
- Participate in regional training and tutoring events
- Advise on hardware and software standards
- Liaise between translation and publishing teams
- Liaise with SIL on development of software tools and translation notes
- Coordinate use of computer technology in translation.

This was all developing just as I was coming on staff as a consultant with the group. Harold was the Director of Scripture Translations at CBS. Now, added to that responsibility, he took on the role of Chair of the Translation Computer Resource Group (TCRG) in the United Bible Societies. In this role he explored how computers could be harnessed to assist with Bible translation and publishing.

Harold had hired a few people to assist him with this task. In some ways, the group was a motley crew, an unlikely group of skills and personalities. Ed Peters came from Rockway Mennonite Collegiate in Kitchener, where he taught history. Ed was a dynamic and creative teacher, who loved exploring new horizons with his students. He had made an agreement with the Apple Computer company, which was just a fledgling operation in the 1980s, to experiment with the use of their computers in the classroom. Ed's visionary nature and unbridled enthusiasm in everything he did brought him to the point of burnout in his teaching career. Harold calculated that with his supervision, working in a more structured office environment, Ed's gifting could be maximized while avoiding burnout.

At Rockway High, one of Ed's brilliant young students was Jeff Klassen. Jeff had an innate bent toward technology. Jeff had not pursued post-secondary education. His computer knowledge was gained from hands-on experience. He loved technology, but not the classroom. Jeff thrived in an experiential, hands-on learning environment. It seemed there was nothing about the rapidly emerging computer and software technology that he could not learn. Even though CBS had instituted a hiring freeze to try to bring their budget into balance, Ed somehow persuaded Harold to bring Jeff on board as a temporary hire with no guarantee of long-term employment.

At the time, SIL also had a very ambitious project of developing computer support for all the academic areas of SIL engagement – translation, linguistic, literacy and anthropology. As the chair of UBS' TCRG, Harold maintained a close relationship with SIL and kept abreast of what they were learning. With Ed and Jeff's help, he implemented a lot of this technology into the work of the United Bible Societies. The most immediate payoff seemed to be typesetting and printing.

As my health and energy improved and I got involved in projects that were aligned with my natural bent towards extroversion and pastoral care, Harold and I began to discuss my longer-term future with the Bible Society. Harold was turning 65 years old in 1997, the age at which the Bible Society's consultants were required to retire. Harold's preliminary plan was to have me assume the role of Director of the CBS Translations office while he would continue on in a part-time consulting role.

I discovered later that senior leaders in UBS Translations strongly objected to his plan. In their view I was totally unqualified. One of the academic requirements for serving as a Translation consultant in UBS was completion of a PhD. Remember, I had not gone on to complete this degree after my graduate studies in Dallas. Harold responded that my years of experience and the skills I had demonstrated should be counted as a doctoral equivalent.

In 1995, Harold was diagnosed with bladder cancer. Although the initial prognosis for full recovery was very hopeful, his cancer did not respond to

207

treatment as anticipated. By 1996, Harold's health was in steep decline and CBS began making plans for the future of the Translations office post Harold. During the last six months of Harold's life, I was asked to assume the role on an interim basis. I enjoyed this role, but my future in it was far from assured.

When Harold passed away in 1997, there was no one else to assume his leadership role, so CBS kept me on as the interim Director of Scripture Translations. It was another five years before the "interim" designation was removed. The person in UBS assigned to assume the TCRG role that Harold had played in the UBS fellowship was Dr. Kees DeBlois, a Dutch translation consultant my age. I immediately found him to be a kindred spirit. The work that our office, especially Ed and Jeff, was doing was now under the overall direction of Kees as the fully qualified UBS consultant, but under my supervision as Director of Translations for CBS. This was the beginning of a most enjoyable and productive journey.

With Harold's passing, I now carried the responsibility for planning and implementing the Canadian Bible Society's support for Bible translation. This included 12 projects with First Nations and Inuit communities in Canada, as well as the Haitian Bible. To my delight another one of the projects was with the Plautdietsch Bible, my mother tongue.

I was supported in my responsibilities by a dedicated staff team which initially included Ed Peters, Jeff Klassen, Hardy Schroeder, Barb Penner and Heike Walker. Later when Hardy retired Nicole Jiminez joined the team as our administrative assistant. Still later Heike's departure left room in our budget to bring Ruth Spielmann-Heeg, the SIL translator for the Algonquin language project, onto our staff as a translation consultant. Later still when Nicole left, Sharon Peddle joined the team as our administrative assistant.

As our work in the area of publishing support in Canada and around the world ramped up, we recruited Thomas Ortiz, an employee of the Bolivian Bible Society with expertise in desk-top publishing. With Ed's premature passing in 2009, we were able to recruit Sean Morrison, a capable young computer programmer to join our team. When the United Bible Societies' IT Infrastructure Manager moved from Kenya to Canada, UBS asked us to provide space for him in our office. We also embraced Dr. Debra Shadd, a Canadian hired by the American Bible Society as a translation consultant.

She preferred to stay in Canada rather than move to the USA, where her ancestors had lived in slavery before fleeing to Canada. She was given space in our office, where she became a much-valued colleague.

Two years after Harold passed away, our family decided that it was no longer possible to handle my responsibilities as Director of the Translations office in Kitchener while continuing to live in St. Catharines. So, we moved to a new home in Waterloo.

A year later our entire family experienced a great sadness when our mother was suddenly taken from us.

Tuesday, October 3, 2000, was a particularly happy day for our parents. Mom had celebrated her eightieth birthday just two months before, with several celebrations hosted by her loving family and dear friends. Just two days earlier, she and Dad had celebrated their sixty-second wedding anniversary. It hadn't been a large celebration like their sixtieth two years earlier. But Mom was becoming increasingly aware and grateful for how she and Dad were bonding in their senior years and how their marriage was becoming a mutual blessing to them. Dad was even beginning to respond to her romantic nature with tender gestures of his own, like the way he had taken her out for dinner on her eightieth birthday in a rented limo.

The morning of October 3, 2000, even before Mom got out of bed, she reached over to her bedside table and picked up the dented old box of Scripture verses. She knew all the verses by heart, but each morning she drew out a verse for her own encouragement and then drew one for each of her children and let that be her prayer for that day.

What made this day such an exciting day to look forward to was that their dear friends, Herb and Marg, had offered to take them on a drive around the Niagara area to enjoy the brilliant fall colours. This was their friends' anniversary gift and Mom couldn't imagine a more enjoyable way to spend a gorgeous autumn day. They would stop for lunch in one of the many country restaurants they had discovered in their senior years.

As she hurried to prepare breakfast, she thought once more of her family and remembered all the birthdays coming up before Christmas. She had remembered my birthday with a lovely card less than a month before. She had an incredible memory for birthdays. Growing up, I remember how she would remember the birthdays of so many people, even people she did not know. "Today is Queen Elizabeth's birthday," she would say. Even Hitler's birthday was remembered. On this day, before setting out on their special day with Herb and Marg, she made a quick mental calculation of how many cards she needed. She would stop off later in the evening to buy these cards, and then address them and have them ready for mailing at the Grantham Plaza Post Office the next day.

The day turned out to be everything that Mom had hoped it would be. When their friends brought them home in the late afternoon, Mom prepared a quick supper. Whenever they had activities planned for an evening, Dad and Mom would have their devotions together right after supper. Since Mom had a variety of things planned for this evening, they read the text for the day and then joined in a prayer of gratitude for this special day, for their marriage, for their family and their many dear friends. Life was good and they thanked God for this. Dad marveled at how Mom could so easily recall the names of all their 42 grandchildren, their spouses and even the 18 great-grandchildren. They thanked God for each one by name and interceded for them.

Having poured out their overflowing hearts to God, Mom prepared to hurry across the street to get her cards before dark. Dad wanted to drive her, but she assured him that she would be fine walking. Besides, she knew that he wanted to watch the news with details of Pierre Trudeau's funeral. They agreed that Dad would come pick her up in half an hour. They would then stop at the grocery store to buy the turkey and trimmings for Sunday's Thanksgiving celebration with the family.

Dusk was approaching as Mom stepped from the curb to cross Scott Street in front of their Tabor Manor apartment. She saw a car approaching in the distance but, even at her slower pace due to recent hip surgery, she was confident that she could make it across the four lanes of this busy street. What she did not know was that the driver of the approaching car was drunk and was traveling at almost double the speed limit. She was within a step or two from safety when the speeding white Chevrolet Celebrity struck her with full force. He did not even apply the brakes.

Her death was instantaneous. Even as her white loafers flew through the air, landing several meters away, her spirit flew into the arms of her loving heavenly Father. Her crumpled, broken body came to rest beside her cane at the far side of the road. As Dad approached the street on his way to pick her up, he saw the flashing lights of numerous emergency vehicles and his heart sank. "Abe, this is about your life," a voice warned him.

Mom's death brought the family together. The impact was powerful as we formed a solid circle of support for our devastated and grieving dad and for each other. The two-day wake at the Tallman funeral chapel brought hundreds of mourners from the community, across the province and from across Canada. Nori, our house helper from Bagabag, saw the accident report in the newspaper and came from Toronto to grieve with our family for the loss of the one who had challenged her to think about the welfare of her soul and seek a personal relationship with her Lord.

Endless testimonials from young and old alike were given as people shared about the impact that our loving Mom had had on their lives. Surprising and inspiring stories were shared from former neighbours and many friends. Even the staff of the Grantham Plaza postal station, where Mom mailed her many cards and care packages, told of the joy they experienced at the many delicious offerings of baked treats Mom brought them along with her cards to be mailed.

When we considered her good health, with her positive, optimistic spirit and the history of longevity in her family of origin, it seemed to all of us that her death had come far too soon. One of her grandchildren remarked, "She still had at least fifteen good years left in her."

But it was the words of our grieving Dad that took our breath away. Before closing the casket for the last time, he bent down for a final kiss on the cold lips of the life partner who had brought so much love and joy into his life. Then he turned and said to us all, "kiss the lips while they are warm."

Her smiling, energetic presence is sorely missed in family gatherings. There is no one now who calls us together to sing as a family. But her life continues to be an inspiration and a blessing, and will continue to be so for future generations. In final remarks at her graveside, grandson Pastor Jeff Lockyer challenged the family with these words, "She lived a life that is an example to us all; her legacy is up to us."

Family celebrations never were the same without her. But in spite of this painful loss, our family would not let bitterness and anger set in. Guided by our strong faith in God's grace and the power of love over hate, we determined to meet with the offender and offer forgiveness. Dad said he had to do this to let go of any pain, bitterness and anger that would only consume him if he did not reach out to offer grace to the young man responsible for her death.

Dad did find another prayer partner in his life when he married Susie Enns. For Dad this brought him great blessing in the final decade of his life. Susie was by his side in every way until his passing on April 5, 2011, two days after his 93rd birthday. From the perspective of our family, there was no way to replace the mother who had brought so much love, joy and song to Dad's life and to our family. For me, Mom's death marked the end of a significant chapter. Through most of my career at the Canadian Bible Society, the conscious awareness of Mom's daily prayers for me would be missing. Yet, I would never forget that my more than 40 years of ministry in Bible translation was in some sense the fulfilment of her prayers at my birth and through the ensuing years.

We were now living in Waterloo to be close to the CBS Translations office. This made life much easier from the perspective of my work, but it was a difficult move for our son Allan, who was in his second year of High School. He found it challenging to transition from Eden High School in St. Catharines, where he had so many good friends and cousins, to a public high school where he had to make friends all over again in a climate with many temptations and challenges. It seemed Allan found it much more difficult than the rest of us to forgive the person who took the life of the grandma who had always extended such grace and unconditional love to him.

My work at the CBS Translations office was extremely rewarding. And, I can honestly say that everyone on our CBS Translations team was smarter and more talented than I was. Perhaps my past inferiority cropped up from time to time.

Each team member was detail-oriented and superbly talented in their area of experience and expertise. I am much more of a generalist and less focused on the details. Unlike in my early days, this did not discourage me.

Rather I celebrated the potential in this group and looked to my own skills and how they contributed to the team.

I came to see my role as clearing the track of encumbrances and debris so the "thoroughbreds" could run and win. Given the superb giftings of my team members, the management style I chose to emulate was one called "Leaderful Practice." This style is described as follows: "... *a compassionate approach, a 'leaderful practice' that exhibits humility and seeks to serve others rather than power for its own sake. As a result, people learn to count on others because they have learned that each member, even the weakest, will be kept in mind when decisions are made.*" [3]

In this leadership style, every member of the staff is seen as a leader and given freedom to act and make decisions in their area of expertise and responsibility. This leadership style is "collective" in that everyone can serve as a leader. It is "concurrent" in that different people can lead at the same time. It is "collaborative" in that all members of the team are in mutual dialogue to determine what needs to be done and how to do it best. It is "compassionate" in that all members commit to preserving the dignity of each other member and each individual is considered when decisions are made and action is taken.

Our staff excelled in this style. My gifting was more suited to be a shepherd, not a boss. There was a harmonious atmosphere in the office. Retention of talented staff was exceptional, morale was high, and there was very little need for me to intervene or take corrective measures.

One of the Canadian language translation project assigned to me by Harold had been the Algonquin New Testament project. Ruth Spielmann was the SIL-assigned translator. As this project was nearing completion, and we were preparing to publish the New Testament at CBS, I took Ed Peters with me on supervision and checking trips. Ed was processing the text in digital format to ensure integrity and consistency as a preparation for typesetting and printing by our staff.

Having Ed with me was always an enjoyable adventure. Ed was so creative and energetic in everything he did. I remember one trip where we were

[3] https://iveybusinessjournal.com/publication/the-bottom-line-of-leaderful-practice/

puzzling over the product the computer was generating. We got bogged down and couldn't find the solution we were after. Finally, we decided that we might be able to do better after some sleep, so we went to bed. Suddenly, well after midnight, I woke up to find Ed hopping on my bed like Tigger. "I found it! I found it!" he was shouting. The solution had come to him in his sleep and our work was back on track.

My translation experience in the Philippines and my experience as a teaching assistant during my graduate studies in Dallas were put to good use as I came alongside some of the SIL translators in their work with First Nations languages. When I started my work with Harold, Bill and Norma Jean Jancewicz were just beginning their work with the Naskapi people in Schefferville, Quebec. They were working in close partnership with the Anglican Church and were determined to involve people from the language community as much as possible in the translation work. An early assignment Harold gave me was to travel to Schefferville to assist Bill and Norm Jean in a workshop to train local translators for the project. This was the kind of assignment I loved.

The team of Inuktitut Translators: Jonas, Bishop Benjamin, Bishop Andrew and Joshua.

This is St. Jude's Cathedral in Iqaluit.

The largest translation project supported by CBS was the translation of the Bible into the Inuktitut language. A key partner in this project was the Anglican Diocese of the Arctic. For many years, Anglican missionaries assigned in the high Arctic had inspired the work, giving it a good start.

The new project was initiated in the late 1970s. The Church approached the Bible Society about assistance with a totally new project. But, at that time, CBS lacked the capacity to support indigenous Bible translation. The American Bible Society sent Dr. Eugene Nida to conduct training and begin the project. Dr. Nida is considered by those of us engaged in Bible translation as the father of the modern Bible translation movement.

He believed very strongly that translation should be done by people who were first-language (native) speakers. He had published his views on "dynamic equivalence" translation in his volume, "The Theory and Practice Translation," one of his many books.

The Anglican diocese of the Arctic convened a workshop attended by Anglican missionaries, as well as Inuit pastors. Until then, all Bible translation in the Arctic had been done by missionaries and the expectation was that missionaries would again carry the bulk of the load and the leadership in this work.

Nida was determined to apply his wise views on translation. At the end of the training, he selected four gifted Inuit priests who were to become the primary translators. When I came into the picture three of the original four priests were still working on the project. They were Andrew Ataguttaaluk, Benjamin Arreak and Jonas Allooloo. Benjamin's brother Joshua had been added to replace another translator who had left the project. Both Andrew and Benjamin made history by being chosen as the first Inuit Bishops in the Anglican Church.

The translation of the entire Bible took 34 years, as the translators still all continued their parish duties and were only able to work on the translation a few months of the year. Usually this work was done in workshops. Initially we had workshops in various communities in the Arctic. Because the Arctic diocese was short of experienced clergy and hungry for ministry, the translators would be called on to minister in the communities at night after full days of intense work on the translation. Later we agreed that we could be more productive and have access to more support by holding the workshops at our Translations office in Kitchener.

Initially Harold carried most of the consulting load on this project and it is a project in which he would have liked to continue to be involved after his retirement. Due to his passing, I became the consultant on the project. My involvement in the translation workshops was to bring relevant knowledge from the original languages and commentaries, to ensure that the translators were understanding the text well as they were doing their work.

In one workshop in the high Arctic, Joshua Arreak was working on the book of Samuel, which has a number of references to Joab and his brother Abishai. Suddenly Joshua called over to me with a question: "Who is older, Joab or Abishai?" I replied, "I don't know. Why does it matter?" It turns out that Inuktitut does not have a generic word for brother. It has to be an older or a younger brother. I sent word to my colleague Hardy in the Translations office in Kitchener and asked him to do some library research on how to answer this question. I began to realize that these kinds of questions would become commonplace. I was grateful that my team in Kitchener had excellent research skills!

The entire Inuktitut Bible was finally completed and dedicated in 2012. The ceremony and celebration were held in Iqaluit, together with the dedication of a new Cathedral built in the shape of a giant igloo. The Inuit, like all of the indigenous people I have had the privilege of working with, are very generous people. I received many gifts from them, including intricately carved antlers, but the gift I treasure most is the soapstone carving of an Inuk holding the Bible. It speaks of the enduring nature of the work to which I have dedicated my life in answer to my mother's prayers.

This precious soap stone carving of an Inuk holding a Bible was given to me in appreciation for my help with the translation of the Bible in Inuktitut.

It felt like the icing on the cake of my career in Bible translation when I got to assist as a consultant on the translation of the Bible into Plautdietsch, my mother tongue. A New Testament had been produced some years earlier by J. J. Neufeld, a radio preacher. When he preached, he used the German Luther Bible. As he spoke, he translated the Scriptures from German to Plautdietsch on the fly. His listeners expressed interest in his translation, so his work was published.

In the 1990s, a missionary, Ed Zacharias, working with Plautdietsch speakers in Mexico, felt called to expand the early work of Preacher Neufeld to produce a complete Bible. At his initiative, a group of Plautdietsch speakers was convened under the name "Friends of Plautdietsch." The Bible Society was invited to join this group. Many of the people were from Canada, and the Canadian Bible Society expressed an interest in assisting them in their work. We invited UBS to assist, citing the wider Plautdietsch communities in Latin America. The UBS survey confirmed the need and a UBS consultant was assigned to assist with the project as well. Supervision and support were to come from our office at CBS.

When the project was finally completed, the Bible was dedicated at services in Winkler and Steinbach, Manitoba. One enthusiastic supporter commented on a Plautdietsch social media group that November 22, 2003, should be acknowledged as the Independence Day for Plautdietsch, because speakers of our language would no longer be dependent on the German Bible for their spiritual nurture.

For me, this project was so exciting. It felt like coming full circle in my career in Bible translation and in the experience of my wider family and my ancestry. Plautdietsch is a unique language, forged in the crucible of the pain and suffering of my ancestors. Because of the persecution and dispersal of Mennonites coming out of the radical reformation in the Netherlands and Northern Germany, Plautdietsch is the most widely dispersed language in the world today. There are still vibrant communities speaking this language from Siberia to Argentina. This was the language my mother spoke as she nursed me. To this day there are things I can say better in Plautdietsch than any of the other eight languages in which I can communicate.

Another project that was not primarily spoken in Canada, but which CBS supported, was the Haitian Bible project. Haitian is a French based Creole language. Because French is one of Canada's national languages, it seemed like a natural fit. More than that, over the years there has been considerable migration from Haiti to Canada. Our support for the Haitian project was carried out through workshops held either in Haiti or in Canada, and through publishing support by our computer support staff.

The completed translation work in the various languages we supported was typeset by our very capable staff to prepare it for printing. Ed and Jeff ran the translated text through computer programs to check for consistency and accuracy using various checking tools. They also maintained the typesetting software and ensured that it was up to date and functioning well.

Thomas Ortiz came to our staff from Bolivia, where he had gained training and experience in desktop publishing. He became our primary support for typesetting software being developed for the Bible Societies. Barb Penner expertly ran the final text through the typesetting software. Hardy, and later Ruth, did a final very careful examination of the result. They both had an eagle eye and would pick up tiny details, like missing punctuation or spelling errors that had been missed in the pre-publication computer checks.

When the Algonquin translation project was completed and published, most of our team travelled to the area near Amos in Quebec where the Algonquin people lived, to celebrate the completion of this chapter of the work with Ruth and her children. The SIL goal established for this project was the completion of the New Testament and some Old Testament selections for liturgical readings for the Catholic Church. With her part in the project completed, Ruth felt at loose ends. We had come to know her as a dedicated and highly capable translator, so I approached Ruth about joining our team in Kitchener. Initially our budget only allowed for a part time salary for her. She was able to maintain a role in SIL, as a consultant for other First Nations projects, while also serving part-time on our team as a consultant. In addition, she was able to complete a graduate degree in biblical studies at the Lutheran seminary in Waterloo. This included studies in the biblical languages. Ruth is the only person I have ever known to receive a grade of 100% in Hebrew. We were delighted to add her to our staff.

For many years, Hardy carried the primary role of final editor on text being prepared for printing. As Hardy was approaching retirement, we wondered who could fill this very important role. Then we discovered that Ruth was an exceptionally capable editor. With Hardy's retirement we now had the room in our budget to bring Ruth on board full time and she added the editing duties to her consultant role. It turns out that Ruth even had an advantage in that she had competence in the indigenous languages. Ruth was so focused on detail that she was able to find spelling errors, even in languages she did not know.

In my position as Director of Scripture Translations, I was also frequently asked to write material to help our colleagues in the publicity department. Given Ruth's exceptional editing capabilities, I determined not to allow anything to go out of our office that had not been passed by Ruth's eagle eyes. Although neither Ruth nor I met the United Bible Societies' eligibility as translation consultants because we did not hold doctoral degrees, I felt we were able to hold our own in ensuring high quality translations in Canada, as well as in the annual international gatherings of UBS consultants. Ruth was especially recognized for her editing capabilities and appointed to an editorial board for UBS scholarly publication.

Harold's prophetic insight came true beyond everyone's expectation. When he invested $10,000 in that first computer, no one foresaw that impact.

Our CBS Translations office shone. We were recognized throughout the global Bible translation community in the area of our work on computer support for Bible translation and publishing.

I had to chuckle at God's sense of humour. None of us, not one, met the academic qualifications that UBS required. By any estimation we were an unlikely team. Harold's insight in choosing a team with skills, motivation and passion paid off. The CBS Translations office staff delivered beyond what Harold imagined when he launched CBS into the computer age with the purchase of that first expensive computer.

At one point, CBS engaged an outside consultant to establish the "case for support" with respect to various aspects of the CBS ministry. At the top of the "case for support" this consultant established was the work of the CBS Translations office in Kitchener.

When Harold passed away, his role as Chair of the UBS TCRG was assumed by Dr. Kees de Blois, a Dutch colleague who had been a close associate of Harold in the UBS community of translation consultants. He had followed Harold in several other UBS responsibilities in the Africa Area, the Americas Area and now in the area of computer support. He was very current on what had been done in the area of computer support for our work both in UBS and in SIL.

Kees has a younger brother, Reinier, who is also a UBS consultant and exceptionally computer savvy. Reinier had produced a computer tool he called PARATEXT to help him in his own consultant work. It was essentially an editing platform created to allow numerous windows to be displayed simultaneously. With this tool, he could be working on a text in translation, with windows open on the same screen displaying the Greek or Hebrew text, other language versions, and commentaries, with all the windows scrolling simultaneously.

When we saw this tool, we all agreed: this tool would be extremely helpful for all translations. The UBS TCRG agreed that this should be made the first major deliverable as evidence of the usefulness of the TCRG. It fell to the computer support staff on our CBS team to implement this goal. UBS assigned Nathan Miles, a core member of their computer staff, to the role of lead programmer on the PARATEXT project.

Through his children at the University of Waterloo, Ed Peters had befriended Clayton Grassick, a recent graduate of Waterloo in engineering. Clayton was an exceptionally gifted computer programmer and also committed to living out his faith with integrity and purpose. He had no shortage of opportunities to earn money practicing his computer programming skills, but when Ed approached him and challenged him to assist our team in the development of the PARATEXT program, he agreed.

The goal was to reprogram Reinier's early work into a highly stable version with intuitive functionality that could be easily rolled out to people engaged in UBS translation projects around the world, including those who were not necessarily early adopters of computer technology. We established a goal to have a release version available for the UBS consultants' forum scheduled for Merida, Mexico in the summer of 1997.

Unfortunately, Harold passed away before the Merida event, but the goal was accomplished and the first official version of Paratext (Version 4.0) was delivered. With the help of all the UBS colleagues who were early adopters of technology, we rolled out the program and held classes at the translation conference in Merida to teach every consultant how to use it.

We calculated that adoption of this tool by at least a third of the UBS consultant staff would constitute a critical mass and could be considered a success. As it turned out, the design of the program and the thoroughness of the training was successful beyond our wildest dreams. Almost immediately the tool became a runaway success.

Now we found ourselves with a new challenge. Any widely used computer tool requires constant support and ongoing development to keep current with technological advances and to assist users who encounter problems in its use. The need for additional coordination and discipline around development, maintenance, and distribution of our new software tools had grown exponentially. The UBS fellowship asked CBS to assign our office to anchor the support role that this new development demanded. We were given the responsibility, but there was no budget to increase our staff. We would need to be creative. We had to rely on staff that other Bible Societies were able and willing to relinquish on at least a part time basis to deliver the needed support all over the world.

Gradually, a coordinated effort was achieved through the collaboration of Computer Assisted Publishing (CAP) practitioners from various national Bible Societies, translation consultants, and publishing staff, as well as staff from partners such as SIL. This group operated under the guidance of TCRG (Kees de Blois) and the support of the CBS Translations and CAP Department in Canada, where I was the Director and Ed was the manager of CAP. This support community eventually adopted the name Institute for Computer Assisted Publishing (ICAP).

The goal was not only the development of software. We were intent on adequately training and supporting users of our software tools. We chose not to assign any leadership titles in ICAP. The leadership was shared collegially by Kees, Ed and myself.

As the success of ICAP became known in Canada and around the world, our office was given opportunities to advocate on behalf of our work with people eager to invest in Bible work. I recall an occasion where Ed and I were given the opportunity to host a major Bible Society donor at our office. The donor listened with rapt attention as we grew eloquent and enthusiastic on the impact that ICAP was having on the Bible ministry around the world. At the end of the session the donor pledged a million dollars for this work.

The impact of our work was far beyond what people expected when they visited our office. Based on what they had heard about us, colleagues from other agencies and Bible Societies around the world would visit, expecting an imposing office with a large staff. They were always surprised to see that the work they had heard so much about could be done by a skeletal staff in a small and unimpressive office. One of the CBS National Directors became a little jealous when he attended a global gathering and continually heard CBS' work identified with Kitchener rather than the national office in Toronto.

One of the greatest pleasures and sustaining aspects of the ICAP network of developers and supporters was the experience of working among people who actively expressed their responsibility and deep commitment to the Bible mission. The genius of the arrangement we had was that through ICAP we were able to generate mutual sharing of gifts among various Bible Societies. We were also able to identify Bible Societies which lacked the necessary resources to implement their own computer support program, and come alongside them with assistance.

We held yearly conferences in Canada and around the world to discuss priorities and maintain currency in the software. Continued efforts were made to coordinate greater levels of technology use within translation projects, to implement technical standards and encourage best practices, to provide collections of quality translator resources in digital formats, and to work towards smoother integration between translation and publishing tasks, seen in the development of tools like Publishing Assistant.

In 2011, Kees officially retired from his position in UBS. With his retirement, ICAP, which until then had been a very informal collective, became an official entity within the Global Bible Translation (GBT) Department of the renewed UBS Global Mission Team, working under the leadership and direction of Kees' younger brother, Reinier de Blois.

The early activities of ICAP occurred prior to the digital technology and publishing revolutions, which were fueled by increasingly widespread access to broadband and mobile internet. Paratext Version 7 development began in 2007, the same year that the first iPhone was released.

With the release of Paratext 7 in 2009, for the first time Paratext was "in the cloud." Having a web-based solution opened up numerous new possibilities. So many things have changed in such a short time. When we began our translation work in the Philippines, we were using pen and paper. A manual typewriter was the extent of our technological reach. In the internet age, we were able to share information easily in real time world-wide. We created a global registry of translation projects. More than that, we were now able to develop a global archive of digital scriptures.

For the first time we were able to work quickly with the help of the computer, increased technological knowledge and the internet. Translated texts and audio could be activated and distributed through digital formats and mobile devices. We could distribute texts to remote regions more easily than ever before.

Jeff Klassen was appointed leader of a team to create a digital Bible library, with the goal of eventually encompassing all biblical texts in all languages, and using a standard format easily accessible by applications such as digital and audio Bibles available on personal computers and phones.

One of the things I appreciated about the legacy that Harold left at the Bible Society was the willingness to hire staff based on their innate qualities, capabilities and experience, rather than insisting on paper qualifications. More than that, Harold left a history of working in partnership with others. Throughout the Bible Society's engagement in the development of computer tools, it was our consistent practice to partner with other agencies in many activities, including in this technology development work. Fostering these partnerships became a core value for the ICAP team.

Over the years, Bible Societies had benefited greatly from the pioneering software products and computer training offered by Wycliffe's SIL organization. The year 2010, five years before my official retirement from CBS, was a banner year in the collaboration between UBS and SIL. In a joint conference in Chang Mai, Thailand, we celebrated a special milestone in our ongoing work together through an agreement of joint ownership and shared maintenance and support for Paratext and Publishing Assistant projects.

There were significant benefits to combining the resources of both agencies, but it required new methods for collaborating on the work, and establishing project direction and priorities together. I consider the achievement of this agreement as a personal high point in my leadership of the CBS Translations Department and a fitting culmination to my 40 years of engagement in Bible translation. Appropriately, the young man leading SIL's computer development work at the time was Mike Cochran, the son of Pat and Joanne, who had recruited us to join the work in the Philippines more than

30 years earlier. The Global Director for Language Program Services at SIL, was Charles Sanders. I can't say enough about the inspired and humble way in which both Charles and Mike worked with our team to accomplish this historic collaborative milestone.

I believe that my years of experience in SIL, and the credibility I had established through my leadership there, contributed greatly to the environment in which sufficient trust could be established between SIL and ICAP to be able to come to such a historic collaborative agreement. Although there had always been collaboration between our two great Bible translation movements, there were also some mutually fostered misunderstandings that had been passed down through suspicion and lack of trust. It was so rewarding to see how two groups that had invested a great deal in parallel paths of computer development could come together and work harmoniously on a shared path.

During my career I also served on several boards. Already before our return to Canada, I was appointed to the board of Wycliffe Canada. Later I served a term as Chair of this board. In Canada I served on the board of our Church in Niagara and then two six-year terms on the board of our Church in Waterloo. I also served a term on the board of Shalom Counselling Services and another term on the board of Community Justice Initiatives.

18: The Final Layer

Yes, I have layers. They go deep into the soil of many lands and deep into the annals of time, but deeper even still into the faith forged out of Scripture, prayer and the experience of God's grace. Faith was a given in my family. The fantastic narrative of blessing, demise, escape and seeking peace was woven with examples of God's grace and leading.

My mother and father were forever grateful to God for protecting them and guiding them in the harrowing escape from the terror and deprivation they had experienced in Russia. The faith and prayers of those who went before me, especially my mother, Anna, paved the way for me to make my own commitment of faith and obedience to God's call on my life. God's call on my life itself has many layers, but the common thread throughout has been my mother's prayers, accompanying my birth and guiding my choices throughout my life.

I am so grateful that God answered my mother's prayers and allowed me to serve and exercise leadership roles in two of the greatest organizations dedicated to Bible translation in the world. I believe this is a legacy that Mother Anna would be proud of.

The ability to all asleep anytime and anywhere is a family trait demonstrated here

by Jason and me.

And so, I hand the baton to the next generation. Looking back is an act of Passover – for we are often unaware of God's grace in the moment, but as we live out our life, we begin to see the pattern.

I celebrate my children and grandchildren … and their children.

As we grow old, we watch for hints of our past in the lives of our future.

We see patterns. Like my mom and her father, Grandpa Jacob Wiens, I can fall asleep at the drop of a hat, no matter where I am. In public spaces, church (a nudge from Ginny), anywhere. It's been a blessing to me, especially as I travelled in unusual and exotic places. Even when the road was rough, I could sleep. Our friends sometimes ask why I pay money to go to the theatre when I am often sleeping through much of the performance.

I have a tendency for being in a hurry. This is another pattern repeated in my family of origin and in my offspring. At home we called it "Schwind, Schwind." Over and over again I resolve to slow down and pay attention – but the urge to hurry is strong. I am who I am. Those who share this trait tend to be big-picture people who rush over the details. God made me and led me into the precise places where my own unique personality would thrive.

Without a doubt, this characteristic comes from my mom, but I am prone to chatter, sometimes exposing even personal and embarrassing details, so eager to build a connection. It really doesn't matter if I know the person or not. Like I've said, I've watched my mom move from community to community to community, chatting her way into strangers' hearts. Some people find it endearing. My own children laugh when I introduce someone I have just met as my new best friend. I have no hesitation to share the stories of my family – often revealing more than is necessary or called for, to the chagrin of my more introverted family members.

I learned to be helpful at my mother's knee. I'm eager to pitch in, even if I haven't been asked. My family laughs that if we see someone stopped on the side of the road, I will be likely to stop and offer to help.

My mom and I share all these and more characteristics in abundant measure, and now we see various manifestations displayed in many of the next generation.

The Last Words

We cannot predict our final days. My days of formal work are over. But I'm not done with life. I take great pleasure in nurturing the generations that follow me. There are children and grandchildren that have been added to our family by birth, by adoption and by marriage. Some of those we consider our children are not adopted in any legal sense. They come out of our experience in the Philippines or our heritage as refugees. We embrace them all as our own. We love them all and pray that the love and grace of our God will sustain and guide them, as it has guided us and the generations that went before us.

As I grew into my role in administration and field supervision, I began to see how God had blessed me with the gifts of encouragement and service to others, something I felt I had inherited from Mom. I began to identify with the first century apostle Barnabas who seemed to have had an aptitude for encouraging and serving others in the ministry.

As a helper and servant at heart, I find joy in my retirement in joining other staff at Lee Valley Tools to serve our customer base. I love to serve.

Each morning I get up early to teach English to a bunch of eager students in China. How rewarding to know that in this small way I can give back to the nation that extended such tremendous hospitality to my parents and grandparents so many years ago.

I worked on writing this story during the greatest global pandemic of our time. Our children and grandchildren have never before experienced the boundaries imposed during COVID-19, much less the poverty and deprivation of the generations that went before us. Telling my parents' story and my own story during this time has stunned me. It's hard to believe we experienced and lived through so many adventures.

My parents were dirt poor – yet, in the end, they thrived. Every step, even when they were stepping over the edge of an unknown chasm, was done in faith. I had many more opportunities, but, like them, each step I took was a step of faith.

When Ginny and I left for the Philippines we could not have imagined the friendships and the joys we would experience there. Nor could we imagine the heartbreaking challenges we encountered. Our lives are uniquely orchestrated by God.

Looking back, I see that God led the way. Who knew that Abram and Anna Wiens would end up in the same village in Siberia, just in time for the great escape? Who knew that they would end up in the same village in Paraguay? Who knew that in her fourth pregnancy Anna would feel the urge to pour out her anxious heart to God in a prayer dedicating me to God's service? Who knew as she sailed past the Philippines in 1932 that 41 years later the son for whom she prayed would end up serving God there? Who knew that Ginny would need a date for graduation? Who knew I would have such a heart for language? Who knew?????

Like a shepherd, God has led us. If I could give my children and grandchildren just one piece of advice, it would be this: follow well.

I don't know what the next decade will look like for us, but I pray we may walk with grace, generosity, love and faith, bringing glory to our God, freed from the old "sin management" theology. I pray for wisdom to understand and contribute to the building of the Kingdom where Jesus is Lord, secure in the knowledge of God's mercy, love and grace toward all.

Jesus loves us!

World Map
Anna & Abram's circuitous journey from Russia to freedom and opportunity in Canada

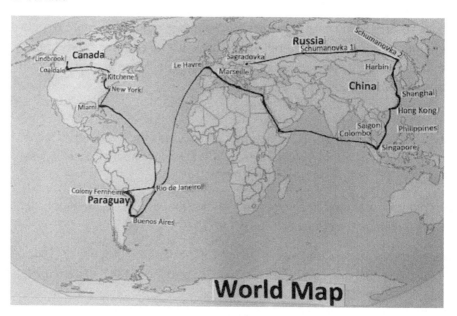

Abram's journey begins in Sagradovka, Ukraine on April 3, 1918 and Anna's on August 8, 1920 in Schumanovka 1. In 1927 both families moved to Schumanovka 2, in Eastern Siberia. They escaped to China in December, 1930. From there they travelled through Shanghai, Hong Kong, Saigon, Singapore, Colombo, Suez Canal, Marseille, Le Havre, and Buenos Aires, to Fernheim Colony in Paraguay. In 1948 they immigrated to Canada via Rio de Janeiro, Miami and New York. They stopped in Kitchener, Ontario on their way to Coaldale, Alberta. After 11 years in Alberta, our family moved to Ontario in 1959.

Ancestry and Family

I have records of my ancestry in Brother's Keeper, going back more than five generations in some lines. Here I will go back just three generations to my great grandparents on both sides of my family. The Wiens genetic line dominates as both of my parents were Wiens.

Mother's side

Anna Wiens (August 8, 1920 – October 3, 2000) was the daughter of Jacob Wiens (January 2, 1880 – November 25, 1961) and Elisabeth "Liese" Friesen (February 16, 1882 – September 8, 1947).

Her paternal grandparents were Isaak Wiens (January 19, 1855 – April 24, 1919) and Ida Janzen (June 6, 1855 – 1887).

Her maternal grandparents were Daniel Thomas Friesen (August 17, 1844 – October 1, 1909) and Elizabeth Thiessen (September 4, 1847 – February 1, 1922).

Grandpa Jacob Wiens' mother passed away when he was 7 years old. He had one sister, Anna. Grandma Liese Friesen had 5 older siblings – Jacob, Daniel, Justina, Johann, and Heinrich – and five younger siblings – Aganeta, Abraham, Maria, Katarina and Helena.

Mother Anna had 7 older siblings – Liese, Isaac, Daniel, Jacob, Justina, Maria and Abram.

Father's side

Abram Wiens (April 3, 1918 – April 5, 2011) was the son of Franz Johann Wiens (February 1, 1892 – July 23, 1980) and Anna Fast (September 28, 1890 – August 10, 1940).

His paternal grandparents were Johann Julius Wiens (January 31, 1856 – August 14, 1933) and Katharina Krueger (October 15, 1861 – February 8, 1908).

His maternal grandparents were Abram Fast (August 22, 1857 – January 20, 1930) and Agathe Boldt (February 14, 1857 – December ?, 1895).

Grandpa Franz Wiens had three older siblings – Susanna, Liese, and Johann – and four younger siblings – David, Tina, Heinrich and Abram. Grandma Anna Fast had four older siblings – Katarina, Abram, David and Agatha – and a younger half-sister Susanna.

Father Abram had two older siblings – Johann "Hans" and Susanna and – six younger siblings – Helena "Lena", Franz, David, Heinrich, David and Jacob. The first David and Heinrich were twins born in Siberia. David died at birth and Heinrich died in Harbin, China. After Grandma Anna died, Grandpa Franz married again to a widow, Justina Nachtigal and they had one son Heinrich together.

Hart's siblings

My younger brother Henry died when he was 18. I now have seven siblings and each one is married. My siblings are: Ernst "Ernie" (Marie) with three children, Erwin "Erv" (Marian) with six children, Hugo (Lydia) with four children, Mary (Peter Warkentin) with three children, Betty "Betts" (Peter Loewen) with four children, Margaret "Muggs" (Ferdinand "Ferd" Klassen) with two children and Dave (Debbie) with four children.

Ginny's siblings

Ginny had an older brother Ron (Linda), who passed away at 55. They had two daughters. She had a younger brother Billy (Marilyn & Mary Jane), who passed away at 43. Billy had two children. She has a younger brother Bob (Brenda), who have twin daughters, and a younger sister, Pat who also has two daughters.

Our Children and Grandchildren

We gave birth to 2 children. They are Jason (Mary Ellen "Emmy") and Andrea (Scott Moore). We adopted Allan (Josée). In addition, we consider the following as our children through informal adoption. Syrine (Rambie Bernardino) is the daughter of our Kalinga friend and co-worker Pedro who gave his life for our team. We brought Syrine to Canada where she lives now with Rambie and their daughter Sophia. Syrine has 2 older sisters in the Philippines who also think of us as their Canadian parents. They are Christy (Eduardo Sacayle) and Beverly (Alex Balnao). We also brought Christy and Eduardo's niece Joi (John Gregory Madrid) to Canada where they are now living with their daughter Simoune. We also consider Martha and Fabian

Garcia and their daughter Valentina as part of our family since they lived with us for 7 years after coming to Canada as refugees.

We are blessed to be Opa and Oma to 15 children. They include Jason and Emmy's 6 children Elenor, Moses, Beatrice, Abram, Simeon and Laylah. Then Andrea and Scott's 3 children Kiley, Dylan and Jaina. Then Allan and Jose's 3 children Kayleigh, Rose and Soleille. Martha and Fabian have Valentina, Syrine and Rambie have Sophia and Joi and Gregory have Simoune.

In the Philippines we are Lolo and Lola to 8 children. They include Desiree, Hannah Mae, Cheridelle and Hart from Christy's family and Xyrielle, Aprielle, Averly and Urielle from Beverly's family.

Our family at Muskoka Bible Camp in 2019.

We celebrated 50 years of marriage on August 29, 2020.

234

This is a portion of my family tree. The branches go up three generations to my Great Grandparents on both my mother's and my father's side. I have genealogies available in "Brother's Keeper" and "Grandma" databases going back at least five generations on both sides of my family.

Appendix A: Grandpa Jacob

Grandpa Jacob's Life Story
Beginning in the Year 1901
(Anna's Father, my Grandpa)

I was born in the village of Karassan, Crimea on January 2nd, 1880. I was married in Kaltan, on October 23rd, 1901 in Kaltan, Samara. In my 13th year I found my Lord and I was baptized when I was 14 years old on September 28, 1894 and was accepted as a member in the Mennonite Brethren Church.

As I mentioned above, my marriage took place in the village of Kaltan, 7 Werst (kilometers) from my home village of Podalsk. After the wedding we began our married life and lived with my parents in the so-called "Summer room" until September of 1902, for which (assuming he means the wedding) our parents gave us the harvest from 2 Desjatin (Hectar) of wheat as a gift.

Since I had lost my dear mother at an age which was much too early for me, my sister Anna and I became heirs to our grandparents, instead of our mother. This inheritance helped us then acquire our own "Wirtschaft" (farm) in the village of Kubanka in the Orenburg settlement, for 18 hundred gold rubels. This settlement was 100 Werst away from our settlement in Samara. We had already purchased 1 wagon and 2 horses. I had received 2 horses from our parents. Our parents lent us 1 wagon and that is how we left on our trip in September, in good spirits and full of hope, bringing with us 2 cows, one with a calf.

We had made our beginning to become farmers. Now we had to struggle and work. Our house was small. In a big snow storm that winter, the little house disappeared under the snow. So, we made plans to build a bigger house, but our means were small.

We planted our first crop in the spring. Our farming life had begun, but the work was very difficult, especially for the horses, because we lacked adequate feed for them. Our harvest was modest, but with God's help, the house was built in time for the winter. It was 14x8 meters.

From November 11, 1902 we were already a family of 3 as the Lord had given us a daughter. Now I got the inner urge that I would rather live in the Samara settlement, because our farming business was not very productive. The outlook for the sale of our farm was not very hopeful. Yet, in February of 1904 an Isaak Funk came around to buy our farm, but he took it on credit to be paid after the harvest.

We accepted the deal and set out on our second trip; now back to the old settlement (Samara), to live with my wife's parents in their "Summer room."

Right away, we were able to rent 10 Desjatin of plowed land which gave us a good harvest. During the ?? harvest in the summer I got the fever (I'm assuming this refers to the flu). In October 1904 the Lord sent us a son and our family grew. Then we also received the payment (from the farm we had sold in Kubanka) and were immediately able to buy a farm here in Kaltan.

In 1905 we had a small harvest. In 1905-1906 Russia was at war with Japan. And then in 1906 we had another crop failure. So, the feed for the animals had to be purchased. We had to drive 25 werst to a place where we could buy the feed. We hauled 3 rubels worth of feed on one wagon load. Those were hard times, and yet we were hopeful.

In September of 1906 the Lord sent us another son, Daniel who sadly died on November 27th, 1907. Our farm was at the end of the village where we had a small stream. We had it dammed up so that we could wash our horses and where we could bathe as well.

On May 18th, 1908 the Lord sent us another son, Jacob. Now in the spring, we were able to move our farming operation to the middle of the village, across the street from my wife's parents. As my parents-in-law didn't have any of their sons at home anymore, we could run the operation together. I was responsible for overseeing the work of the servants. Together we purchased a grain binder. Those were good times.

In the spring of 1909, my father-in-law came down with an illness on his right foot. More of the supervision of the farming operation fell to me, but I enjoyed it. Then I bought a threshing machine for us alone from the Franz & Schroeder factory. We could do the threshing with 4 or 5 horses.

My father-in-law died on October 1st, 1909. After the funeral on October 8th, I travelled to the Crimea in response to an invitation from my dear uncle Peter Janzen to attend their house dedication and their silver wedding which was celebrated on October 12th. That was my first trip, travelling alone by train. I was away on this trip for one month. On October 24th, 1910 the Lord gave us a daughter (Justine). In the same year, on the last day of Christmas celebrations I left with brother Abram Neufeld for Siberia to look at land there. On the 1st of January we got off the train at Isilkul. There I was the guest of "Geschwister" Franz Doerksen. Then on the 6th of January, 1911 we arrived at the Orloff settlement in the area of Slavgorod where we got some land. We got an inexpensive fare and travelled back home. The farm was already sold. We had our auction sale right away and then left on February 16,1911 with our family to the Slavgorod settlement where we settled on the barren "steppe" land, in the village of Schumanovka in April. There we built a large house 24x9 meters with a metal roof. In 1912 I made another trip back (to Kaltan) to get some more of our belongings.

In 1914 the world war started. In September, 1916 I was drafted as a medic. With the medical corps I travelled through the Samara settlement to Tiblisi (Georgia). In May of 1917 I came home on furlough and then returned to service in the medical corps in July with a 3 day stop in Samara to visit my parents. On the first day of Christmas celebrations in December of that year I arrived at home in good health.

(Flashback) I need to go back now to 1913 when the Lord gave us a daughter, Maria. On February 18th, 1915 the Lord gave us a son, Abram. In 1914, I was given responsibility for the missions account for the entire MB Church in our colony. It consisted of 13 files. In 1918, I was given the responsibility over our cooperative for one year. In 1919 I was selected as a deacon in the Alexanderkrone MB Church and I was ordained a deacon by "Altester" (Bishop) Jacob Wiens on August 29, 1920.

On August 8th, 1920 the Lord gave us a daughter Anna. In 1921 we had a good crop while in southern Russia there was a total crop failure almost everywhere. My father had died in April, 1919 and we had had no interaction that year, not even by mail. Then in September, 1921 I finally got a letter from my stepmother that I should come there (home to Samara). I left in October with two other men, but the trip was almost impossible. It was very difficult, even though I had already travelled a lot by this time. I didn't get back home until December, for Christmas. The trip which would normally only take 4 days had taken 5 weeks.

Because of the famine (in Samara) we could not settle the estate of my father then. That was delayed until 1923. Just before harvest then, I was summoned again. This time the trip was easier. I arrived there and everything got settled. Then, I and my stepmother travelled to the Orenburg settlement with her "Fuhrwerk" (I assume horse and buggy) to the home of my wife's brother Daniel Friesen for 3 days and then back. Then I returned back home (to Siberia).

I skipped the year 1922. When I got home in 1921, my brother-in-law Abram Unruh had already died and soon after that my brother-in-law H. Buller died as well. There was a typhoid epidemic. In January, 1922 my wife's eldest sister Justine Wittenberg died. On February 1st my wife's mother also died and then also the children of some of her siblings. Finally, it hit home in our house as well. Almost all of us were ill and my wife had to take care of us. Jacob and Marichen were barely able to manage the chores. It was a very difficult time. In the end my wife went down (with typhoid) too. Since so many in our village had died, we thought she would be taken from us too. She had to endure a lot more than we did. The Lord was testing us greatly! She even wanted to go (die) but we couldn't let her and our dear Father (in heaven) restored her to us. To Him be the Glory!

On February and March, 1924, our children Liese and David and Isaak and Liese were married. Both couples lived at home with us for a while. In 1925 we wanted to immigrate to Canada and we sold our farming operation, but due to eye disease we had to stay back, so we bought another farm in the same village. I just don't know how to express my inner feelings at the time. I felt as if the rapture had happened and we had been left behind. (Note from Hart: most of Grandma Liese's Friesen siblings moved to Canada in that great migration.) Our children, Isaak & Liese had also gone as far as Moscow, but also had to return due to Liese's eyes. So, we took courage and continued on in our earthly pilgrimage. We did what we could to heal our eye disease. Then in 1926 we celebrated our silver wedding anniversary. At this celebration we were given new courage through the message of our former "Altester" (Bishop) Franz Friesen who had left us a little more than a year earlier and had returned.

Even though our dear brothers and sisters were now no longer with us in person, we were glad to stay in touch with them by mail. Then in March, my dear wife became very ill. The doctor could not diagnose whether it was stomach cramps or gall stones. For 30 hours she lay there so ill that we had lost hope of being able to keep her with us. And yet, our dear Father in heaven restored her to us yet again for the second time. The Lord still does miracles today!

In 1927 many people were moving to the region of the Amur River in far eastern Siberia. We tried once more to get permission to go to Canada, but again the permits were denied. Then I was also sent to the Amur region with some of our neighbours to find out if it might also be possible for us to move there. Four of us left April 1st. The area looked good to me and the government gave us land. There also seemed to be more freedom here. Full of hope, we returned home. We had been gone for exactly one month. My wife and children had already gotten rid of our cattle and other belongings through auction.

So, on May 22nd we left our home in Schumanovka in Western Siberia. This was our fourth move. We moved to the new settlement in the Amur River region. I want to remind us of how the Lord promised the children of Israel a land flowing with milk and honey! Good and productive land. Too bad that we were only able to live there for 3 years. Soon our freedom was taken away here! There is nothing in this world that can fully satisfy our longings. Soon we were living in constant fear here and looking for greater freedom again for which we were given to understand that there might be opportunity in China. In January, 1930 my dear wife fell very ill again with typhoid for the second time. Our dear father in heaven showed us grace again. Praises be to him! Then we were ready for our 5th migration.

This time on December 17th, 1930, the whole village escaped across the Amur River border into China. The escape as refugees had already been told as part of our family's story.

Then we settled in a small area in the Fernheim colony of Chaco, Paraguay. There were 20 families in our village which was named Orloff. Our group of settlers (the Harbin China group) consisted of 80 families divided into 4 villages. Nearby there is a village named Auhagen with immigrants that came through Germany. Right away that same year we organized ourselves as the MB denomination together with Auhagen. Brother Johann Schellenberg was chosen as the leader and I was given the position as his assistant. I was also given responsibility for the finances. Even though we had left all our earthly goods behind in Russia, we were glad that we once again had a home and freedom.

Our home is not anywhere in this poor world. Where can our souls find home and rest. And still we had many happy times as a congregation, especially in the early years when we had a choir in every village! And there were Christian youth gatherings. "Those were the days!"

In 1937 there was an out-migration from Fernheim to Frisland (a new colony in East Paraguay). Through that migration many hearts were broken. Many villages were restructured and many houses demolished. There was a rift in the community. But thanks be to God, this rift in the community could be restored again and care in the community could be restored. On December 22, 1938 my dear wife became very ill again to the extent that she had to be admitted to the hospital from December 27 to January 15, 1939. Those were difficult days for my dear wife because she could not keep any food down. Some speculated that she had stomach cancer. The doctor diagnosed stomach ulcers. For almost one year she lived on cooked milk and cheese. Thank God, the Lord helped us!

In October of 1940 I resigned my position in the community cooperative. I received 5000 pesos from the cooperative board in recognition of my years of service. I had been appointed to serve the cooperative in 1933 as our house was a division of the community cooperative.

After my retirement from the Co-op, I took a trip with my dear wife through Asuncion to Friesland where we made home visitations among many brothers and sisters for 3 weeks. Then we returned home on December 27th.

In March of 1943, we sold our farm to our children, the Isaak Wiens family and we built a new house on the property of our other children, Abram & Anna at the end of the village. With that we began our retirement. The Lord granted health to my dear wife again too and we lived many happy days with and for one another.

On August 26, 1945 we, together with the congregation, celebrated my 25 years of service as a deacon. We did have some very difficult work in the congregation, especially in relation to our relations with the indigenous ethnic community in the Chaco. As we had lost our balance in our immigration, we ourselves suffered much inner trauma as did many around us. Especially in the year 1944, there was great confusion in the whole colony around distribution of various positions and responsibilities. One day the God the righteous judge will give the right and final verdict. Thanks be to God that those of us who have examined our own lives here do not need to fear that final judgement.

On April 20th, 1946 we received a letter from H. H. Rempel (Grandma Liese's family) living in Canada. It was a response to our letter of March 2 asking about the possibility of our moving to Canada at the suggestion of our children Jacob and Maria Wiens, living in village #16. I and my dear wife had long been contemplating such a move. My dear wife could not tolerate the heat and it was the same with Jacob and Isaak's wives. So, we asked the Lord to give a clear sense of what we should do. We were at peace but some of our children couldn't understand this and wanted to proceed. But, mother said, we have come to peace about this. If Canada opens the doors we will go. Now in March, the "revelation" came and then there was no more correspondence.

On February 16, 1947 four of us families received applications from our siblings in Canada. They said they would send the authorizations when these were approved. The "revelation" was put on hold for six months. There was no further response until August 26th. Then my dear wife, our dear mother, fell ill again. We hoped that she would soon recover as had been the case before and we were still waiting for the travel documents. But our dear heavenly Father had other plans and ideas for us. From August 26 until September 6th, she lay in bed. Four of those days were especially difficult. She was in such pain that our children had to be called to help. We cried to God in our distress, but it seemed God was not hearing us. Then on September 6th at 9:00 in the evening we went to the Bethesda hospital in Filadelfia with her. The night nurse admitted us and called the doctor. But the doctor did not come until Sunday morning at 9:00 AM. He determined that her gallbladder was enflamed. He gave her injections and medicine so that she became calm and soon she got a little sleep.

That Sunday, September 7, the MB congregation was gathered in Filadelfia seeking unity and reconciliation among the congregation again. All our children had come too, except Abram & Sara. They immediately wanted to know how it was going for their dear mother in the hospital. They all returned home, hopeful that she would recover. But the next morning, Monday she deteriorated and her heart was giving out. That evening we still prayed together. She thanked the dear Lord that the

Church had prayed for us and she laid our entire big family on the Lord's heart – children and grandchildren. In the morning when I sensed that there was a change in her condition, I told her that if it would get too difficult for her the Lord would be there for her. "Do you think I am dying?" she asked. I said I didn't know and those were her last words. About 9:00 the doctor came and asked if she had a lot of pain. She didn't answer. There were still 4 very difficult hours for me and for her until 1:00 PM. Then she breathed her last and her heart stood still. I so wanted to hear another word from her, but no! – I had already sent word to the children at 9:30. But, Isaak and Jacob came about 1:30 – a half hour too late. The doctor examined her again and found gall stones. We immediately ordered her casket and other arrangements. Then the 3 of us with our deceased mother made our way home where all the other children were already waiting. What would be the news? Seeing that I was on the wagon too gave them a sense of what the news would be. Mother is dead! On September 8, 1:00 PM death took her from me. The funeral and burial were on September 9 in the afternoon in the village of Karlsruh. Her body was brought back to Orloff where she was buried. Her obituary was printed. Mother's last hospitalization and funeral expenses came to 8,270 Paraguayan Pesos. At her grave there is a picket fence and a headboard with the inscription: "God will wipe away all tears from their eyes." Revelation 7:15-17. "Resting in peace here is Liese Wiens, nee Friesen, born February 16, 1882, deceased September 8, 1947. Aufwiedersehen. Jacob Eitzen donated the wood for the fence and the headboard as a Christmas gift. For the hardwood (polosander) posts and gate, son Jacob also contributed. Also, son-in-law Jakob Siemens contributed steal and nails and bolts and payment for work done – 1,500 Pesos.

Christmas 1947 was celebrated without mother. All of the children and grandchildren were with me, their father on the yard of Isaak Wiens under a huge Paraiser tree. Before noon we were all together at Church in Karlsruh. For dinner we were here. We ate cold beef and Ploomemoos. Our 7 children and their spouses were here with 39 grandchildren. (There were also 5 refugees, the family of Mrs. Penner).

On January 7, 1948 we received word that our immigration visas had been granted. On January 8 we had our medical examination and were declared healthy. Then on January 18 I had an injury to my right eye. On January 29 Isaak came from Asuncion with arrangements for our travel. In February we prepared for our trip and on March 10 we had an auction of the belongings of our 3 families. March 14 our congregation in Karlsruh had a farewell. Wednesday, March 17 we left Orloff in a vehicle for the railway station. We arrived in Asuncion on March 20. March 23, we went with Ernst Harder to the travel agency to complete and sign forms. March 26, we had medical physicals for travel and all were declared fit for travel. March 31, we received our exit permits. April 1, we went to the British consulate for our

Canadian visas and transit visas for the USA. April 7 everything was finally ready. We left Asuncion by air on April 8 and arrived in New York on April 10. On April 14 we arrived in Tabor, Alberta and were met by Abram Friesen.

After this there is some book keeping about payments to MCC and who owes what to whom. It's hard to sort this all out and it may not be that interesting.

Appendix B: Tante Lena

☐Tante Lena's Story
(Dad's sister, my Aunt)

Introduction:

Tante Lena was two years younger than my father. I've translated her story as close to her words as possible. I have not polished the written, but rather attempted to capture her voice.

The story fills some of the gaps in my telling of my father's story. She is looking at a different perspective.

Tante Lena writes: In 1930 several Mennonite families left Russia via China.

Beginnings In Russia

My grandparents from my mother's side were Abram and Katharina Fast (nee Boldt). As a young married couple, they came from Molochnaya where they were born. They were landless and settled in poverty in the new settlement of Sagradovka. Grandpa Fast told how difficult it was for them to settle with small children and little capital. As the soil was very fertile and the climate favorable, the harvests were good. With the help of the old colony in Molochnaya, things improved gradually. Their grain was threshed with the flail and stone. But after just a few years there was an upswing. They had good men in the colony administration. The men looked after 18 villages and built an orderly colony. Grandpa Fast, as a young farmer, also helped build all the branches of the colony. They had sons and daughters. Their sons were Abram and David. Their daughters were Katharina, Agata, and Anna. Anna was my mother.

When my mother (then Anna Fast) was 12 years old, her mother died of cancer. Grandpa Fast was left as a widower with 5 motherless children. After a short widowhood, Grandpa Fast married an elderly spinster, Suse Unrau. From this second marriage there was a daughter Susanna and a baby which died. With this second marriage, Grandpa Fast received more capital and their economic situation expanded greatly. So, he became a wealthy man. Already with his first wife they came to faith in God, were baptized, and joined a small Mennonite Brethren Church in the colony.

The years passed. The sons and daughters grew up and thought of getting married. Johann (Julius) Wiens lived in the same village (No. 14), which was called Steinfeld. His family belonged to the Mennonite General Conference church. He had a big family too. Their sons were Johann, Franz (later to be my father), David, Heinrich, and Abram. The daughters were Susanna, Liese, and Tina. There was a friendly relationship among the youth of these two families. Franz Wiens made a marriage alliance with Anna Fast. These were my parents. Then Abram Fast (my mother's brother) married Susanna Wiens, (my father's sister). And then again Abram Wiens, (my father's Brother) married Susanna Fast (my mother's sister from the second marriage).

The couple on the left are my grandparents Franz & Anna Wiens, Dad's parent. Next to them are Abram & Susanna Fast. Susanna was Grandpa's sister and Abram was Grandma's brother. The couple on the right are Abram & Susanna Wiens. Abram Wiens was Grandpa's brother and this Susanna was Grandma's half-sister.

Franz Wiens and Anna Fast who became my parents celebrated their green wedding (i.e. got married) in 1912. After the wedding, they moved in with Grandpa and Grandma Fast (my mother's parents).

My grandpa and grandma had decided that they wanted to have Franz Wiens, their son-in-law to live with them on their big estate because by now they had only one daughter left at home. They wanted my father Franz Wiens to take over the management of their estate when the grandparents got older. Grandpa Fast, my grandfather, was so pleased with his son-in-law (my father) that they agreed to live together as one family and that they would have everything in common. His motto was "What is mine is also yours". Soon the last daughter, Susanna Fast, born to the second marriage was to marry. My parents, Franz and Anna Wiens, joined up to become one family with my grandparents, grandpa and grandma Fast. In this family, Grandpa Fast was the head and my father, Franz Wiens, was an advisory member of the family. Grandpa could rely on my father. Because he was hardworking and skillful, he was highly regarded by Grandpa. That aroused envy among the other children of Grandpa and Grandma Fast in Siberia, where two of his sons and the oldest daughter lived with their families.

In 1914 the first son, Johann, was born to Franz and Anna Wiens. In that same year, 1914, the world war erupted and our father was conscripted to serve in the forestry service. During this time, Grandpa Fast had to manage the Estate with a Russian worker. On January 6, 1916, while the political situation in Russia was worsening, a daughter, Suse, was born to my parents.

When the Russian Emperor was overthrown in 1917, there was anarchy in Russia, and the good and pleasant days of our ancestors were over. After 150 years of life in an empire, where the Mennonites had become prosperous, the entire empire of the Romanov family collapsed. Now two parties formed in the country, red and white. The reds were the communists and the whites were the democrats. During this time, bands of robbers emerged, inflicting great terror and harm to the Mennonite settlement of Sagradovka which suffered badly. Terrorist captain, Nestor Machno, was the one who with his gang, brutally robbed and murdered the inhabitants in 1919. Our grandparents along with my parents with their small children, left everything and fled from the robber gangs into the surrounding fields where they stayed for the night. When they came back to their farm in the morning, the gang had withdrawn, and there was temporary calm. Again, one night another gang came into their farmyard, smashed windows and shouted that they should open the doors immediately. That caused them great shock, and Grandma and my mother cried out in fear. When the doors were opened, armed men came in and demanded money. Because there was no money Grandpa and Father had to stand facing the wall. A bandit had turned to Mother with his gun, and mother then screamed as loud as she could out of fear, while the bandits ransacked the whole house and took away valuables. In the morning my mother had lost her voice and couldn't speak a word out loud. Her hair was also a good deal greyer.

Here is a little explanation: When the imperial government fell in March 1917 and then in November 1917 the Bolsheviks came to power, the good days with peace and security were over. The surrounding Russians demanded and received land, horses and farm implements. Every Mennonite farmer had to give up some of his belongings and land. That wasn't easy. For a while the young people stood watch day and night, to keep the bandits out of the settlement. But it got harder and harder. In the Spring of 1919 bandits kept coming into the villages and robbing them. The gang had grown big and strong, and in the summer, they invaded villages and took horses, clothes, buggys - in short, everything they wanted. The people of Sagradovka always went to bed in fear. Life was very insecure. Armed gangs roamed the countryside, robbed and murdered with impunity. The worst of these was the Makhno gang. The days of greatest horror in the settlement of Sagradovka were on November 29th and 30th and December 1st, 1919. In November 1919 a part of the gang raided six villages in this settlement. As a result of this many became widows and orphans. The whole village of Munsterberg, (No. 11) and 75 Estates in other villages were burned to the ground. All around, the sky glowed red. Also, one could hear gunshots and the devilish screams of the terrorists. Finally, the fiends left the village of Tiege (No. 8) and moved on to another village. In the morning, when it was light, people went around shouting fearfully. Only then did they discover the terrible reality, namely that many residents in Tiege (No. 8) had been brutally murdered. Besides murder, arson and robbery, numerous women and girls 12 and over were shamefully raped. Often, they were then also brutally killed. This all happened in Tiege (No. 8) on the first night of terror, November 29, 1919. When finally, after a seemingly endless night, the morning dawned overcast, they saw more clearly the devilish marks of devastation. In Tiege the best Estates were incinerated. Now the people believed that the gang had withdrawn from this area satisfied. But early in the morning, November 30th, they came back from the surrounding villages. Countless wagons came to pick up loot. Now the post office in Tiege was robbed, the cash register broken into, and the telegraph machine destroyed and much more. After this, homes were looted and the wagons brought along for transport were loaded high with loot. Besides money and valuables, flour, grain, food, and clothes, more than 40 horses were taken from Tiege. On December 1st, a large number of stragglers came to Tiege to continue with their predatory activity, while a large group of them moved on to Schoenau (No. 13) where they also burned, robbed, and murdered. Six villages were affected by this historic disaster: Gnadenfeld (No. 12), Reinfeld (No. 16), Orloff (No. 6), Tiege (No. 8), Münsterberg (No. 11), and Schoenau (No. 13).

These six villages experienced the atrocities in a similar way. Most terrifying however was the diabolical devastation in Munsterberg and Tiege. From the evening of 29 November on, the fire raged there; almost all residents, from children in their cradles to the life-weary old people, were butchered and a large number burned – over 100 people. The whole village with belongings and lots of live cattle were torched. Of the more than 100 dead, it was only possible to bury 37 corpses in a mass grave (the rest were incinerated). During the nights of the murderous rampage, Samagonka (home-brewed brandy) was being brewed continuously for the gang in the village of Schesternja. Finally, finally on the evening of the third day of the murderous rampage, December 1st, the robbers in Schesternja were frightened by the flashing of a spotlight coming from the local defense forces with the approaching "cadets" (Denikinzy).

An eyewitness describes this moment: the robbers were immediately signaled to leave, and in a wild escape, the fiends left the village of Schesternja and thus also our broken community. From here they headed in a southeasterly direction to Kronau and from there to Nikopol. Rumor has it that most of the terrorists were killed by the pursuing cadets. This happened on December 1, 1919. (I have taken some of this from the book Sagradovka.)

What follows is about my grandpa and grandma Fast, my parents Franz and Anna Wiens, and also my uncle and aunt, the Abram Wiens. This is what I heard from the older generation. My parents lived with Grandpa and Grandma Fast in their summer room, and my uncle lived nearby, in the village of Steinfeld (No. 14). In such troubled times, nobody can take their life for granted. So it was that Grandpa and Grandma Fast, my parents with three small children, and our Uncle and Aunt with a baby sometimes had to leave their homes, hiding somewhere. They had to hide somewhere out in the fields at night and during the day they spent their time in the cornfields, as long as the gangs were in the village. One night the gang came into the yard and smashed the windows with a long pole. There was the flashing of light and loud crashing, a lot of scary feelings. Then they threw a hand grenade through the window into the room. My Father threw it back out as fast as he could and then it exploded. Another time Mom was about to bake bread. The dough was ready to be baked. The fire in the stove was also ready. Then came the announcement that the gang was approaching our village. Everyone tried to get to safety as quickly as possible. Mutti then quickly put the bread in the oven and ran out into the cornfield, where the family was.

Here is an explanation: at the end of every village there was a guard on horseback. Because there were open fields around the village, they had a wide view. So, when such a gang was approaching, word was passed from house to house. My grandpa and grandma Fast and parents often had to escape, sometimes in great danger. They lived in fear day and night. During this difficult time my parents had three young children (5, 3, and 1 year old), and that was very difficult. (Note from Hart, the youngest was my father Abram).

Under the Soviets

The Soviets took all the land and distributed it evenly among all rural residents who wanted to farm. The original land owners were always seen as criminals and evil doers. The poor, whether guilty or innocent, were always seen as noble and oppressed. They were continually incited against the wealthy. This caused a lot of annoyance and anger. In the autumn of 1921, the men were mobilized. They had to perform their service to the homeland, some in forestry and some in legal firms. The oppression continued at home. In these circumstances the fields could only be worked very poorly, some not at all. Since 1921 was a very dry year, the crop was almost a total failure that year. As a result, there was a great famine. In the spring of 1922, the houses where there was still bread were almost always surrounded by starving people. There were people laying down and dying under hedges and along fences. My grandpa and grandma Fast and parents Franz and Anna Wiens still had something to eat. My parents also fed many hungry people. But they couldn't feed everyone. Thousands of unemployed and starving people flooded the area. During this time the American kitchen was established. This was in the early summer of 1922. It really helped in this time of great need. In this same year, a typhoid epidemic erupted, and many more people died of this disease. As already mentioned, during the spring of 1922 these villages were swamped with hungry strangers. Home invasions and theft of food became so overwhelming that something had to be done to keep the settlement from being taken over by the bandits. There were no police or even authorities to whom residents could turn for help. Commissions for the fight against banditry were established. The idea was good in and of itself, but the way it was carried out in several villages was not good. It was a very nasty time.

In 1922 the harvest was poor, but at least good enough to provide bread for the people again. But frequently not as they had been accustomed to before. Still the killing and robbery went on. The Forster's family was miserably slaughtered. Even if people who had some grain were on their way to the mill, their wagons would be robbed and the people cruelly murdered – some were strangled with their harnesses. Even children and old people were killed. In the autumn of 1922, a little more security returned to the country. Assaults and murders became less common. The government grew stronger. Now the people were robbed and bullied by legal means. More and more communists from outside the area were sent into the villages. They assumed control everywhere. These people who were now in charge, almost all belonged to the terrorists, and many of them were common criminals.

In such circumstances many people wished to leave Russia. When such an opportunity arose, many went to Canada and South America from 1924 to 1927. In 1924 things started to get a little better. The government gave the people more freedom, and it was easier again. But then the government suddenly changed their tactics again in 1928. They strictly implemented collectivization. The people were regarded as enemies of the state. Nobody was allowed to emigrate anymore. A great many families were exiled to Siberia in the cruelest of circumstances. With hard work and very little to eat, many; perhaps most, died. We learned about the situation of the exiles in Siberia from letters. People were driven to their death by slave labour. They had to work day and night for 200 grams of bread. Old Women with their feet swollen from hunger, young girls with bleeding shoulders from dragging wood ...

A 16-year-old boy wrote in February 1932: "Today I almost despaired of my life because I am so alone here surrounded by Tatars and Kazaks, without food and almost without clothes. I was thrown into a cold room where I shivered in the cold for five days and was given no bread. Then I was released, and I was pursued by riders on horseback with no food or water and I still had to carry a heavy load." He wrote much more about how people were viciously tortured to death.

Grandpa Fast and my father Franz Wiens felt threatened because they were landowners. Emigrating legally was no longer possible because exit permits were no longer being granted. Now our grandparents and parents decided that our father should go to Siberia to find out whether the political circumstances were better there. So, our father took the opportunity to go and scout out the Amur area, where Mama's sister, the wife of David Friesen had just settled. When he had surveyed the region and the people living there, he made up his mind that if Grandpa Fast agreed, they would liquidate their Estate in southern Russia and move to the Amur region. We had a very large and beautiful Estate, with a large garden and an orchard with sour cherries, apples, apricots, and many varieties of plums and mulberries. There we children sometimes would eat to our hearts' content. We could eat whatever we wanted. I can still remember the day when everything was sold and then how grandpa and my father felt so very insecure. At night they were in hiding somewhere out of fear that they would be robbed.

In late autumn, of 1927, my parents with 6 children, and grandpa and grandma, along with my uncle, Abram Wiens, with their 5 children (father's brother) bade farewell to the beautiful Sagradovka. We had lived there in the village of Steinfeld (No. 14). My siblings were Johann, Suse, Abram (Hart's father), I (Lena), Franz, and David. So, Grandpa and Grandma and our parents went to the train station with heavy hearts and much fear. It was a dangerous journey because so many were attacked along the way and brutally murdered, even children and the elderly. We traveled by rail to the Amur region, (a distance of more than 8,000 kilometers) where Uncle David Friesen picked us up from the train station. That winter Grandpa, Grandma, and our family with 6 children lived with the Friesens, who were also at the very beginning of their new life in the Amur region and living in makeshift shelters.

My father made preparations for us to settle on new land, which was 20 kilometers from the village of Schumanovka (where the Friesens lived). I was 7 years old then. Once we were settled, my parents lived here together with Grandpa and Grandma. Grandpa was still considered the Head of the family. Grandpa sometimes punished us children too. In short: Grandpa believed even here, that he had to decide everything and he did not even consider leaving decisions to his son-in-law. This was often not easy for my parents. But I never observed any big arguments between my Grandpa and my father. By the spring my father had finished the house on our new settlement in the village of Osorne to the extent that we could move in. This was in 1928.

In the spring of 1929, our parents had twins born to them: two boys, Jacob and Heinrich. Heinrich only lived 10 days before he died. Grandpa Fast and my father had bought a steam threshing machine together which my father used to thresh grain in the Russian villages as a means to earn some money. My brothers Johann and Abram (note from Hart: this is my dad) often helped with this. Because in the Amur region it always rained a lot in the autumn, the grain had to be threshed at the beginning of winter when everything was frozen solid. In the late autumn of 1929, my grandmother suffered a stroke, which made her severely disabled. She had to be cared for like a baby. So, my mother had her hands full now. Because my father was not at home, Grandpa helped to look after our sick grandma.

In January, 1930 Grandpa died after almost 10 days of illness. Then grandma died on March 20, 1930 at the age of 69. Grandpa was 73 years old when he died.

In 1929 there was a flood in our village of Osorne. So, we had to move and we bought an abandoned Estate in the village of Friedensfeld. My uncle Abram Wiens moved in there. My parents moved to the neighboring village of Schumanovka and stayed with David Friesens (mother's sister) again that winter. In the winter of 1929, the steam threshing machine was moved to the village of Schumanovka. Grandpa Fast and my father then contributed the threshing machine to the Schumanower communal enterprise. My father then worked in this communal enterprise with the steam threshing machine.

The leading men of Schumanovka set December 15 as the departure date for the escape from Russia through China. The inhabitants of Schumanovka were informed. Whoever had close relatives in the neighboring villages, was allowed to invite them to participate in the escape. Our family arrived in Schumanovka just in time to join in with the escaping group. Everything was prepared for the escape. The sleds were packed, except for the food and a few other objects, which the people could hardly bear to leave behind. The leadership had chosen the well-known Chinese peddler/smuggler, Alexander as its guide. Already, he had taken two scouts from our village Schumanowka (Note from Hart: my Onkel Isaak and Mr. Fehderau) safely over the border and back to scout out the situation. They negotiated a deal. They made an agreement with the Chinese guide that every family would give him their best horse once he had brought them safely to the Chinese side of the river. If the escape would be successful this would be a great business opportunity for one night of work. He gladly accepted this.

Now the much-anticipated day, December 15th, had arrived. In feverish excitement the father of every family sees to it that everything is ready and prepared for the escape. In great impatience and excitement, the people can hardly wait for the evening to come. As night falls, a number of men go to the village teacher, as well as to another farmer. These two are considered unreliable and are seriously suspected of being compromised by the G.P.U. (secret police). To their utter astonishment the whole undertaking is presented to them and they are urged to join in the escape across the border. The citizens of Schumanovka feared that they would refuse to go with them. Then they would have been forcibly taken along. This seemed very necessary so that the whole group would not be betrayed to the G.P.U. by these two. But force was not needed. The teacher and the farmer promptly agreed to come along and they quickly got ready after they were given some clothes needed to join the group to escape across the border. But a young 7or 8-year-old boy from the neighboring village had come to visit his uncle. To prevent betrayal, the poor boy also had to participate in the escape.

Now the much-anticipated evening is here. The plan is to set out around 9 p.m. When the announcement is sent around: "Get ready," that would be the time to harness the horses and set out. Everyone is sitting and waiting with great excitement and with hearts thumping. They have no appetite for their supper, which has been prepared in a hurry, because they are too excited and agitated to eat. Now the message is suddenly passed from house to house that the plan won't work for today. What Disappointment! So, what's going on? A delegation from the nearby village of Newjork has arrived at Mr. Jakob Siemens place and has demanded that the departure be postponed for eight days, since Newjork has not yet finished their preparations for the escape. Mr. Siemens tries to make it clear to them that such a long delay is very dangerous. He explains that the whole plan could be betrayed and then they would all be lost. The men, however, stick with their demand for a delay, and they can't be persuaded. "If you don't wait for us, we'll report you to the authorities," is their threat. It is big enough to intimidate Mr. Siemens and persuade him to give in to them. So, the escape must be postponed for better or worse.

The people of Newjork are suspicious, so they are constantly watching the bustling of the people in Schumanovka with guards posted at the end of the village. Because the preparations must remain very secret, everything in the house has to be put back in its place in the morning. My grandfather's big clock also had to be hung back on the wall. Should someone suddenly come to visit us there should be nothing to make them suspicious. My uncle, Abram Wiens, from the village of Friedensfeld was here that night to take part in the escape. Because it was now delayed, he had to go back home with his family and the children were back at school the next morning.

So, my parents really got, should I say, unwanted visitors from the village Friedensfeld. They were there for lunch and supper.

During the day, that is now on December 16, the leaders of Shumanovka held a secret meeting on how to proceed in this critical situation. Since postponement of the escape for eight days was too big a risk and almost a crime against their own life and the lives of their families it was agreed, despite the promise they had made, that they would leave without the people of Newjork after all. The departure would be that night. The announcement went from house to house again that they should be ready for that evening. The evening is approaching, again we are eagerly waiting for the announcement: "Get ready." Today, at around 10 p.m., it should happen. Again, we have lost our appetite at supper out of fear and anxiety. We look forward to the daring escape plan with heavy and fearful hearts. The spies from Newjork are back and are watching carefully up and down the street to see what is going on in the individual yards. We sit and wait.

There is a knock at the door. Is the announcement being made yet? No, it's our neighbour Isaac Wiens. He's been instructed by the leadership to take charge of the group's security. He asks if someone could go to the end of the village and listen to see whether there is anything that can be heard on the main road leading to the headquarters of the G.P.U. Twin brothers Abram and Gerhard Friesen willingly go out of the village and listen and peer attentively in the direction of Konstantinovka, where the headquarters of the G.P.U. is located. It is bitterly cold. The thermometer goes down to 40 degrees below and lower. In the direction they are watching, it is very quiet, and they want to go back to the village. Suddenly they hear the crunch of snow from a great distance in the other direction. A great shock goes through all their limbs, and they stand still as if they have been nailed to the ground. Who can still be out this late at night? Have we been betrayed? Is it perhaps the G.P.U. that wants to thwart our plan? But no, it is just a sleigh from the neighboring village of Friedensfeld that is driving at a brisk pace to join the escape plan.

With the shock of this late visit, it is now 12 o'clock midnight. Because it is so bitterly cold, the Newjork guards have now left their stations and gone home. Now that the shock is over and everything is quiet again, the anticipated announcement comes: "Get ready." Now there is a mysterious running back and forth throughout the village. The cattle are released and driven out of the barns. They are now given complete freedom. The heart of everyone in the group is beating as if ready to burst. In our house, too, everyone is on their feet and getting ready in feverish haste. Everyone packs what they want to take with them in the sled in order to suppress their inner turmoil. Our cattle, too, are given the golden gift of liberty at father's command. The lamps are not to be extinguished, and the uneaten supper is to be left on the table. Everything that was dear to us is left behind. A prearranged sign is given, and the line of sleds starts moving. Through every courtyard gate the sleds drive out into the street. There is now a long row of sled after sled. Around 60 sleds in all. The Chinese guide Alexander strides at the head of the line. All the other sleds follow one after the other. Several men are riding alone beside the caravan. They ensure that everything is orderly and see that nobody is left behind. Many men walk next to the sleds to keep warm. Word is sent from sled-to-sled warning everyone to keep calm and to avoid breaking the silence so as not to cause a disturbance.

The group moves forward, and everyone is preoccupied with their thoughts. "Well goodbye my dear Homeland!" That is what is going through every heart, and everyone is experiencing more or less in the same way what it means to leave their dear homeland in anticipation of such an uncertain future. Some send up a silent prayer. In the present moment an entire village is on the way to the Amur River to escape across the border. And if we get across safely and if we don't drive straight into disaster, what will be our destiny on the other side of the river? The sleigh caravan proceeds out of the village as silently as a funeral procession. We drive for a stretch on the straight road out of the village, but then we turn off the road and begin to plow through knee-deep snow across the wide-open fields, to keep as far away as possible from the border guards.

Apparently, the cold is still increasing and it's almost unbearable. The hard-frozen snow crunches so loudly under the sleds that we are afraid to be betrayed by this sound. The lead horses that have to break a trail in the knee-deep snow have a particularly difficult time pulling their sleds. It is about 18 to 20 kilometers to the Amur River. This puts a heavy demand on the horses pulling the sleds across these pathless, snowy fields. After some distance, we come to a Russian village, the first base of the border guards. We made a detour around this village. There is fear of being discovered and that doom will overtake us from this village. But everything stays calm and soon the village is far behind us.

The further we go now, the harder the journey becomes. There are deep ravines and steep hills. This is now very difficult for the rearmost sled, because the snow has been packed down solid into slippery ice. The horses then have to use all their strength to climb these hills. Often the sleds bump into tree stumps. Some also tip over, which is unpleasant and causes delays. My uncle David Friesen's horse suddenly becomes stubborn and doesn't want to continue. Love doesn't help, nor do blows. It bends over and breaks the sled. It is close to where the border guards make their daily ride. What will happen now? Won't the guard show up suddenly? We tremble all over with fear. And yet action must be taken. The sled is quickly moved aside tinkered together as best as possible. The frost penetrates mercilessly, and we have to continually examine our limbs to see if there is still life in them, because all too quickly fingertips, nose, ears, or toes become frozen. Then they must be aggressively rubbed with snow to bring life back into them again. In such circumstances the work moves forward very slowly. They manage to repair the damage to the sled, and the travel can continue again. The sled of our neighbor P. Janzen also breaks. He had loaded his family, along with a whole butchered beef onto his sled. The load was too heavy, and so the sled broke up and could no longer be repaired. The family members were quickly loaded onto other sleds, which was not that easy, because all the sleds were quite overcrowded. The broken sled was just dragged to the side and left behind with the beautiful, fresh beef.

After a long, arduous journey and many stops along the way, with extreme nervous tension over the danger of colliding with the border guards, we come close to the Amur river. We still have to pass the Russian village of Orlovka. The journey almost seems like an eternity to us. And now the dangerous Orlovka, where a border patrol of 20 men with machine guns are guarding the border. It was already getting dark and we could hear dogs barking and roosters crowing in the village. Won't the machine gun suddenly rattle, mowing through our ranks? Here the road gets worse and worse and more and more sleds break down under the load and are then somehow patched together. It's not very far from that dangerous village where the sleds had to be patched up. It's a miracle that the border guards seem not to see or hear anything, as if their eyes were kept from seeing.

The front sleds finally arrive on the bank of the river. The bank drops off steeply here about three meters high. It is very dangerous to jump down that high.

The horses now become unwilling to move and they hang back. But they must be forced to go down, because there is no other way out. So, the men are called together. While some help at the top to push the sleds down the slope without much thought, the others pick them up at the bottom. It is arduous, hard work, and the men sweat in spite of the bitter cold. Even if the men below work together to grab hold of the falling sleds, several break apart on the hard ice. The things packed on the sleds fly out and are all jumbled together. Women and children have to get out at the top and slide down the slope. The broken sleds quickly get repaired again. Everyone is up and at it. Everyone has to somehow help along. Even so, it is a tedious and laborious job. It's getting lighter and there are still several sleds up on the bank.

The dangerous Orlovka village is only one kilometer away from us. How is it possible that the border guards are so mild and sluggish today? Will they suddenly ambush us due to the delay? There is no time to ponder. Everyone has to work as hard as possible and do their part so that we can leave this dangerous riverside as quickly as possible. Finally, the last sled is down on the ice and the foremost sleds are already far away on the Amur River. Our armed riders now form the rear guard and look back anxiously at Orlovka, wondering whether the border guards might suddenly rush up to attack us. But through a miracle of God no guards appear. Everyone is off at a full trot on the firm ice, which is covered with a light blanket of snow. Now the distance between us and the Russian bank keeps growing. After going straight forward on the ice for a stretch, we then had to meander between islands and open spaces. The horses are urged to go faster. As my siblings Johann, Suse, and Abram were further forward on another sled, they were on Chinese soil sooner than we were. We were among the last and were still on the ice at sunrise. That was nerve wracking. Will the G.P.U. maybe catch us even now? But thank God we also reached the Chinese shore safely. Soon we were surrounded by curious Chinese. But the parents can't breathe a sigh of relief just yet, because the fear of the cruel G.P.U is too great. Even now they could not suppress the thought that we could still be sent back even from here.

We drove into the Chinese village of Kani-Fu, where we were given a friendly and accommodating welcome. With a deep sigh of relief, heartfelt thanksgiving prayers are sent up to heaven. Two hundred and seventeen people have escaped the communist land in a wonderful way, and under divine guidance. Of these 175 were from our village Schumanovka. It is almost unbelievable that we are actually finally in freedom and no longer living in fear of the G.P.U. Or is all we went through that night just a dream? But no, it is not a dream. It is real. We are saved! Praise and thank God, and we cry tears of joy.

On China's soil

Although we had escaped communist Russia, all sorts of very serious inconveniences and obstruction still stood in our way even here on Chinese soil. It would take all our willpower to overcome these. Here we were homeless in a foreign, pagan land, among people speaking a foreign language. Everything became almost unbearable for us at times. The Chinese distributed us among their houses as best they could. Since there was not room for all of us refugees, quite a few had to be accommodated in the neighboring village. The neighboring village was fortunately not far away. First everyone warms up their frozen limbs by the warm stove. Quite a few men have frozen toes on their feet, and warming up their feet causes them terrible pain. (Later, in Harbin these men's frozen limbs had to be amputated). Soon a hot breakfast was prepared and eaten hungrily. How wonderful after such an adventure and tension filled night in below minus 40 degrees temperatures to be in a heated room, enjoying a good warm meal. Now our leaders negotiated with the Chinese guide Alexander for his compensation. He was promised a horse, the best from every family. Now they try to persuade him to be satisfied with fewer horses. The horses are all the wealth we have and we would need the money we can get from them for our onward journey. The Chinese guide is open to negotiation. The negotiations end with success for our group. The Chinese is content with 22 horses, which includes pretty much all of the best horses of our group. We also found it necessary to put our horses under guard at night, otherwise the horses could easily be stolen by bandits. Now all the heads of families are called together for a consultation. At this meeting, Mr. Jakob Siemens, the former manager of our collective, is elected as the group leader. Then it is decided to send three men to the Chinese authorities in the city of Sijiazixiang to obtain visas or residence permits for our group. Sijiazixiang is about 80 kilometers from Kani-Fu. They were also tasked to negotiate with an automobile company there to arrange, if possible, vehicles to drive us to the city of Zizikar, 580 kilometers away. From there we would be able to get to Harbin by rail.

Three men left Kani-Fu that evening accompanied by the Chinese guide Alexander. They only traveled at night to avoid being intercepted by the police. On the third night they arrived safely in Sijiazixiang. Negotiations with the automobile company are difficult. Finally, they agree to rent us 8 buses. But they ask 1000 Chinese dollars for each bus up to Zizikar. Because many families are short of money those who were better-off had to help out with loans, which would later at some point have to be paid back. So, we helped each other out and we managed to get together enough money for the trip to Zizikar and for the visa.

All human activity has its time. There is a time to be born and a time to die. That is how it was after the difficult, almost endless night, where everyone had to be as quiet as possible, including the children. In Kani-Fu, when the women and children were helped to get off the sleds, one couple was horrified to discover that their two years old daughter had suffocated (died): This was our group's first burial on Chinese soil. Another couple also had a baby here. This was not easy for the woman in the crowded rooms of the wretched Chinese huts. But nature claims its rights and the child was born. Everyone in the group was restless, waiting longingly for the time to continue further into the country. They feared that Russian border troops would attack us at night and drag us forcibly back to Russia, or that there would be Chinese traitors, who would extradite us to the Russians. But despite the danger, we had to stay there for a full eight days, waiting to receive the residence permits from Sijiazixiang.

With all that was going on, the Sacred Christmas day is approaching. Because our minds are absorbed with all the unfamiliar conditions on Chinese soil and are waiting for things to come, little attention is paid to the holidays. Never before had we spent Christmas in such a way and under such extraordinary circumstances as we did in this year 1930. How and when will we finally be able to continue, and will we be able to reach our preliminary destination, Harbin?

But finally, the residence permits are granted with the permission to go further into the country. So, we quickly get ready to travel again. We leave Kani-Fu by sled on December 27th and go to the larger village of Kochuricha, 8 kilometers away. From here the buses coming from Sijiazixiang are supposed to pick us up to take us to Zizikar. Again, we have to wait three days. Our accommodations are in a large inn.

The place was teeming with Chinese. This was not pleasant for us girls and women because they would gaze at women with lustful looks. It was also dangerous for the small children there because the Chinese might kidnap them. The Chinese don't just steal valuables or money, but also children. One child from our group almost disappeared there. Someone saw it happen, ran after the Chinese, and snatched the child from him. On the advice of the landlord, we now locked our suitcases and boxes in a secret room to protect things from the gangs. Afterwards we discovered that the boxes had been rummaged through and some things had been stolen. Because every hour costs money here, and our money was very limited, we waited impatiently on the vehicles that would bring us closer to our destination.

Finally, the eight big buses arrived, and it was time to board. But it's not that easy to accommodate the 217 people in eight buses. The buses get overcrowded, so that over time it becomes almost unbearable. The last, for whom there appears to be no space, are unceremoniously taken hold of by the bus drivers and pushed in and then the bus door is closed. There we sit in the bus, like sardines in a can, and we have to ask each other repeatedly to move over a little, as the heavy burden of the person beside us threatens to paralyze and cut off the circulation in our limbs. The luggage, such as boxes, beds, suitcases, is packed and firmly tied up on the fenders. Every spot on the bus is loaded and covered with something or someone. Our family with three other families - 32 people in total – is locked into the largest bus. Even though it is very uncomfortable to have to sit so tightly packed together, we are glad that we are moving forward again, further away from the dreaded Soviet Russian border, and we are able to move closer to Zizikar, where the hardships of this arduous journey will come to an end. The engines of the buses are cranked, and with terrible howls and one violent jerk the beasts get in motion. We are travelling in the direction of the town of Aigun about 32 kilometers away. When we arrive here, we stop for the night. To our astonishment we meet a refugee group of 87 people here who crossed the Amur border one day before us (i.e. December 16, 1930). This group traveled with 13 sleds. After a simple breakfast the next morning, everyone has to get back in their bus. Our driver tells us that we have a long way to go to our next stop so we have to get ready for a long journey. It's ten o'clock in the morning. The buses get into motion with a great deal of noise and in an extremely cumbersome manner. In our opinion, they are too heavily loaded. The road is very slick, and the drivers have to work very hard to keep the vehicles entrusted to them on the track. Every now and then they go very close to the edge of the road. The buses lean sharply to one side and we fear that there might be an accident. But things are going pretty well for a number of hours, and we are happy that we are making progress. But our joy is only brief.

Suddenly the largest bus, precisely the one in which our family with the three other families is riding, slides away. In the next instant it falls into the ditch and tips over on its left side. Since we're so tightly pressed together, luckily, there are no injuries. Only now everyone has to change their position because we have come to rest on each other due to the tipping of the bus. That required more than a little effort. With great effort, the men manage to get out of the bus to help. Somehow the bus is turned back on its wheels and after the driver cranks the engine, we push with all our might. However, it is no use. The bus does not budge even a little. We find a post lying along the way and lift and push around the bus with it until we manage to get the monster slowly back onto the road. Now the vehicle can be set in motion again. Then we hear that the engine is not running very smoothly. Something is wrong. After a short distance we come to a stop again. We get out, and the driver examines the bus. Soon he realizes that the tube on one of the wheels is damaged, and the tire is going flat. The damage is repaired and the journey can continue. How happy we are when the bus starts moving again, because when the bus stops the bitter cold is almost unbearable. The young children are particularly to be pitied. Now the engine rattles in an alarming manner, and we realize that we will not go far like this. And truly, after we've driven a stretch in this miserable fashion, the motor comes to a halt again. The driver becomes annoyed and won't give any answers to our urgent questions. Apparently, he tries to convince us that we will be leaving again soon but it is obvious from the expression on his face that he himself does not believe what he is saying. Irritated, he pounds on the engine, unscrews things, examines them, and puts them back together. Time goes by and it seems like an eternity to us in the bitter cold. The sun is about to set and it becomes more and more clear to us that we will not continue our journey today. But what can we do in this desolate wilderness where all we can hear is the crashing sound of the frost in the trees for miles around us? The other buses had driven past us when we tipped into the ditch earlier, and who knows where they are by now? Far and wide we see no place where we could find shelter for the night, and warm up; no village, no huts around. We can't possibly spend the night here in this bitter cold. What should we do? We think about it together. We ask the driver whether there is a village nearby. But he doesn't answer and pretends he doesn't understand a word of Russian. Night falls and there is bright moonlight. The frost torments us mercilessly. While we find ourselves in great concern, we now see that the driver and the bus conductor casually wrap themselves in their furs, and head to the front of the bus behind the wheel, getting ready to go to sleep. Our patience is at an end. We make it clear to them that we can't possibly stay here overnight. We press him to show us the way to the next village and to tell us how far away it is. Now he finally relents and answers our questions. He shows us the direction and says that it is about three to four kilometers to the next village, although he doesn't know for sure. Our men consult on what to do and they agree to send a number of men to find out whether there really is a village there, and whether we might find shelter there for the night. Now three young men volunteer to take on this assignment. They are Abram and Bernard Ratzlaff and Abram Friesen. The driver generously assigns his assistant as their companion. So, they set off to scout out the area. The frost penetrates us all mercilessly. The men wander around for hours in the bright moonlight and are beginning to think that there is nothing to be seen or heard all around, and that the driver has deceived them. His assistant, the companion of the three men, also does not know the area and becomes perplexed. They are ready to turn back and return to the bus. Suddenly a loud barking of dogs reaches their ears. They notice that they are close to a hut surrounded by sheds and a large yard. They realize that it is a kind of inn. The innkeeper responds to the loud shouting of these men. He hurries, ready for duty, opens the gate and invites them to come into the house. With Chinese courtesy, he sets the table and has them to eat and drink. The food consisted only of millet porridge, and the drink was just boiled water. But they eagerly attack the meal in order to renew their strength and warm up. They negotiate with the host and he agrees to accommodate our group and to provide us with lodging in the house. They can tell from his demeanor that in his mind he already sees the dollars flowing from our hands into his pocket.

After they have eaten something, having rested and warmed up, they quickly return to the bus, where we are freezing and waiting impatiently for them. They report on their experiences, and we all get out of the bus quickly. Food and bedding are gathered up. The men take the children in their arms, and off we go to the "friendly inn", where we look forward to a comfortable night's sleep, in warm rooms. But it was an arduous hike in the bitter cold and in the dead of night, where all the body wants is to rest and sleep. Every adult had a burden to bear. On the one hand there were 6 children who had to be carried because of their lack of warm footwear. Warm blankets and some food were also taken along. It was particularly difficult walking for our mother, as well as for my sickly uncle David Friesen, as well for my seriously ill sister. She was so weak that she could not walk alone. She had to be supported on both sides while walking. Again, and again, we had to stop to rest. Finally, we arrived at the inn. We dropped our burdens and tried using the bedding we had brought with us to make a place for us to sleep on the cold floor. Instead of being able to rest, the parents had a lot of work to do with the children. Some of the children had serious frostbite on their feet from the walk to the inn. As their feet began to get warm, they experienced unbearable pain. There was a lot of screaming and yelling, which completely spoiled our night's rest.

After the uncomfortable night we were thankful that we were now at least able to stay in the warmer place, and no longer out there in the barren wilderness exposed to the bitter cold. It was a very simple, dirty, Chinese inn. It was situated close to the big road, and everyone who passed by could stop to warm up or have a drink of tea. That is how it went from early morning until late at night. Dirt and clutter were the order of the day, and vermin were rampant. We believed that the next day the bus driver would be able to repair the bus and that we would again be able to be on our way and get closer to our desired destination. We just could not afford to stay here, eating, and paying for lodging, as our food was only enough for a short time. The length of time for the trip had been calculated and supplies measured out accordingly. Our cash had already been used up to the last penny. The Chinese innkeeper had already made it clear to us many times that he would not let us linger free of charge for a single day or night.

How disappointed we were when the next day a team of oxen came into the yard driven by our bus driver and towing our bus. The bus driver examined the engine again and finally established that one of the cylinders had burst. It could not be repaired. But where could he get another one? So, the driver's assistant had to go to the town of Naun as soon as possible to buy a new cylinder. During this time, we settled down as well as we could in our great scarcity. Our bread was soon finished and we had to exchange clothes for food. We got some small-grained Chinese millet grain called Tschumisa from the innkeeper in exchange for clothes. This Tschumisa was only cooked twice a day with water and without salt. We were completely infested with lice which plagued us, day and night. We struggled against the lice by killing them from morning to night. Our host made it look very easy to battle the lice. When the plague was too great for him, he took off his shirt, and with both hands he pulled the seam taut, and then passed over it with his teeth so that it crackled. With that he was then reconciled with the pests for a while.

The lice plague and malnutrition meant that my uncle and my sister became so sick that we thought they were dying. It was a desperate situation for us. After a few days the driver's assistant finally came back from town and brought a new cylinder for the engine of our bus. But oh no, the cylinder was too small. We had waited and hoped in vain. Now the driver decided to go to town himself, to get the right part, but he had to wait for a ride. Several days passed again. Finally, after a few days, he returned and brought the necessary part. But no matter how hard he tried with all his tools and skill; he couldn't get the engine running again. The bus stayed standing defiantly in its place. Our men talked to the driver, asking him to have another bus come from Naun or Zizikar as quickly as possible. But apparently, he didn't pay any attention to their suggestions. He pretended not to understand what they were saying. So, we had to surrender to our fate. We had to wait some more and content ourselves with the Tschumisa, and every day we had to fight the vermin, so that they wouldn't drag us away. We had more lice than food. But what were we waiting for? For some gracious coincidence? We didn't know.

Fortunately, our sick people slowly got better and began to recover. This inn was a long, low house. It was divided into three rooms. The middle room was the kitchen and one had to go into the house through the kitchen. Instead of doors there were just large openings from one room to another. In two rooms there was only one window on the courtyard side. The window was covered by a beef belly (the skin). In the middle was a hand-sized piece of glass. You could look out there. In the evening a lantern burned in the middle room and it had to light the whole house. We spent a full 13 days here, fighting the lice. I was 10 years old then and had a sick brother who was one year old. He was sick from birth and had to go through all these experiences.

Finally, on the fourteenth day in the morning while we were having our millet porridge, two buses approached and stopped in front of our hut. What is this then? Our driver strides in with determination and makes it clear to us that we are to get ready for the onward journey. In our great joy at this turn of events we forget about the Tschumisa on the table and quickly get ready to go. But then the landlord rushes in and angrily demands his due in payment for our lodging. However, since we have nothing left, we offer the Chinese innkeeper one fur as compensation, trying to make him understand that all of our money has been used up. The landlord likes the fur very much, but he had been expecting cash and demands money from us. At last, he comes to realize that there just isn't any cash to be had from us, and so he contents himself with the fur. Soon we are ready and we board the buses. One bus is filled with Chinese passengers except for three available spots. David Friesen has to get into this bus with his wife and son. My very ill uncle David Friesen boards this bus and the last passenger to board was Abram Friesen, wedged in by the driver who then closed the bus door behind him. He had to stand at the door in a completely stooped position so that his back ached terribly. How happy he was when a compassionate Chinese passenger offered to let him sit on his knee. Then we finally got in the other empty bus, 27 of us in all. Now the buses started moving.

Finally, we were on our way again. These two buses left at the same time. During the day the buses would stick together and we spent the night in the same village, only in different houses. The next morning, we left almost simultaneously again. Our bus followed close behind the one in front of us. Our journey together continued undisturbed for several hours. But then our bus got into trouble again, which separated them from us and we had to stay behind. Our bus broke down in such a way that there was no possibility of keeping going with it.

Once again, a bus breakdown in the wide-open countryside in the bitterest cold, where you don't know what to do. Just snow and ice all around and a long way to the next village. What should we do? The men paced back and forth helplessly, discussing with each other, racking their brains. They couldn't find a way out of this desperate situation. Our mothers sat in the bus with us children, helpless and freezing all over. Our driver says a few words in broken Russian, "If you can walk, go", and he points along the road with his hand. Now we set out walking, everyone who can walk. Even my eight-year-old brother Franz comes along. Better to walk than sit in the bus and freeze. The fathers, mothers and the small children stay behind in the bus.

Then, what a benevolent stroke of fate! From a distance we could see a Chinese sleigh and a two-wheeled cart approach. They were going the same way and soon caught up with the broken-down bus. They stopped the cart and after a lengthy negotiation with our bus driver and our fathers they were prepared to take these refugees they are meeting on the way and load them onto their sled. The mothers and children are helped up onto the tall two-wheeler, and the men walk behind. There is not much room on the sleds as they have no fenders. On the high two-wheelers the passengers get tossed about on the bumpy road. We experience an extremely arduous and difficult ride on these strange vehicles. Added to that there is the icy cold that mercilessly tortures us riding in the open sled and on the two-wheelers.

Finally, we reach the next village. We think we can't go any further because of the cold. We have to warm up and have a hot meal first. We haven't eaten any food all day, but we have had a long walk already. Everyone is very tired and frozen and doesn't want to go any further. But the drivers don't want to stop. They seem to be in a hurry and want their passengers to go further with them to make even more money. In desperation some of our people throw themselves off the sled, which forces the drivers to stop. We pay the caravan drivers what we owe them and leave them. Our fathers then look for a warm shelter where we can warm our frozen limbs.

My mother now wants to cook a warm meal (it's in an Inn). We and my uncle

Abram Wiens and our families are always together as one family on this journey, and so we are a group of 18 people. But my mother is not allowed to cook in the inn. We have a little flour. She gives it to the cook at the inn and tells him this little bit of flour is intended for 18 people. He takes the little flour and it doesn't even take long before he brings us a huge, tasty noodle soup with small chunks of meat in it. We can all eat our fill. I haven't eaten such a tasty soup before or after. But how do we get on with our journey? This anxious question comes up again after we are full and warm. We look for a Chinese in the village who speaks Russian and whom we can ask for advice.

Finally, they find an old Chinese man who speaks a few bits of Russian. He tells our men that there is a bus company in the big neighboring village, where they could rent a bus for the onward journey. We spend the night here, and early in the morning one of our men goes there and actually comes back after a few hours in the bus he has found. Now the journey can be continued again. It's a relatively good and comfortable ride that continues without interruption. At night there is a stop in a small village. We now bring our last groceries together to cook a hearty meal. But we are not allowed to cook, so we have to ask a Chinese to prepare the meal for us. He is done with it soon and puts the soup on the table in a large clay bowl. It tastes wonderful to us.

Early the next morning we drive on, and after several hours of good driving our bus stops suddenly. It is in the open countryside again, and it is also a very dangerous place because of robberies, and the bitter cold. The driver and his helper both get out. What's going on again? The two men quickly get to work. The one wheel of the bus was loose and needed to be screwed on tight again. Out of fear, the two work with their bare hands and without a coat in this bitter cold. It doesn't take that long either, and we are on the way again. We reach the city of Zizikar on the same day, safe and happy. Emaciated, we arrive there dirty and full of vermin. Here we are greeted with a hearty welcome by our fellow refugees who have been here for a long time already (about two weeks), waiting for our arrival.

Finally, we are together with the other refugees again. They cannot hide their astonishment, at our shabby and emaciated appearance. We are then immediately presented with a hearty, warm meal because we have not eaten anything all day and are also very frozen. We aggressively and eagerly attack the food. After we have bathed and dressed in clean clothes, we feel like newborn. Now the questioning and recounting begins, which apparently does not want to end. The long and arduous journey is finally over, and Harbin, the final destination of our journey seems to be noticeably closer. Now we are all united again in Zizikar and we are heartily grateful that the Eternal Guide has directed our fate up to this point.

Even if we had to endure difficult things, yet we have been protected from the worst, namely a total collapse of the escape plan and the revenge of the Soviet Russian G.P.U. In this an authentic Chinese city, we have to wait another two weeks when our fellow refugees have already waited two weeks, as we have no funds for the rest of our journey. Our Schumanovka Group has sent a representative to Harbin to arrange the entry permits and also to get in touch with the committee for German refugees. In the big city of Zizikar we don't find any opportunities to earn money and therefore we have to limit ourselves extremely, as we have almost no funds available. Our diet mostly consists of skimmed milk, fine rice and the Chinese Tschumisa porridge. Now and then we have a piece of bread. We have to be content with this.

In Harbin the German committee issues international calls for help for the refugees in Zizikar. Then various organizations put out calls for help and collect funds for the needy. The Committee for German Refugees can provide us with several hundred dollars. In this way it is possible to put together the necessary money for the journey of the refugees from Zizikar to Harbin. The food for the first while in Harbin will also be provided. The authorities also issue entry permits for us. The committee now sends their employee, Mr. Peter Penner to Zizikar, to greet the refugees on behalf of the committees and escort them to Harbin. We arrive safe and sound in Harbin on February 12, 1931. We give our heartfelt thanks to our Heavenly Father for his gracious guidance. We are also very grateful to the German committee and the other organizations for their friendly support. We get a warm reception from different quarters.

In Harbin

The Committee for German Refugees had already made all the preparations for our reception and lodging in Harbin. It had rented a big three-story building from a Japanese and set it up as a home for refugees. In this home we all found accommodation; our Schumanovka group, as well as the Pribreshnoje group. Here in Harbin, we met up with many acquaintances from the various German colonies of the Amur area. Most of them had been in Harbin for many months, some even a year or two before we crossed the Amur, and they knew their way around in the big city of Harbin very well. First, we were provided with food by the committee. But soon there was competition among young men in search of employment. Employment was very difficult to find, and one had to be content with the lowest category of work, for which there was only a low starvation wage. Young women and girls were far better off in this regard. These were sought after by rich people in the city, and therefore they were also paid more.

So, it happened that the financial support from the committee was withdrawn. It also happened that some men stayed home because of a lack of work for them. They stay with the toddlers while the mothers went to work in order to earn support for the family. Some employers were also very hard on their employees, and when a maid had an accident and broke a saucer or bowl, that was deducted from their low wages. My husband who was then only 12 years old also experienced similar things. He worked as an errand boy for rich people (in short: "A Girl Friday"). He once broke a saucer and that was deducted from his wages. For many families, 'Schmalhans' was the cook (means living was very meager). We were also very poor. My mother couldn't leave home because she had a baby who was sick from birth. My father got a very low wage job and my (15 years old) sister Suse's wages were similarly very low. Her job was in a restaurant where she had to do everything. In addition, my uncle Abram Wiens was also seriously ill. Nobody thought he would get well. My aunt's work was to care for her sick husband (also her baby). So, her 11-year-old daughter Lena got a job as a housemaid. She had to do all the work that came up around the house. As I have mentioned already, we (together with my Uncle Abram's family) were always a family on this journey. It was very difficult for my parents to take care of 18 people. Because my uncle was so malnourished and anemic, the doctor prescribed for him to go to the slaughterhouse and drink the warm beef blood. After having done this for a while, he slowly got better and made progress toward recovery. It was like this with drinking blood: he had to start with little and each day drink a little more. Soon he had to consume a large cup, then reduce the dosage again. That is how he had to take this cure and afterwards, praise and thanks be to God, he was well again. (I forgot how small and how big the cup was, but it was bigger than an ordinary cup.) After we got to know the city better and were better acquainted with the employment opportunities, the men also managed to find better places to work and earn a living, where they made more money. One could not hold back from any work, of course or consider any service too low. You just had to accept the work that you were offered. So, our young people got to know a wide variety of jobs. They served, for example, as night watchmen, bakers, gardeners and served in large hotels and restaurants, as illegal workers. They worked in the various factories, and whatever other work was available. In the majority of cases, our ability and diligence earned us the trust of our employers who appreciated our work and showed us respect. But there were plenty of high-class people who tried to take advantage of their workers, refusing to pay them their wages under all kinds of pretexts, and sometimes treating them like cattle. In this house, where we were housed as refugees, we were crowded together with as many as 32 people in one room and this for over a year.

On February 12th, 1931 we arrived in Harbin, and on February 22nd, 1932, we were able to leave Harbin. The Refugee Committee with its capable chairman, Mr. Peter Wiebe from the United States at the helm, Prof. B.H. Unruh from Germany, along with other Organizations tried their best to get us out of China. Because China was overpopulated and unemployment was high, we were undesirable guests to the Chinese government. If an opportunity could not be created soon, we were in danger of being sent back to Russia. When Prof. B. H. Unruh (Karlsruhe, Germany) learned of the danger we faced in Harbin, China, he drove to the Chinese Consulate in Bonn Germany to establish the truth for himself. In Bonn he was then told that China was suffering great unemployment and that China could not afford to accept refugees. "If they do not leave the country soon, China will be forced to send these people back to Russia." Now Prof. B.H. Unruh begged the Consulate to be patient with the refugees and he promised to do everything he could to bring them out of the country and overseas as quickly as possible. Now the M.C.C. made it their goal to get the refugees out of China as soon as possible and bring them somewhere overseas, be it to North America, Germany, or anywhere else in order to restore orderly living conditions for us. Germany was out of the question for us at the time because it was already overpopulated. We wanted to go to Canada because there were so many Russian-Germans living there. Many of our refugees would also have been happy to go to the United States. Individual families succeeded to emigrate there through the mediation of their relatives. But the U.S.A. remained closed to our larger group. Also, there were no open doors in Canada for us. My father had a brother in Canada too, but our Aunt didn't want to take in their relatives. So, the committee was in collaboration with the Mennonite Central Committee in the U.S.A. and Prof. B. H. Unruh in Germany made every effort to find a new home for these German refugees anywhere else in the world. Even Mexico and Brazil were out of the question for us refugees. It was a very arduous undertaking, because it looked as though the Earth was too small. It seemed that nowhere in the world was there an open door for the homeless who had put their lives and everything they owned at risk because of their faith. We had our lives but we had lost what was necessary for life. Homeless and without rights we had to struggle in utter poverty in a foreign country. Nobody knew how and when these unregulated living conditions would end for us. The work of the M.C.C. and negotiations with various countries in the world continued without success. The only and last option was to settle the refugees, at least the first group consisting of about 300 people, in the Paraguayan Chaco of South America.

Several years ago, Mennonites had immigrated from Canada and had established the Menno Colony there, and later refugees from Soviet Russia (Mennonites who had immigrated via Moscow and Germany) had founded the Fernheim colony in Paraguay. The Mennonite Central Committee then decided to bring the first group of Harbin refugees to Paraguay, where the government promised that the refugees would have the privileges they wanted (i.e. freedom of worship and freedom from military service). This first transport of Mennonites from Harbin was supposed to go to the Russian-German settlement of Fernheim. Most of the cost of the trip was paid for by the M.C.C. but only as an advance loan. The money was to be paid back by the settlers in later years. In Harbin my 2-year-old brother Jakob, who had been sick from birth, was buried in February, 1931. Our uncle's baby, Suschen, (one year old) was also buried there. The committee also issued calls for our material support to various foreign organizations in major Chinese cities such as Hong Kong, Beijing, and Shanghai. The committee also, reached out to the M.C.C. in the United States of North America for help. This is how various donations came to the Germans Consulate for our support. The support consisted of clothes, school supplies and cash. It was a great help to us, especially our sick people and their care, as well as for the construction and maintenance of the school for our children.

Now the necessary negotiations and preparations were done, and the first transport could be organized. For this first transport almost all the Schumanovka Mennonites and the Pribreshnoje group were included. Several families from other groups were then added to this. It was finally a group of 373 people who formed the first transport. Two hundred and seventeen people escaped over the border from Russia to China on the night of December 17, 1930. Of these 175 were from our village Schumanovka. Here our parents showed great courage. On the one hand it was their big families with the small children, and then again, the journey in the cold through the wilderness where even children were born. The choice was very clear to us: either perish miserably in Russia, or risk this great escape. Because the escape was so very difficult, our parents fervently prayed for divine assistance and guidance every day. He, our great God helped. Praise and thanks be to him for that!

Appendix C: TRANSLATING THE GOSPEL

Preface

"For God so loved the world that he gave his only Son, so that everyone who believes in him may not perish but may have eternal life."

As long as I can remember it was my ambition to be a missionary, to participate in spreading Good News. My wife Ginny grew up with a similar ambition. So together, we set off for the Philippines, to live with the Kalinga people. They were known as "headhunters" in the anthropological literature. We learned to know them as kind, generous, hospitable people. One night they even threw a party and adopted us into their tribe, giving us a whole new set of family relationships. One of our new "sisters" took her responsibilities so seriously that whenever I was not home, she would stay up at night to ensure the safety of my family, although she had 9 children of her own to care for. Ultimately one of our new "brothers" and our best Kalinga friend actually sacrificed his life to protect our translation team from cruel bandits who were terrorizing the village. No wonder the priest who helped us get settled in our assignment told us that he had learned more from the Kalinga people than he would ever be able to give them. For our part, we gained a whole new understanding of what Jesus meant when he said, "the greatest way to show love for friends is to die for them (John 15.13)."

God himself is a friend like that, because in Jesus he paid the ultimate price to give us life – life in all it fullness – life without

end. That is the Good News we have to share. The message is stated most succinctly in John 3.16, a verse from the Bible that many of us have learned by heart.

In the 14 chapters of this booklet, I profile some of the challenges that translators face as we seek to restate this Good News from God in other languages. Words that seem so simple and straight forward, as we read them in our familiar language, can suddenly take on an unexpected complexity as we struggle to make them plain to people who speak entirely different languages.

I hope that as you read this booklet you will gain a new appreciation for the profound beauty of the Good News we have to share with the world and also a deeper understanding of the ministry of Bible translation. As partners with you in this task, we hope that you will be inspired to join with us to ensure that more and more people can access this wonderful message in words that can penetrate and change their hearts.

The famous theologian, Karl Barth, was once asked what he thought was the most profound truth of the Christian faith. Thoughtfully he responded, Jesus loves me this I know, for the Bible tells me so.

This truth is succinctly expressed in John's Gospel, chapter 3 verse 16. This verse has often been called the Gospel in a nutshell. In a series of articles reflecting on this verse word by word, I will use this great affirmation of God's love to illustrate some of the challenges Bible translators face as we seek to restate God's Good News in every language spoken on earth.

The first fact that a person used to reading the Bible in English must face is that this verse was originally written in Greek. To fully understand and appreciate all of the nuances of the text we must look at what John actually wrote.

Here is the text in Greek with an English gloss under each word

John 3.16

Οὕτως γὰρ ἠγάπησεν ὁ θεὸς τὸν κόσμον,
Thus   for   loved   – God the   world

ὥστε τὸν υἱὸν τὸν   μονογενῆ   ἔδωκεν,
that   the son the   unique=one he=gave

ἵνα πᾶς ὁ πιστεύων εἰς αὐτὸν
that all – believing in   him

μὴ ἀπόληται ἀλλ᾽ ἔχῃ ζωὴν αἰώνιον.
not may=perish but have life eternal (for the age)

Since this series of articles is written for the benefit of English readers, we will follow the order of words as it is found in a more familiar form of the text taken from the Revised Standard Version of the Bible.

"For God so loved the world that he gave his only Son, so that everyone who believes in him may not perish but may have eternal life." (John 3.16 NRSV)

Issue 1 - Translation in Context

The first word in our English version is "for." In the Greek this is actually the second word. It is a small word, but it brings with it a number of issues that the translator must consider. This little word is used to signal that John 3.16 was not written in isolation. It is part of a larger text. In fact, the chapter and verse numbers found in our Bibles were not in the original text. This is an important point, not only for the translator, but also for the reader or student of the Bible. Every verse of the Bible should be read and studied in its wider context rather than as a verse in isolation from the larger text. We violate the integrity of the text when we read, study or translate a verse of scripture in isolation. Yet how often have you been to a Bible study where participants are each assigned to read one verse? Such a process results in a serious loss of continuity, especially when different versions are being used. Reading Bible verses in isolation should be avoided, both when studying and when translating the Bible.

The Greek word **gar** (γὰρ) may be translated by a number of different English words, depending on the context in which it is used. It is found eight times from John 3.16 to 4.8 and in those eight occurrences the translators of the NRSV have used 6 different

ways of representing it. In 3.16 it is "for," in 3.17 "indeed," in 3.19 "because," in 3.24 "of course," in 3.34 it is left untranslated in its first occurrence, and in 4.8 it is represented by parentheses around the whole verse, to set it off as parenthetical. In linguistics, we call this little word a discourse particle. It has no specific meaning alone, but in conjunction with other words it helps to connect what is being said in the overall context. English versions frequently do not translate this particle by any single word, but rather let its meaning come out in the way that sentences are put together in the overall flow of the text.

In this particular context, the word translated "for" signals that verse 16 amplifies the statement made in the previous paragraph. There we read that, "just as Moses lifted up the serpent in the wilderness, so must the Son of Man be lifted up, that whoever believes in him may have eternal life."

Verse 16 elaborates this statement by telling us how and why God offers us this life. Translators must choose the most effective means at their disposal in the particular language for which they are translating to signal the connection between verse 16 and the preceding context. Even within the same language there may be a variety of ways of accomplishing this. I encourage readers to look at different English versions to see how they have done this, especially some of the newer, meaning based versions such as the Contemporary English Version or the Good News Translation. Also, if you know another language, see how translators have accomplished the discourse connection in that language.

In the next section we look at one of the biggest challenges a Bible translator faces – how to translate the word for "God."

Issue 2 - Translation or Transliteration

One of the most important challenges a Bible translator faces is the translation of the expression for God. In fact, in the Expository Dictionary of Bible Words, Lawrence O. Richards says: "Multiple volumes have been written to explore this short word."

The Bible assumes that God exists. It opens with the words, "In the beginning God...." But to the Hebrew people, in whose language the book of Genesis was written, the names and titles used for God were extremely significant. They communicated a lot about the people's understanding of who God is. In view of the multiple volumes that have been produced on this short word — God, it is obvious that one brief article is inadequate to really do justice to the topic. Consequently, I will limit myself to a discussion of the Greek expression **theos** (θεὸς) found in this verse.

In cultures where the Christian tradition is already well entrenched, there is often not much of a decision left because an acceptable way of referring to God has already been established. However, in those languages where Christian teaching is new and the Scriptures are

being translated for the first time, the decision about <u>how</u> to

translate the Greek θεὸς in this verse can be quite far-reaching. I recently heard a speaker from one of our First Nations express the pain his people have suffered as a consequence of the decision made by early Christian missionaries to reject the common term for the Creator in their language in favour of a borrowed word. As a result God has always seemed like a foreign God to them.

Our two official languages in Canada help illustrate the two basic approaches that translators have tended to follow. The French language uses Dieu for God. This is essentially a borrowed adaptation of the Latin Deus. French is one of the Romance languages with roots going back to Latin and most Romance languages follow this pattern of borrowing or transliteration. In the Latin Vulgate, the word Deus, is consistently used to translate the Greek θεός. On the surface the two words even appear to be derived from the same source but linguistically they are not related.

Martin Luther, John Wycliffe and others who translated the Scriptures into the Germanic languages such as German and English, followed another common approach. Following the precedent set by Ulfilas in his Gothic translation of the New

Testament they used the native English and German words, God and Gott. These were the terms commonly used among pre-Christian Germanic tribes to refer to the supreme or ultimate reality.

Translators, who choose this solution of using a common native term for God, frequently face the reality that the indigenous term may have meanings associated with it that are at odds with the biblical understanding of who God is. The awareness of this has

generated sharp criticism from some Christians toward Bible translators who have chosen to use the common word for God in languages of people who are feared as enemies. On the positive side, this solution has the advantage that the term is already familiar and allows people to learn about the God they encounter in the Bible as one who is already known to them by another name. The apostle Paul modeled this strategy in communicating the Gospel in Athens: "That which you worship, then, even though you do not know it, is what I now proclaim to you" (Acts 17.23 GNB).

When translators choose the solution of transliterating or borrowing a word for God from another language, they must face the possibility that the God of the Bible may seem foreign to the people for whom the translation is being prepared. At the same time, this option is more likely to avoid the tendency of inadvertently introducing an understanding of God that is not supported in Scripture.

No matter which route a translator follows to translate **theos** (θεός) the term will not really be totally adequate to convey all the aspects of God as revealed in the Bible. Ultimately the meaning of the term chosen will need to be filled out by a study of what the Scriptures reveal about this supreme being – the creator of the universe.

No revelation of God is more complete than Jesus Christ – God made real to us in human form. That is why the writer of the Gospel according to John says, "In the

beginning was the Word, and the Word was with God, and the Word was God"
(KJV, NRSV, NIV, ESV). In Jesus, God became one of us and demonstrated in the

most dramatic way possible how much God cares about each one of us. That is the
great Good News which John 3.16 expresses so succinctly. That is why it is such
good news and why we go to so much effort and expense to ensure that all people
have the opportunity to discover it in the language they understand best.

Issue 3 - Translation and Interpretation

"So" – such a tiny word! Surely it can't present much of a challenge to the Bible
translator!

The length of a word really has nothing to do with the degree of difficulty a
translator is likely to face in accurately representing its meaning in another
language. Also, the fact that this word is tiny in English obscures the fact that
Houtōs (Οὕτως) in Greek is a word of normal length and just as complex in meaning
as most. The structure of the English language, which tucks this tiny word between
the powerful words "God" and "loved," also tends to downplay its significance. In
the Greek **Houtōs** (Οὕτως) comes first in the sentence. It establishes the context for
what follows.

A paraphrase representing one meaning of this word might read something like,
"God loved the world so much that ...." Many modern versions have done just that.
We tend to understand "so" as an adverb used to express the degree to which God
loved the world. Many Greek scholars, however, interpret the word **Houtōs** (Οὕτως)
as an adverb of manner and most interlinear Greek texts

render it as "thus." Another way of paraphrasing it is, "This is how God loved the
world ...."

Often the intended meaning is so rich that it is impossible to capture it fully in any
one version. In this case, John may well have intended to express both the degree
to which God loved the world as well as the manner in which that love was

expressed. The challenge for the translator is to capture both thoughts in a way that is clear and natural.

I believe Dr. Eugene H. Peterson's "The Message" comes about as close as possible to expressing in English what John intended. He accurately captures the complexity of the little word "so" when he says, "This is how much God loved the world: He gave his Son, his

one and only Son. And this is why: so that no one need be destroyed; by believing in him, anyone can have a whole and lasting life." (John 3.16 The Message)

The Bible is like a precious multi-faceted diamond. The different versions are like the different surfaces that a skilled jeweler cuts into the gem to bring out the light. Reading the Bible in different versions helps to expose the brilliance of its eternal message.

Issue 4 - Translation Across Cultures

"Love" is the heart of the Gospel message. Greek and Hebrew have many different words for "love." The Greek verb **ēgapēsen** (ἠγάπησεν) used here is just one of several. By contrast most languages, including English, are impoverished in their "love language." So we face huge challenges when searching for suitable ways to represent what the Bible says about love.

The love of a mother for her child is quite different from the love expressed by a man for his wife. Yet in English we use the same word – "love." The Greek language has two very distinct words to express these different kinds of love. The Greek-English Lexicon, edited by world renowned translation scholar Dr. Eugene A. Nida, lists 25 entries under the topic of "love," based on at least seven different Greek root words.

The Gospel message is about the love God has for us. Conveying this is complicated in cultures where the concept of a god who loves people is not familiar. Animistic cultures are more concerned about the many "gods" who might harm them. In Kalinga, a language spoken in the Philippines, the word used for love really means "to want or desire." It may also carry sexual connotations. In one African language the only word available for love means "to please."

This would imply that the world pleased God so much that.... In such circumstances, we struggle to find ways to minimize the likelihood that people will misunderstand the Gospel message.

With complex and loaded words like love, it is almost always impossible to discover the precise equivalent in another language. English has only one word for a range of concepts requiring a number of different Greek words, so it cannot possibly express the meaning as powerfully as the original. We translators do our best to express the intended message clearly and precisely. People benefit from access to the Bible in many versions as well as the opportunity to learn more through teaching and study in the community of faith. Each one helps to illuminate the rich meaning of the original.

Issue 5 - Primary and Secondary Senses

"The world" – this phrase is challenging for Bible translators because the Greek word **kosmon** (κόσμον) is used with at least five different shades of meanings in the New Testament. Depending on the context, it may mean "the universe," "the earth," "the inhabitants of the earth," "the way people live in the world," or "everyone and everything that is alienated from God." John 1.10 illustrates three of these meanings in one verse.

When translating words used in a variety of ways, we must distinguish between primary and secondary senses. For example, the English word "run" has the primary meaning of "motion with quick steps on alternate feet." It also has literally dozens of secondary senses. When used with "nose," "motor" or "stocking," it has three very different meanings – none of which would be translated by the word for "run" in French, Spanish or most other languages. It is the secondary senses of words that create the most challenges for translators, because they are rarely transferable from one language to another.

In Scripture, words are commonly used in such a way that the whole stands for one of its parts. For example Luke uses "Moses" to stand for the writings attributed to Moses in the Bible (Luke 16.29), and in

Acts 2.4 "tongues" represent the languages spoken with the tongue. The technical name for this rhetorical device is "metonymy."

The Greek word **kosmon** (κόσμον) as used in John 3.16 is a clear example of metonymy. Here "the universe" stands for the people who live in it. God's love is focused on those who inhabit the world. The book of Genesis represents the Creator as expressing pleasure with all of creation ("it was good"), but not love. The agape love in John's Gospel focuses on people, the only beings capable of responding to God in faith.

Translators who fail to consider the secondary sense of the Greek word **kosmon** (κόσμον) used here may end up with a rendering that represents God's love as focused on the earth, a lifeless lump of clay, rather than on the people with whom he identified supremely in the incarnation. The Contemporary English Version ensures that the intended meaning of the original is conveyed clearly with the rendering, "God loved the people of this world so much that...." Although "the people" are not stated in the literal Greek text of the original, they are clearly the intended objects of God's great love. Newer translations of the Bible such as the Contemporary English Version can help the reader to understand more clearly what the original authors wanted to communicate.

Issue 6 - Collocational Clashes

Here we concentrate on the sixth element in this fabulous message, "he gave." The verb "to give" in its primary sense, has to do with transferring possession or ownership and normally implies material objects. In contexts such as the abhorrent institution of slavery, people can also be objects of possession and transference. In English, "his only Son" as the direct object of "he gave" is not incomprehensible.

However, in many other languages it would constitute a serious collocational clash – two elements that do not naturally go together.

The unusual nature of this collocation highlights and draws attention to the statement. To readers steeped in Bible knowledge, it helps to evoke images of Jesus' birth and his death as a sacrifice for the sins of the world. Readers familiar with Old Testament Jewish history are reminded of Abraham and his willingness to sacrifice his only son Isaac. Most contemporary readers may need an explanation such as those offered in study Bibles.

In other languages, the clash between "he gave" and "his only Son" may be even more pronounced. In the Kalinga language of the Philippines, there is no context for readers to understand the

concept of giving one's son. In this case it was decided to borrow the verb "sent" from the following verse which, while not retaining the rich imagery of the original, is necessary to help readers who have very little biblical background.

Perfect translation is not possible, and even very good translation requires difficult choices. Sometimes the choice is between two or more possible renderings, each of which provide only an imperfect representation of the originally intended meaning. At other times

the choice may be between a rendering that is not quite accurate and one that would convey no meaning at all. As Bible translators we value the prayers of God's people so that the choices we make will help people understand the message in a way that will draw them to Jesus – God's communication wrapped in humanity (John 1.14).

Issue 7 - Metaphorical Language

Now we come to the words "his only Son." Webster's primary definition of son is "a male offspring especially of human beings." In John 3.16, the pronoun his links this phrase back to God making it clear that the reference is not to a human being but to God. The notion of God having offspring is extremely difficult to grasp. To the Islamic mind it is sacrilegious since it appears to bring God down to the level of humans. Christians interpret this as an

anthropomorphism (using human images to explain something about God). Obviously the word son is being used to communicate something different than is conveyed by its primary sense in our language.

There is a rich tradition in Hebrew and Greek literature both inside and outside the Bible with respect to the usage of this word. This background helped the original readers understand the reference to Jesus as the Son of God in a metaphorical rather than a literal sense. It signals a relationship of intimacy and respect similar to the ideal relationship between a human father and son. It also reinforces the traditional Christian understanding about the special circumstances surrounding the conception and birth of Jesus. There is no implication of a sexual union between God and Mary, the

mother of Jesus. Incorporating all this background in a translation is impossible!

John helps a little by adding "only." The English language is inadequate to capture the full range of meaning communicated by the word **monogenē** (μονογενῆ) in Greek. For centuries this word was incorrectly translated in English versions as "only begotten." Scholars today are virtually unanimous that this is an unfortunate adherence to the Latin Vulgate by translators of the KJV and other early English versions, rather than an accurate representation of the meaning of the Greek. All now agree that it means "only" in the sense of "unique." John reinforces his special use of the noun "son" clarifying that the relationship between Jesus the Son and God the Father was unique. In the English written text we use a capital "S" on "son" to highlight this unique use of the term.

Translating the Scriptures into the thousands of languages spoken in our world today is complex. Translating this concept of Jesus as the Son of God is especially challenging in Islamic contexts where such a concept is scandalous. Translators in every age and in every

language do their best to communicate concepts that are sometimes too difficult for words. In such circumstance translators are thankful we are not alone but that we work in partnership with the Holy Spirit and with the Church. The prayers of God's people play a crucial role in Bible translation.

Issue 8 - Logical Connections

The little Greek conjunction **hina** (ἵνα) is represented by the two English words "so that." In translation we refer to tiny words like this as "discourse particles." Few Bible Commentaries discuss them. They are generally relegated to the Grammars and Lexicons where only the most serious Bible students are made aware of how complex and full of meaning they are. However, as translators we are very much aware of the large freight of meaning that these "particles" carry. They are the glue that holds a discourse together, connecting separate units into a meaningful whole. To translate them properly we must have a clear understanding of how they are used in Greek and then research grammatical possibilities which will make comparable connections in the language into which the translation is being done.

Since these particles function to link parts of a discourse, their precise meanings can only be discovered by examining them in context. The Greek Lexicon produced by Arndt and Gingrich, one of the best available resources, identifies at least 4 major areas of meaning for this particle, each with its own complex variations.

In the present context it is used to introduce the purpose for which God sent his only Son. The Judeo-Christian view assumes that

God's actions have meaning and purpose. Other cultures may not share this view. For example, in many animistic cultures the activity in the spiritual realm may be viewed as arbitrary and capricious.

The challenge in translation is to find the word or combination of words that will most clearly establish the logical connection of purpose. Traditional English versions attempted to capture this with one word, "that." Unfortunately this is somewhat ambiguous and not as natural as it could be. Most newer versions use the phrase "so that." This is an improvement both in clarity and in naturalness. Eugene Peterson's paraphrase captures the clearest rendering of all. "This is how much God loved the world: He gave his Son, his one and only Son. **And this is why: so that....**"

The English-speaking world is fortunate to have a large variety of versions which all contribute to the clear communication of God's word. As Bible translators we invite those who have such ready access to the Bible to participate in the ministry of making it available to people in languages that still do not have even one word of the Bible in their language.

Issue 9 - Lexical Equivalence

everyone who

The little Greek word **pas** (πᾶς) is represented by the two English words "everyone who." The translators of the King James Version, writing in an older form of the English language, were able to use just one word, "whosoever." The Canadian Oxford Dictionary labels this word "archaic." More recent versions such as the New International and the Revised Standard have also tried to retain one-word equivalence, with "whoever." Unfortunately, in contemporary usage this has become a rather flippant slang expression for the youth culture in the same domain as "whatever." This contemporary usage of the term tends to diminish its appropriateness to convey the meaning intended by the original Greek term.

The term used in the Greek actually means "all" or "every." In this grammatical construction it means "everyone who." This is exactly the rendering that the New Revised Standard Version and other meaning-based versions such as the Good News Translation and the Contemporary English Version have chosen. The term extends the invitation as widely as possible. Using "everyone" challenges our human tendency to be ethnocentric.

The early followers of Jesus were Jewish. They had grown up with the view that they were God's chosen people and therefore superior to the Gentiles, who, according to them, lived outside of God's blessing and providence. They held this view even though in the covenant God made with their ancestor Abraham he had specifically indicated his intention to cause them to "be a blessing to all nations on earth" (Genesis 22.18 CEV). This sense of superiority is a natural element in our human nature. We tend to define God in our own image and to believe that he cares about us more than he does about others. Jesus challenged these assumptions. He made it clear that he came to earth to love and rescue all people, regardless of their social, religious or ethnic origins. That's Good News!

It is the universal implication of the Good News about Jesus which motivates his followers to go to great lengths to ensure that this message is made available to all people in the language and style of communication that speaks to them most clearly. This is why Bible agencies such as the Canadian Bible Society, along with its many partners, focus significant resources on the support of Bible translation in Canada and around the world, where people speaking over 3,000 languages still lack access to this Good News in a language they can really understand. We rely on the prayers and support of God's people to help make this happen.

Issue 10 - Key Terms

The next word **pisteuōn** (πιστεύων) is translated "believes" in our English text. In translation we consider this a "key term" because of the critical role it plays in communicating the message. In the Gospel, belief is the channel through which salvation by grace comes to people (Ephesians 2.8). This core word occurs 240 times in the New Testament. The Greek root is variously translated as "believe" or "faith" depending on the version and context.

The translator's challenges are to first understand the concept in the Greek and second, to express it in the language receiving the new translation. It's critical to go to the source text for key terms, ensuring faithfulness to the original.

The problem with our English verb "to believe" is that for those not very familiar with the Gospel, its meaning may be limited to a dictionary level understanding of accepting something as true. That is belief at the intellectual level. In the context of the Gospel, the original term carried a deeper meaning of acceptance, not just at the head level, but also in the heart. Whenever the original Greek term is used in conjunction with the preposition "in" or "into" as it is in this verse, it carries the meaning of faith or confidence in a person to the extent of acting on that faith.

We struggle for the right word to translate key terms such as "believe." Sometimes a language has a unique word that captures the full meaning. The common word for believe in Kalinga is "manuttuwa." It goes back to the word for truth which is "tuttuwa." When used as a verb this term is commonly used to mean "believe" as well as "obey." The Kalinga understand intuitively that to believe in Jesus implies obedience as well. This does not make the road to discipleship any easier for them, but it does bring their understanding of the Gospel more directly in line with the teachings of our Lord's brother James who maintains in his letter that faith without works is dead.

Translation is never easy. Often it seems downright impossible to simply and accurately convey some of the teachings of the Gospel in other languages. But at other times we experience the serendipity of finding concepts in a new language that convey the message about Christ with a clarity that almost transcends the original. There is always something to be learned by reading or hearing the message in a new language.

Issue 11 - Grammatical Issues

The tiny word "in" following the verb "believes" is the preposition εἰς (pronounced like "ace" or "ice") in Greek. As with many grammatical terms, this preposition carries little intrinsic meaning of its own. Its function is grammatical rather than semantic. Its significance can vary considerably depending on how it is used in context. Strong's Greek dictionary gives it the primary glosses to or into, but then goes on to give an entire paragraph of other glosses depending on how it is used. In combination with the verb "believes" the most natural rendering for this preposition in English is "in".

What is really interesting in this verse is to observe how the addition of this tiny grammatical particle, with no real meaning of its own, impacts the meaning of the verse. We could leave it out and still have a perfectly meaningful sentence, but its thrust would be quite different. To say "everyone who believes him…" is very different from saying "everyone who believes in him…." The first kind of belief is merely mental assent and as James 2.19 points out, even the demons have that kind of belief in God. The addition of the small preposition "in" transforms the verb "believes" into something that involves a deep personal relationship with and trust in the person on whom the belief is focused – in this case, Jesus.

English has an abundance of prepositions compared with many other languages. For this reason, teachers of English as a second or foreign language frequently encounter serious problems when they try to teach the English use of prepositions. For example, Spanish has one preposition "en" that serves as the equivalent of three prepositions in English: in, on, and at. Then there are many languages which do not use prepositions at all. Canadian Algonquian languages for example, attach directional or location markers to nouns where English uses prepositions. What English expresses through the use of prepositions, many other languages accomplish through the use of different cases which are grammatical markers attached to nouns or verbs. A language like Estonian has 14 different cases.

Because of such differences in the grammatical structures of languages, it is important for translators to explore and understand the grammars of both the source language from which they are translating and the receptor language into which the translation is being made. Lack of understanding of differences in grammatical structure is one of the most common reasons for awkward and unnatural renderings in translation.

Issue 12 - Pronominal Reference

The little pronoun "him" **auton** (αὐτὸν) in this verse profiles a particularly pesky issue in translation – the proper use of pronouns. Languages commonly substitute pronouns to take the place of nouns as a kind of communication shorthand. However, not all languages have the same pronouns or use them in the same way.

For example, the Kalinga people in the Philippines have 3 different forms of the first-person plural pronoun. So, every time the pronoun "we" or its Greek equivalent occurs in Scripture, the Bible translator must determine for the Kalinga language whether the communicator intends to include the audience or not and if so, whether the audience consists of just one person or more than one. In Matthew 8.25 Jesus is asleep during the storm and the disciples shout, "Lord, save us! We're going to drown!" Here the Kalinga translator must decide whether the disciples are intending to imply that Jesus will drown along with them or not. The Kalinga translator must make a choice where Greek and English do not.

English, on the other hand, requires us to make a choice about gender in our use of the third person singular pronouns "he" and "she" while many other languages, including Kalinga, have only one generic third person singular pronoun. So the English language

presents a problem for translators in a verse like Matthew 16.24. The NIV quotes Jesus as saying, "If anyone would come after me, he must deny himself and take up his cross and follow me." Yet it is quite evident that Jesus' invitation is given to anyone, not just to males. In the past the English pronoun "he" was understood to refer to a person of the masculine gender as well as generically to any person whether male or female. This is how the NIV intends to use it here. However, in contemporary English people no longer understand the pronoun "he" as generic. So most newer versions of the Bible avoid the use of the third person singular pronoun and find a way to ensure that readers will interpret Jesus invitation as including them, regardless of their gender. The CEV has, "If any of you want to be my followers, you must forget about yourself. You must take up your cross and follow me."

Another kind of ambiguity occurs with the use of pronouns when it is unclear what the antecedent is. In the statement, "Peter went to John because he owed him money" it is not clear who is meant by the pronouns "he" or "him." Either pronoun could refer to Peter or to John. There is a similar ambiguity in the use of the pronoun "him" in John 3.16. It could refer back to the Son or to God. The Translator's Handbook produced by the United Bible Societies to alert translators to potential pitfalls, profiles this problem as follows: "It is important to indicate clearly that **everyone who believe in him** refers to the Son, not to God."

With tools such as these it is possible to achieve higher standards of quality in Bible translation today. The Canadian Bible Society is deeply involved in making tools accessible to translators world-wide

through computer resources being developed under the Institute for Computer Assisted Publishing. These tools help ensure that the Bible can be translated into many more languages at higher quality – bringing them the Word in the language of the heart.

Issue 13 - Rhetorical Figures

may not perish

The phrase "may not perish" is part of a bold rhetorical figure which the writer uses to highlight the ultimate destiny of the person who believes in Jesus. The figure profiles the desirability of that destiny by first emphasizing what it is not. In this issue we deal only with this first part of the figure – "may not perish."

In the Greek, this phrase consists of the word **mē** (μὴ) translated as "not" followed by **apolētai** (ἀπόληται) which is translated in some English versions as "perish." The primary meaning of the Greek word actually has to do with destruction and is glossed in Greek lexicons as "to destroy" or "to ruin." In The Message, Eugene Peterson has "be destroyed." Other recent version such as Good News, God's Word and The Contemporary English Version try to capture the fact that what is being dealt with here is a life and death matter and translate the Greek word into English as "die."

The variation that we find in our English versions illustrates the difficulty of translating rhetorical figures in a way that fully and accurately captures the meaning of the original. Peterson is certainly right to translate this verse in a way that shows that believing in Christ keeps us from destruction. However, his rendering is so general that many readers will have difficulty knowing what type of destruction is being referred to. Older and more literal versions tend to use the English word "perish," which is accurate, but also archaic because contemporary English does not use "perish" with the meaning "to die" anymore. By making this a life and death issue, newer versions are more easily understood, but people may take these translations too literally as referring to physical death.

Our Translators Handbook published by the United Bible Societies warns translators that this verse has frequently "been misinterpreted to imply that if people simply believed in Jesus that they would never experience physical death." The Contemporary English Version tries to avoid this misinterpretation by saying that those who have faith in Jesus will "never really die," implying that there is a kind of death other than physical death from which they will be spared.

Ultimately as translators we must recognize that in the case of difficult rhetorical figures such as these, our work is not enough. The work of the translators must be supplemented by the work of teachers and preachers and group study in the community of faith. The Bible Society is keenly aware of the need for partnership with the Church. The work of Bible teachers, preachers, and even parents and Bible study groups is critical for followers of Jesus to understand the Bible so they may grow and become true disciples in the Kingdom that Jesus came to bring.

Issue 14 - Limitations to Translation

One of the reasons Christians love this verse so much is its promise of life – eternal life. According to this verse we have this life through a combination of what God has done and our response. God sent his Son to save us and the anticipated response on our part is faith that results in action.

But what is this "eternal life" that we are promised?

The original Greek is **zoen aionion** (ζωὴν αἰώνιον). The first Greek word is the source from which we derive our English word "zoology." It is generally translated in English as "life." The second word is frequently translated into English as "eternal." We get our English word "eon" from this Greek root. Unfortunately in our English translation, as in many languages, the focus in a word like "eternal" tends to be on the length of time – time without end. However in Greek and in the context of the Jewish culture in which the Gospel was written, the focus is as much on the quality of life that is promised as on the length of time. The Jewish people viewed history as consisting of two ages – **aion** (αἰών) in Greek. There was the present age in which God's people were waiting for the coming Messiah. Then there was the age to come when all promises and

covenants would be fulfilled. Messiah would come and God's promised blessings would finally come in full measure.

Those of us who just read this verse in our English translations without understanding the context in which John lived and wrote, will tend to think of the next age as the time after death when the part of us that does not die goes on to live forever in heaven. However, for Jesus, and for his early followers, that time had already begun with the coming of Jesus, the long-awaited Messiah. Everything that Jesus did and taught was intended to demonstrate that the messianic age – the "Kingdom" had come near. So what John is telling us here is that by believing in Jesus – by believing that he is indeed God's messiah – we are ushered into a whole new age or era with a new quality of life. This life does not just begin at our physical death and then go on forever after that. It begins here and now and goes on after our bodies die. It begins as soon as we recognize and place our trust in the Messiah – the one and only son of God whom God sent into this world because he loves us so much.

The inadequacy of translations to capture the full range of what Scripture is trying to communicate profiles the importance of sound biblical teaching to help convey the depth of meaning that cannot always be captured in translation. As Bible translators we work in partnership with the Church to bring the good news of the Gospel to people with the power to transform lives.